ENCOUNTERS WITH MICHAEL ARLEN

BY THE SAME AUTHOR

Hofmannsthal and Greek Myth (2002)
Sandy Denny: Reflections on Her Music (2011)
Becoming Helen Mirren (2019)
Laura Nyro: On Track (2022)
Instead of a Critic: Essays Written and Unwritten (2022)

Frank Wedekind, *Franziska* (1998) [trans.]
Frank Wedekind, *Mine-Haha* (2010) [trans.]

ENCOUNTERS WITH MICHAEL ARLEN

Philip Ward

Copyright © 2023 Philip Ward

The moral right of the author has been asserted.

Apart from any fair dealing for the purposes of research or private study, or criticism or review, as permitted under the Copyright, Designs and Patents Act 1988, this publication may only be reproduced, stored or transmitted, in any form or by any means, with the prior permission in writing of the publishers, or in the case of reprographic reproduction in accordance with the terms of licences issued by the Copyright Licensing Agency. Enquiries concerning reproduction outside those terms should be sent to the publishers.

Troubador Publishing Ltd
Unit E2 Airfield Business Park
Harrison Road, Market Harborough
Leicestershire LE16 7UL
Tel: 0116 279 2299
Email: books@troubador.co.uk
Web: www.troubador.co.uk

ISBN 978 1 80514 114 3

British Library Cataloguing in Publication Data.
A catalogue record for this book is available from the British Library.

Printed by TJ Books Limited, Padstow, UK
Typeset in 12pt Bembo by Troubador Publishing Ltd, Leicester, UK

To Alex

CONTENTS

List of Illustrations	viii
Acknowledgements	ix
Introduction	1
How (Not) To Write Literary Biography	7
Early Life	28
Success: New York, 1925	47
Encounters	59
D.H. Lawrence	61
Katherine Mansfield	92
Ernest Hemingway	96
F. Scott Fitzgerald	115
Aldous Huxley	130
Rebecca West	150
At the Movies	158
Armenia the 'Courtesan'	165
A Family Photo Album	179
A Detailed Timeline	186
The Extant Letters	218
Two Letters to His Mother	228
Sources	233
About the Author	245

LIST OF ILLUSTRATIONS

Two letters to his family, 1925	6
A literary lion arrives in New York, 1925	49
Filming *A Woman of Affairs*, MGM Studios, July 1928	160
The Kouyoumdjian family, Bulgaria, late 1890s	179
The matriarch: Satinik Kouyoumdjian	180
Arlen in front of the family's Southport home	181
Arlen in middle age	182
Arlen, Michael John and Atalanta	183
Venetia and Atalanta	184
Arlen with his nephew Sarkis, Southport, 1928	185
The High Life, Riviera, 1930s	185

ACKNOWLEDGEMENTS

Some of this material has previously appeared in print or online. I am grateful to the editors of the *D.H. Lawrence Review*, the *Hemingway Review*, the *F. Scott Fitzgerald Review*, the *Aldous Huxley Annual*, the *Katherine Mansfield Society Newsletter* and the *Rebecca West Society Blog*. The chapter on literary biography, in shorter form, was originally delivered as a seminar paper at Wolfson College, Cambridge in 2019. The diverse origins of these pieces mean that some overlap and repetition is unavoidable, as is a degree of inconsistency in style and in the scholarly apparatus attaching to them. For this I apologise – if such things trouble the reader.

Anyone with an interest in this subject is indebted to Harry Keyishian, author in the 1970s of the only previous English-language study of Arlen (which I cite many times in what follows.) He generously passed on to me the impressive personal archive of articles and correspondence he built up while working on his book, and, together with my own additions, this now exists as a resource for future research. Professor Keyishian's book is the place to go for an expert literary-critical discussion of Arlen's fiction and plays: something I cannot pretend to offer. His volume also includes a detailed bibliography of Arlen's published writings and a list of film adaptations of his work.

My personal thanks go also to Michael J. Arlen, Kevin Brownlow, Milena Dobreva, Anna Girling, Andrew Harrison, Gerri Kimber, Lusine Mueller, Christine Ann Sarkis, Suzanne Schuster, Nareg Seferian, James Sexton, and the many archivists and scholars who have helped along the way. The Biographers' Club has been a great support. Above all, thanks to Alexandra Sarkis, Arlen's great-niece, to whom this volume is dedicated and without whom it wouldn't have come into existence.

INTRODUCTION

Michael Arlen (1895-1956) was a literary shooting star among the smart set of the 1920s. The self-styled chronicler of Mayfair society, he published a string of short story collections and novels that made him a celebrity on both sides of the Atlantic. Nothing he wrote was more successful or more discussed than *The Green Hat*, his novel of 1924 (later adapted as a stage play with Tallulah Bankhead in the West End lead and a movie starring Greta Garbo). In Iris March, the book's free-spirited, sexually adventurous heroine, he created an archetype of 1920s popular culture. Flushed with success, Arlen moved among aristocrats and *haute bourgeoisie* and was courted by Hollywood. Marriage to an elegant Greek countess followed in 1928, and the newly-weds set up home in a villa in the hills above Cannes. A son, Michael John, was born to them in 1930; a daughter, Venetia, followed two years later. He tried his hand at other genres (science fiction, the detective story) without recapturing his earlier success. Even if the later books found less favour with the reading public, there was consolation of a kind for Arlen in the companionship of the Riviera *émigré* community. At the start of the Second World War he returned to England, hoping to "do his bit", but, after an unhappy spell in civil defence work in the Midlands, he moved again. By the time he emigrated permanently to the USA in 1941, the stream of inspiration was drying up. There would be no more novels, only desultory work on Hollywood scripts and in TV. Gradually, the shooting star sank into oblivion. In his son's words, by this time "he really wasn't doing a damned thing except having lunch with people". Never believing himself an important writer, he declined to have his best-sellers reprinted. Still he remained, at all times, immaculately tailored, endlessly clubbable...

Yet that outward show was only one of his lives. For 'Michael Arlen' was not what he seemed. Born to Armenian parents who had emigrated to Lancashire from Bulgaria at the turn of the century, he was in origin Dikran Kouyoumdjian, a young adventurer who dropped out of university, made his way to London during the First World War, changed his name and reinvented himself as a dapper man of letters. Consciously willing himself into a new identity, he created a character as exotic as anything in his fiction. Quizzed about his Armenian heritage, he would often bridle and change the subject, reluctant to be the torch-bearer for an oppressed people. His critics, however, would never let him forget it. In the eyes of native-born Britons, from Winston Churchill to Virginia Woolf, 'Michael Arlen' was always an outsider, his loyalty to King and Empire open to question even twenty years after he became a naturalised British subject, his 'swarthy' appearance and knack for making money out of middlebrow taste arousing suspicion and mobilising prejudice.

I first encountered him in the pages of Claud Cockburn's *Bestseller* (1972), a survey of "the books everyone read 1900-1939". Cockburn had little time for Arlen or the celebrity that he so studiously cultivated. He dismissed the baffling plot of *The Green Hat* as "a hurriedly constructed though highly painted vehicle in which the reader is to be taken on the conducted tour through an imaginary England". In a sense Cockburn was right. Let's take a passage from the novel at random, this from the narrator's first encounter with the enigmatic, hat-wearing heroine, Iris March:

> Her eyes were stronger than mine, even as wind is stronger than air, and always in them was the magic of wide open places. I looked down, and far below, like two pearls in the dust, shone two ankles clasped in silk the colour of daylight. I thought of her fate and of her. I thought of corruption, of curses, of death, of life, of love, and of love's delight. I took hold of the sword in my mind with both hands, but was not strong enough to lift it. I thought of the limbs of Aphrodite, of the sighs of Anaitis, of the sharp cries of love's delight. I thought how charming men would be if they could misbehave outwardly as prettily as they can in their minds…

Whether two ankles, however shapely, could possibly inspire this stream of quasi-philosophical speculation in an attentive young man is anyone's guess. For a captive public, somehow it didn't matter. In his own first novel, *Burmese Days* (1934), George Orwell conjured up an image of Arlen's typical reader in typical reading posture:

> Elizabeth lay on the sofa in the Lackersteens' drawing-room, with her feet up and a cushion behind her head, reading Michael Arlen's *These Charming People*. In a general way Michael Arlen was her favourite author…

'Elizabeth' and her leisured kind are no more. Arlen's books are little read nowadays, except as time-capsules of a long-vanished era, and his life is patchily documented. This is a shame, for in his untold story are all manner of connections to other people whose reputations have held up better than his own. A friend of D.H. Lawrence, he turns up in *Lady Chatterley's Lover* (1928) as the playwright Michaelis. One of the many lovers of Nancy Cunard (she nicknamed him "The Baron"), he vied for her affections with Aldous Huxley, who as early as 1915 was writing in a letter of Lawrence's plans to decamp to the "deserts of Florida" with his new Armenian *protégé*. Later, Huxley speared Arlen in print as a character in *Those Barren Leaves* (1925). Arlen's writing had a powerful impact on the young Scott Fitzgerald, an influence that Ernest Hemingway deplored (although Arlen and Hemingway would later bond, after a fashion). Arlen bankrolled the London premiere of Noël Coward's play *The Vortex* (1924): the start of another lifelong friendship. When Anthony Powell came down from Oxford, he was naturally drawn to lodge in London's Shepherd Market because that's where the seduction scene in *The Green Hat* was set. Rebecca West (with whom Arlen allegedly had an affair) spent General Election Night 1929 in his company at an all-night party at Selfridge's, although she was later to write sniffily of his work as "a mixture of the genuine article and advertising copy". *The Green Hat* was among the favoured teenage reading of Simone de Beauvoir; it had a more baleful influence on Nadezhda Alliluyeva, Stalin's second wife, who, her husband believed, was inspired to take her own life after reading Arlen's description of Iris March's melodramatic suicide in the novel's closing pages.

This book, *Encounters with Michael Arlen*, is pitched at the general reader, someone with an interest in the literature and culture of the interwar years. As we enter the 2020s and the centenaries fall in quick succession, there is continuing fascination with phenomena like the 'Roaring Twenties', the 'Jazz Age', the 'Lost

Generation' and the 'Bright Young People', and with Hollywood in its 'Golden Age'. Expatriates living their pampered lives on the Côte d'Azur are always in vogue (see for example, Mary S. Lovell, *The Riviera Set*, 2017). A cast of well-known figures pass through the book, figures better known than Arlen himself is nowadays, and anyone interested by what constituted 'society' in this era may find oblique light thrown on familiar names.

What this is *not* is a full-scale biography of Michael Arlen. For reasons I explore in the next chapter, such a book may never be written. It is, rather, a composite set of essays drawing on unpublished letters in archives, new research in the UK, US and Bulgaria, and the testimony of Arlen's surviving son that reflect how the author was seen by himself and by his contemporaries. Their encounters with him. And *my* encounters, pursuing trails that in most cases have long gone cold. Arlen constantly rewrote his own story; he is the most unreliable of narrators. If the facts could ever be established, a complex picture would likely emerge, of a man whose suave external appearance concealed a conflicted soul: an immigrant who craved acceptance by the host community, a reluctant Armenian nationalist, a writer who recognised his limitations yet longed to be taken more seriously by the *literati* whose company he enjoyed. I neglect to discuss Arlen's books in any detail, you may object. This is because I can only regard them as so many chapters in the history of *taste*. How the books that everyone read a hundred years ago become the books that no one reads today is, perhaps, the topic for another inquiry altogether. In the meantime I offer what follows. An earlier book of mine was called *Instead of a Critic*; the present volume might be cheekily subtitled *Instead of a Biography*.

Book-Cadillac Hotel
DETROIT

My dear,

The play opened here last night to an amazing reception. And they have recieved me here as though I was the Prince of Wales. I can't write, as I am tapped out. I am dining to-night with Mr. Henry Ford and his son. All my love

Dikran.

27 B Charter St.
Mayfair.

My dear Anaïs

Thank you for your translation. It is ~~physically impossible~~ for me now to do anything for them. I am rehearsing all the time and also I'm clearing up a lot of odd jobs before leaving England. I simply cannot cope with the demands on my time, and sometimes I think I shall go crazy. So write them a polite letter in their own language and tell them I am in America and will do what I can when I can. Love...

Dikran.

All right about Cox.

Two letters to his family, 1925.

HOW (NOT) TO WRITE LITERARY BIOGRAPHY

In 1928 an article appeared in *The London Mercury*, an influential arts magazine with a right-of-centre reputation, under the title 'Two Types of Modern Fiction'. In it the author, E.F. Benson, distinguished between what he saw as two trends in the contemporary English novel: 'Dallowayism' and 'Green Hattery'. Both sorts, he argued, aim to "tear off from the characters presented apparel of all sorts, textile or psychical, and to show us flayed humanity, like carcasses in butchers' shops". Dallowayism achieves this, by use of lancet and scalpel, to show us "what we are like inside", which is "something so minute, so withered, so kippered, that we wonder if it can indeed be the genuine article"; its stream-of-consciousness method is "nothing more than skimming off the scum that is continually rising to the surface of the brain". Green Hattery shows us how the "children of the monkey-house" have "cast aside the outworn lendings of morality" to engage in a joyless round of "cocktails and fornication" as "languid martyrs who till their last hour gave their all in the service of what so unspeakably bores them". I won't dwell on the argument, which is convoluted and contrived, but I isolate this moment in 1928 because it brings together three names, whose respective fortunes have been very different in the near-century since. The article's author, E.F. Benson, may still ring bells in the English-speaking world. He is remembered for the Mapp and Lucia novels, genial comedies of village life which have twice been adapted for British television in the last thirty years. 'Dallowayism', of course, takes its name from Virginia Woolf's 1925 novel *Mrs Dalloway*. Woolf is now one of the presiding deities of English Literature studies. She needs no introduction. At Cambridge University disciples can attend a 'Virginia Woolf Summer Course', spend a week studying one or two Woolf texts a day, with lectures, seminars, supervisions, visits, etc. But this other type of modern fiction, 'Green Hattery' – what is that about? It's a reference to *The Green Hat*, a wildly successful novel of 1924 by Michael Arlen. Who was he and why has he disappeared from view?

Well, for a start he wasn't 'Michael Arlen'. That was a pen-name adopted in 1920 at the start of his career. He was born Dikran Kouyoumdjian in Ruse, Bulgaria, in 1895, into a family of Armenian merchants. The family emigrated to England at the turn of the century and their youngest son was thoroughly anglicised at Malvern College. After a brief spell at Edinburgh University, Dikran moved to London, started writing for the Armenian exile press – this was in the wake of the Armenian massacre of 1915 – and for *The New Age*, a literary periodical of leftist leanings, before discovering his true *métier*. This involved remaking himself as a well-dressed man about town and weaving fictions around the fashionable crowd he so longed to join. The trick, as Somerset Maugham observed, was to reflect London society through an outsider's eyes and thus "make it the scene of adventures as rich with glamour, as fantastic, incredible, romantic and vivacious as those with which Scheherazade beguiled her caliph". Over the course of the next ten years, he studied the literary market and by dint of hard work and sheer ambition lifted himself from obscurity to cosmopolitan celebrity.

By writing about Society, Arlen gained admission to it, despite the whiff of scandal that attached to his most successful novel, *The Green Hat*. A word about this book is necessary. It's the story of Iris March, wearer of the eponymous green hat, who is depicted as a *femme fatale*, a "house of men" with a "pagan body and a Chislehurst mind". For much of the book we're led to believe that her first husband, a golden youth in the Rupert Brooke tradition, committed suicide on their wedding night after discovering his bride's pre-marital infidelity. Iris always claims that he died "for Purity". At the end we discover that the golden youth killed himself because he had syphilis and Iris had always lied about this to preserve his sainted reputation, especially in the eyes of her own brother, an indolent alcoholic who idolised the young man. Her second husband, a military hero, dies at the hands of Irish republicans. She dallies with the (unnamed) narrator, resumes an affair with her childhood sweetheart, conceives a child by him and loses it in a Paris clinic. There's a lot more plot and a lot more characters, and a hectic finale in which Iris wraps her yellow Hispano-Suiza around an old oak tree, with fatal consequences. Ethel Mannin, another novelist who made her name in the Twenties, thought that Arlen had set out to establish a point, which was that a *demi-mondaine* like Iris can yet possess "integrity, courage, selfishness to the point of the quixotic". And "gallantry" – one might add – of a sort more usually associated with male heroes. The book's subtitle, 'A Romance for a Few People', hinted at snob appeal; the reader could join, or at least eavesdrop on, an elite. As the *Dictionary of National Biography* puts it:

> Arlen's pictures of London café society were as exact as glossy photographs. 'The Loyalty' – recognisable as the

Embassy club, at which the smartest people, including young princes, then danced to the blues – was depicted almost table by table, with a mixture of mockery and romanticism which delighted those who read of themselves.

But the novel's impact was universal, and sales topped 150,000 copies within a year of publication. Capitalising on his success, Arlen adapted *The Green Hat* as a play, which ran in London and, with a different cast, toured the USA. Both productions generated spin-off merchandise, with green millinery a must-have item of the season (a fashion that Evelyn Waugh later poked fun at in *Vile Bodies*.) The book was filmed in 1928 as a vehicle for Greta Garbo (at Garbo's own instigation), although the studio had to change the title (to *A Woman of Affairs*) and alter the characters' names and some of the lurid plot details in order to satisfy the Hays Code on morality.

To modern readers *The Green Hat* might seem like a farrago of improbabilities, of fatuous dialogue and rhythmic, empurpled prose. It was much parodied, and much derided by the intelligentsia. Such concerns didn't bother his original audience, for what Arlen gave his readers was the illusion of reading about fashionable people leading 'racy' lives, all evoked in a language of baroque ornamentation and narrated with an absolute determination to bring his fantasy world to life – a winning formula that, with the help of sound overseas investments, made him a millionaire, at least until taste started to move away from him in the 1930s.

I became interested several years ago in this forgotten figure. I went looking to see what had been written about him. Not much, it seemed. Apart from a German doctoral thesis in the 1930s and a recent volume in Armenian, there were only a couple of books published in the Seventies. One is a work primarily of literary criticism by an American professor, Harry Keyishian; the other is a memoir by Arlen's son, Michael J. Arlen, recalling his childhood and relationship with his exotic parents. The professor's book is valuable for taking Arlen more seriously as a writer than most people do nowadays. The son's book, *Exiles*, is a lively read but, like any such memoir, highly subjective and, as I was to discover, highly unreliable on facts. Is that a handicap? Ford Madox Ford was once arraigned for glaring mistakes in the articles which constituted his book of memoirs *Ancient Lights*. His response was to reprint them unchanged: "This book," Ford wrote, "is full of inaccuracies as to facts, but its accuracy as to impressions is absolute." What was lacking in Arlen's case, it seemed, was a book that was accurate as to facts *and* accurate as to impressions: in short, a biography. I resolved that I would be that biographer.

I began by identifying four categories of sources: his own published writings, his letters (all unpublished), his press coverage (which at the height of his success in the Twenties was considerable), and what I called his 'crossed paths' (those points where his life intersected with lives better documented and researched than his own – the lives of people, like Virginia Woolf, who for good reasons are better remembered than he is). Taking these in turn… Apart from some whimsical essay pieces in magazines like *The Tatler*, Arlen's own publications, fourteen volumes in all, are works of fiction, novels and short stories, or plays. In the words of John Haffenden, "one area in which the biographer can be a complete *menace* is when he or she reads creative works for factual information about the author's life". Well said. But on occasion Arlen positively invites us in. A couple of works, *The London Venture* (1920) and the 1929 short story 'Confessions of a Naturalized Englishman', employ a first-person narrator called Dikran Kouyoumdjian (Arlen's birth-name). These ventures into fictionalised autobiography, or if you prefer autobiographical fiction, have proved a 'menace'; they form the basis of the Wikipedia entry on Arlen. Here's a passage from *The London Venture*:

> ...I, up at Edinburgh, was on the high road to general fecklessness. I only stayed there a few months; jumbled months of elementary medicine, political economy, metaphysics, theosophy – I once handed round programmes at an Annie Besant lecture at the Usher Hall – and beer, lots of beer. And then, one night, I emptied my last mug, and [...] came down to London – "to take up a literary career" my biographer will no doubt write of me.

This passage is full of studied misdirection. In fact, the mischievous reference to "my biographer" looks like a gauntlet thrown down to the likes of me coming along later. When did he "come down to London"? He appears in the Edinburgh university registers for 1913-14. Elsewhere he implies that he dropped out before Christmas 1913 – certainly he stayed for no more than one academic year, as he does not appear on the university roll for a second year – but it's possible he remained until mid-1914. His reference to Annie Besant, president of the Theosophical Society, may be significant, for she gave only one lecture in Edinburgh at this time, in June 1914, and was out of the country for much of the preceding year. When he applied for British nationality in 1922, he told the authorities that he had left Edinburgh "a few months *after* the beginning of the War". But in the same application, when required to list his previous addresses, the first London address he gives is November 1915. In short, your biographer hasn't a clue where he was or what he was doing for the first year of the war.

Another example is the figure of Iris March in *The Green Hat*. Arlen always denied that this character was based on anyone in particular; at most, she was a composite of society women he had known. However, contemporaries, aware that he'd been in a short-lived relationship with poet, heiress and political activist Nancy Cunard, were quick to see parallels with Cunard. She recognised this and was unhappy with his use of gynaecological intimacies gleaned from their time together. "Part of that novel," she wrote later, "was inspired by the only too real circumstances around me in a hospital in Paris in December 1920 and Jan-Feb 1921. I did nearly die there, and he did hear me scream…" Yet, in other respects, reading fictional character against real-life prototype is frustrating and ill-advised. As Cunard's biographer, Anne Chisholm, has said: "The whole point about Iris [March] is that beneath her dashing, modern exterior and her bold disregard for conventions like chastity, she is a romantic idealist. Nancy [Cunard] certainly had a strong romantic streak, but she was far more advanced in behaviour and attitudes than the luckless Iris, who dies 'for purity.'"

My second category of sources was letters. When I contacted the son, hoping for access to family letters, he told me he had none (despite having quoted letters in his own memoir); he thought there might be a few elsewhere. In fact, by diligent search of archives (mostly in the US) I've found over a hundred of Arlen's letters. This isn't quite the *coup* I would have hoped. While they serve to fill in the chronology – telling me where he was and when – all too many of those preserved are formal responses to or issues of invitations, communications with publishers and broadcasters or discussion of matters now forgotten or difficult to identify decades later. Very little of Arlen's incoming correspondence survives (mostly in cases where business correspondents kept carbon copies of their outgoing mail), so it's like listening to one side of a phone call.

Reading these letters, I rarely get any sense of the man – which is why the absence of family correspondence (with the exception of a couple of letters to his mother and several to his siblings) is so disabling. Writing to female correspondents, he may drop his guard a little. I found three bundles that promised more. Some letters to Lillian Gish, the great silent movie star, that suggested a friendship formed on his first visit to Hollywood in 1925 – but in the absence of her replies, do they amount to any more than 'fan mail'? A series of affectionate letters dating from the Second World War to Republican Congresswoman Clare Boothe Luce; she was notorious for her extramarital affairs; was Arlen loyal to his marriage vows? Perhaps most intriguing were letters arising from a passionate attachment in 1926 to Audrey Emery, one of the so-called 'dollar princesses' who migrated from the US to Europe in expectation of trading their inherited wealth for a title and status. This was the real deal. Perhaps. When George Doran, his American publisher, came over to Europe, Arlen insisted that Doran meet his new *inamorata*. "Impossible not to admire her," Doran wrote later, "equally impossible not to see that she could never be Michael's woman. Michael was not pleased by my reactions to the evening, for I told him that much as he thought himself to be in love with her, she was in love only with life". (Shortly after her affair with Arlen, Audrey got a better offer and married Grand Duke Dmitri, one of the surviving members of the Romanov dynasty.) Here is a sample of Arlen in love:

> …Audrey, it's long since I discarded, in thinking of you, all the small knowledges of life, the little sciences of love that make what is called 'the world.' I've loved you always largely, completely, very sincerely, my dear. And I have been angry with myself for it. I have resented you. But now it is somehow all different. I am somehow washed clean of the vanity of being 'in love.' I love you and that's

all. And all words seem trifling, rather artificial when I want to let you know of my love, Words make such fools of so-called clever men, dear. Oh, how well I know that – how I have suffered for it! Your beauty is the horizon of my life. I see that now. I don't mean, my darling, just your 'classic' features. For, you see, you are a rare and perilous woman – there is no end to you, as there is to the fascinations of most women. That is your glory, my dear, and perhaps your misfortune. Your beauty fills the cup of my dreams because it suggests something even more beautiful than itself…

The kind soul who was first alerted to the existence of these letters commented to me: "Oh, I've been *that* in love in my time. Hope *my* letters don't survive. Well, why should they? I never wrote *The Green Hat*." My reaction was a little more jaded. While not doubting the genuineness of the emotion that prompted them, I saw stylisation, 'self-fashioning'. Michael-Arlen-in-love was speaking like a Michael Arlen character in a Michael Arlen novel. He was once asked what was his greatest success. "Well," the author replied, reaching into his clutch-bag of ready-made aphorisms, "the best thing I ever did was to create Michael Arlen."

My third category of sources was press coverage. It's only when you dip into the newsprint that you realise how, for a few years, in the later 1920s, Arlen was one of the most famous people on either side of the Atlantic. At the birth of the modern 'celebrity' industry, newspapers couldn't get enough of him: where he went, what he wore, whom he saw, how much he earned from his writings. In the hope of attracting publishers' attention, I composed a biographical extract narrating his first visit to the US in 1925. This was compiled almost entirely from news reports, all I had to go on – endless gossip columns recounting how New York's hostesses competed for the privilege of entertaining him, arranging lavish parties "each for the purpose of introducing the author to herself". My effort may have seemed a pleasing *jeu d'esprit*, but it didn't please me. The material basis was plentiful but shallow. I was reminded of an oft-quoted passage in Julian Barnes's novel *Flaubert's Parrot*, itself a meditation on the difficulties of biography:

> You can define a net in one of two ways, depending on your point of view. Normally, you would say that it is a meshed instrument designed to catch fish. But you could, with no great injury to logic, reverse the image and define a net as a jocular lexicographer once did: he called it a collection of holes tied together with string.
>
> You can do the same with a biography. The trawling net fills, then the biographer hauls it in, sorts, throws back, stores, fillets and sells. Yet consider what he doesn't catch: there is always far more of that…

What emerged when I strung together my newspaper reports was nothing but "a collection of holes tied together with string". Too much had escaped the net.

My final source, 'crossed paths', was the most promising. I was delighted to find how my subject turned up, like Zelig in the Woody Allen film, at key moments in history. When Scott and Zelda Fitzgerald were in the midst of another marital squabble in 1930, there he was. When D.H. Lawrence was seeking recruits for his utopian colony in Florida in 1915, young Arlen (not yet called 'Arlen') stepped forward. In 1928 when Lawrence was finalising *Lady Chatterley's Lover* in Florence, up popped Arlen again, so Lawrence put him into the novel as the minor character of 'Michaelis'. When Winston Churchill was reclining on the Riviera at Maxine Elliott's villa in 1935, who should turn up to argue politics with him but Michael Arlen. When Stalin's first wife committed suicide, Stalin (according to their daughter, at least) blamed it on the pernicious book she'd been reading, *The Green Hat*. And so on. Charlie Chaplin. Oswald Mosley. Lord Beaverbrook. Gore Vidal... These were exciting leads to follow up, but as I rarely had Arlen's version of the encounter, they suffered, like the letters, from one-sidedness. Often the accumulating anecdotes told me more about the person he encountered than about the man I was seeking. And when Arlen himself told the story, it was just that – a story. In a column in *The Tatler* in 1940, 'I Knew Dr Goebbels', he regaled his readers with how, once in Athens before the war, he had found himself staying in the same hotel as the Reich's propaganda minister. When Goebbels appeared on a balcony below, Arlen spat on the Nazi's "superb silk hat". He missed, but despite his poor aim he was on the right side of history. By the time this story reappeared in his son's memoir thirty years later, it had been thoroughly Arlenized. Now Arlen senior, spotting his victim on the balcony below, "went to the sideboard, mixed a Martini, very exquisitely called down to Goebbels, and poured it on his upturned face". Well, the history books will tell you when Goebbels was in Athens – which adds some verisimilitude to the tale – but they don't speak of misdirected spittle or the waste of a good cocktail.

So here I had assembled my four source categories: writings, letters, press and famous paths crossed. I collated, cross-indexed, began to write. The life had a convenient 'story arc', from obscurity to celebrity and back to obscurity, which seemed ready made for the conventional cradle-to-grave tomes you see stacked high in Waterstones. But very soon I stumbled. Too late in the day I realised I knew virtually nothing about my subject's childhood. By dint of enormous effort I'd managed to extract a little information from Bulgarian archives about his nineteenth-century antecedents and about the family's business enterprises, but none of this illuminated the life of a child – one particular child – growing up in an immigrant community in north-west England at the start of the twentieth century. More generally, I had no access to his inner life. I couldn't get inside his head. I couldn't tell the story from *his* point of view. So I resolved to step back, to examine my own practice and reflect on the challenges of literary biography and how biographers have faced them.

From the start I had seen my task as 'forensic'. Like a detective I would collect witness statements, compare their testimony, decide on the credibility of witnesses and propose my best estimate of what 'really' happened. No 'fact' should be admitted that was not verifiable. This might work for other subjects; it was ill-suited to Arlen, for here was a man who never let the 'truth' get in the way of a good story, whose anecdotes were polished smooth as pebbles by retelling, who palpably treated himself as if he were a character in one of his own overheated fictions. Alec Waugh, who knew him better than most, remarked that "in 1924 Michael Arlen was a composite production, the writer and the man were one." On meeting him again in the late Forties, Waugh noted that his friend, who hadn't published anything for years, "could now be Michael Arlen more effectively by *not* writing". The persona had replaced the person – if there was ever a person there in the first place. He is not the only writer to present such challenges to the biographer. Arlen's near contemporary Ford Madox Ford is described by one of his biographers as "a living fictional construct" who told stories not just in his novels but in his memoirs, letters and conversations too. Ford spoke of how the writer must "romance a little when he talks of himself. Then that romance becomes part of himself and is the true truth". What is truth, said jesting Pilate, and would not stay for an answer. What, indeed, is "true truth"?

Virginia Woolf wrestled with these questions. She was as interested in life-writing as in fiction. In an essay of 1927 on 'The New Biography' she wrote:

> On the one hand there is truth; on the other there is personality. And if we think of truth as something of granite-like solidity and of personality as something of rainbow-like intangibility and reflect that the aim of biography is to weld these two into one seamless whole, we shall admit that the problem is a stiff one and that we need not wonder if biographers have for the most part failed to solve it.

Woolf was writing in the wake of her friend Lytton Strachey's experiments in biography, beginning with his *Eminent Victorians* in 1918, that manifesto for Bloomsbury's debunking of its fathers and grandfathers. Here facts needed to be deployed selectively; the true life was the inner life. Character, she suggested, could be displayed in "the tone of a voice, the turn of a head, some little phrase or anecdote picked up in passing." By the time she returned to the problem in the late Thirties, she was struggling to write a commissioned life of the painter and art critic Roger Fry. Her diaries record what "drudgery" this was for the novelist in her. May 5, 1938: "How can one cut loose from facts, when there they are, contradicting my theories." In another notebook she is still struggling with how to unite the "granite" and the "rainbow". "Facts have their importance," she writes, but "the biographer cannot extract the atom. He gives us the husk. Therefore, as things are, the best method would be to separate the two kinds of truth. Let the biographer print fully, completely, accurately, the known facts without comment; then let him write the life as fiction."

Woolf's role as both novelist and biographer is intriguing, because the relationship between novelists and biographers is often an antagonistic one. Biographers in fiction get a bad press. In William Golding's novel *The Paper Men*, his novelist hero is woken at night by the noise of his house-guest and aspiring biographer Professor Rick L. Tucker rifling through his dustbin in search of discarded manuscripts. In A.S. Byatt's *Possession*, the biographer Professor Mortimer P. Cropper (another American, I'm afraid) is caught literally robbing the subject's grave in search of a revealing letter he believes was buried in the coffin. Henry James gave us another predatory biographer in *The Aspern Papers*. In that instance art followed life, or *vice versa*, for in the very year the story was published James made a "gigantic bonfire" of his personal papers. As he wrote to his nephew later, "my sole wish is to frustrate as utterly as possible the postmortem exploiter". Principal among such exploiters was what James Joyce called the "biografiend", the biographer who will stop at nothing to get his man.

What, then, is the biographer's ethical responsibility towards his or her subject? If the subject is safely dead, there is no fear of libel suits, but there are still living relatives to be considered, testamentary wishes of the deceased writer to be respected or disregarded as conscience dictates. I found no evidence that Arlen made any provision, for good or ill, against future biographers. His son, who is also his literary executor, made no effort to block my researches, albeit while setting limits to the scope of his cooperation. His attitude was that he had said what he wanted to say in his own memoir. My 'forensic' examination has shown up factual errors in his account but I hesitate to confront him with these. Perhaps, like Ford Madox Ford, he'd respond that his book was "absolute" in its "accuracy as to impressions".

What is special about literary biography – the lives of writers – as opposed to other types of biography? In the early to mid-twentieth century some critics argued that literary biography was a fallacious quest for the origins of works: fallacious, because anything relevant to an autonomous work was by definition contained within it. T.S. Eliot asserted that "the more perfect the artist, the more completely separate in him will be the man who suffers and the mind which creates." However, by the end of the century, with a great upsurge in sales of biography and the arrival of master biographers like Michael Holroyd and Richard Holmes, the genre underwent a renaissance. The notion of biography as a necessary supplement to the author's work was usually implicit. At its best, this means demonstrating what Richard Ellmann, biographer of James Joyce, called the "participation of the artist in two simultaneous processes" – understanding the writing as a source for, as well as the outcome of, the life. At its worst it means crass amateur psychologising in the attempt to map fictional plots onto the novelist's life events. As taboos have fallen away, there is no aspect of the writer's life that is not open for inspection. Evelyn Waugh's biographers are not content to tell us that their subject died in the lavatory: we need all the details. Martin Stannard finds a "faint whiff of the grotesque" in the manner of his demise, a detail consonant with some of the stranger deaths in Waugh's novels. Potentially, anything in the life can be read against the fiction, and *vice-versa*. But we may go to writers' lives for other reasons. Ann Thwaite begins her monumental biography of A.A. Milne by telling us that, while she will put his children's books in context, "there is no question, as there is with the biographies of the majority of writers, of making any attempt to illuminate the most important texts". For illumination on Winnie-the-Pooh (a "foolish enterprise", she calls it) she suggests *The Pooh Perplex*, Frederick Crews's great collection of spoof criticism.

If illumination is not a *sine qua non* of the literary biography, there may even be a market for biographies of writers who led exotic, eventful lives but are no longer read: Joan Hardwick's biography of Elinor Glyn is an instance, a life that makes almost no reference to Glyn's numerous romantic novels, except to note where they were adapted for the cinema. (Perhaps this is the appropriate niche for an Arlen biography?) Janet Malcolm has suggested that what really underlies the genre's popularity is the "transgressive" nature of biography. Readers are tolerant of even the most badly written books because they feel they are colluding with the biographer in "an excitingly forbidden undertaking: tiptoeing down the corridor together, to stand in front of the bedroom door and try to peep through the keyhole". (Or to stand in front of the toilet door, in Evelyn Waugh's case?)

Collusion requires that the reader *trust* the biographer. The reader needs to feel that their self-appointed guide to another person's life is up to the task. If the subject is a major writer, has the biographer the literary sensitivity to lock horns with such a big beast? Biography is often rife with speculation – inevitably so – but as John Haffenden has written in a critique of Peter Ackroyd's life of T.S. Eliot, "speculation is only credible and creditable when the reader's confidence is secured. We do not feel confidence in cliché... or a metaphorical mixture which muddles analysis... any more than we trust unsupported and prejudicial imputations..." Could *I* be trusted? There were so many holes in my net that could only be filled by speculation.

John Worthen, biographer of D.H. Lawrence, has a brilliant essay which came to my aid at this low point in my ruminations. He calls on us to acknowledge what he calls the "necessary ignorance of a biographer", writing: "Not only do biographers necessarily remain profoundly ignorant of many things in the lives of their subjects, but the narrative of a biography is in almost every case designed to conceal the different kinds of ignorance from which we suffer". For example, there is the illusion of omniscience. Publishers market biographies as "definitive"; they'll tell you everything you want to know because the biographer knows everything. If the manuscript comes in too short, it'll be printed in larger font or on thicker paper: omniscience requires bulk. Very often the biographer doesn't know why something happened. He or she circumvents this problem by presenting the event as 'inevitable'. With the benefit of hindsight any event can be presented this way, but in reality we live our lives forwards, not backwards. The authors of the multi-volume Cambridge biography of D.H. Lawrence, of whom John Worthen was the first, eschewed this convention. Where earlier biographies, treating Lawrence's first meeting with his future wife Frieda, might begin "little did Lawrence know as entered that suburban Nottingham drawing-room that the next half hour would change his life", in the Cambridge biography the reader, like the historical Lawrence, accompanies Lawrence into that drawing-room in ignorance of what, if anything, will ensue. Is something lost here? Well, we're accustomed to the soothing effect of imposing order on the sheer randomness of life. The biographer reaches into the toolkits of the novelist and the historian – to build up tension at the end of a chapter ("the next half hour would change the course of his life…") or to tell you that, while the subject was quietly correcting the galleys of his novel, the storm clouds were gathering over Europe and jackboots were on the march. When you examine biographies critically, you notice how often they are organised for the convenience of the biographer. Every biography will depend on the random survival of source materials and the availability of facts. If we had different materials, we could, and would, write a different life. Yet, as Worthen comments, the illusion the biographer must create is that "the facts which we happen to know are also necessarily the important ones"; otherwise, trustworthiness and omniscience are called into question. My conclusion from researching Arlen's biography was that while I had sufficient evidence to cast doubt on his own versions of events, I didn't have enough to substitute a more accurate version. Perhaps I should draw encouragement from Claire Tomalin's biography of Ellen Ternan, mistress of Charles Dickens. After summarising the probable events of the years 1861-5 in the couple's joint lives, she bravely admits: "Some or all of this may be wrong…"

Thus I began to question whether biography was any more than a kind of confidence trick. By sleight-of-hand these dishonest ghouls were concealing their ignorance. Whether they had too much material or too little, somehow it was 'just right' for their purposes. Can we ever *know* another person? They undertook to ventriloquise for the dead, yet often remained silent on their own motives. No wonder novelists portrayed them as villains. What arrogance persuaded them that they could narrate anyone's life but their own? Perhaps all biography is a form of autobiography? And a related question: If a biographer turns autobiographer, how does *that* work? You're accustomed to scholarly research, to the forensic examination of sources. You know that memoirs, by their very subjectivity, are to be treated with scepticism. Do you bring the same critical scrutiny to bear on your own memories? From experience you know how memory rearranges and collapses events, how it suppresses what happened and sometimes invents what never happened. When reading someone else's recollections, you'd make every effort to compare and check their memories against other people's; and whenever they were bystanders at public events or brushed up against people in the public eye, you'd know to check dates and places and published sources to establish The Facts. All this is much easier nowadays, thanks to the all-knowing Internet. Yet, when telling our own stories, these principles fall away. There's a primacy to our own memories. We are ferried along on our own memory-stream and depend upon it for a sense of our continuous identity. If you recount a favourite anecdote from your past and the listener says, "That couldn't have happened – X wasn't in Y in 19--." it's as good as a blow to the solar plexus. Or so it seems to me… By the same token, every memory you preserve is significant to you, even if others might dismiss it as trivial…

If biography is a search for 'truth', then whose truth? It occurred to me that, having turned myself into a 'world-authority' on the life of this now obscure figure, I could assert almost anything about him, without fear of contradiction. This lowers the bar of veracity. To be honest to myself means not telling an untruth, yet is a serial fibber like Arlen worth the expenditure of so much moral capital?

I decided there were, perhaps, five ways out of this impasse. As categories they overlap, but I call them: quest, travelogue, diary, encounter and confessional. Some successful biographies have been structured in the form of a personal quest. My favourite example – and a classic of the genre – is *The Quest for Corvo: An Experiment in Biography*, by A.J.A. Symons (1932). It's a biography of Frederick Rolfe: angry, pugilistic turn-of-the-century novelist, picker of quarrels, embittered failed priest, who called himself 'Baron Corvo'. Symons himself was a dandyish bibliophile and aesthete who was drawn to this colourful character, and his book foregrounds the biographer's search for his subject. Like a detective, he is led from one clue to another, one witness to another, all the time building up and deepening his knowledge, which starts simply from a newspaper obituary. There is no pretence of objectivity, nor of 'definitiveness', although the book reaches a satisfying resolution when Symons locates the last of the 'lost' manuscripts of Rolfe's novels to which he has been alerted by witnesses in the preceding chapters.

The Quest for Corvo is also part-travelogue as Symons's pursuit of his quarry takes him to Wales and Italy. The greatest living exponent of the biography-as-travelogue is Richard Holmes, whose book *Footsteps: Adventures of a Romantic*

Biographer (1985) is a benchmark. Holmes believes that the serious biographer must physically pursue his subject through the past: "he must go to all the places where the subject had ever lived or worked, or travelled or dreamed". For his first book, following Robert Louis Stevenson through the wild Cévennes, he slept out deliberately like his subject under the stars, in a small sleeping-bag without a tent. For his later Coleridge biography he tramped through Devon and the Lake District, took ship for Germany and Malta. This is another perfect match of biographer and biographee: the Romantic poets lend themselves particularly to this treatment. Holmes uses two-sided notebooks. On one page he can transcribe what the poet saw, as recorded vividly in letters and diaries, on the opposing page he notes his personal responses, speculations and questions. "Only in this way," Holmes writes, "could I use, but also hope to master, the biographer's most valuable but perilous weapon: empathy".

My next thought was the diary method. One accidental outcome of my Arlen researches is that I had, effectively, reconstructed a category of documents which, were his effects better preserved, I would have anyway: namely, his appointments diaries. Whom he saw, when and where. Since much of my knowledge came from secondary sources, this would be a 'ghost' diary. There'd be no substantive 'entries', just pages of annotations. I would be relegated from biographer to editor: a loss of status, admittedly, but at a stroke I'd be free of these self-lacerating cogitations about the proper role of a 'biographer'.

Then I returned to my 'crossed paths', those seventy or so figures, many of them still household names, who crossed Arlen's path and lived to tell the tale. Perhaps a composite work could be written, as much about them as about Arlen? Something like Craig Brown's *One on One* (2011), which comprises 101 "true encounters" between famous people, the trick being that, like a baton relay, each chapter reintroduces a figure from the chapter before and introduces a new celebrity whose story is then picked up in the following chapter.

My final solution, the 'confessional', was to come clean, to lay bare all my misgivings about the limitations of biography. As in those maths tests at school where the exam paper instructed you to "show all working", I would show all *my* working; the rough scaffolding of construction would be exposed, necessary ignorance conceded, my own biases and subjectivity confronted. Biography as *mea culpa*.

I've no idea if any of these approaches would be appropriate by itself, but a combination might just hack it. For the conscientious biographer, every such question threatens to become what Sherlock Holmes would call a "three-pipe problem". Perhaps I am over-thinking all this? Or was Lytton Strachey right in saying that "it is perhaps as difficult to write a good life as to live one"?

In short, I am speechless with admiration for the literary biographers who do this sort of thing for a living.

EARLY LIFE

To be an Armenian in the Ottoman Empire was never easy. Officially they were a part of a multi-national, multi-faith realm, but as a Christian minority they had to endure official discrimination and second-class citizenship. To maintain their freedom of worship and sense of community, they had to endure inequalities including special taxes, the inadmissibility of legal testimony and a prohibition on bearing arms. As long as the Empire was strong and expanding, they lived in relative peace, but when an autocrat took charge or the Empire was under external threat, their position became more perilous – culminating in the infamous genocide of 1915.[1] Those who were tenant farmers or sharecroppers remained rooted to their historic homeland, but the mercantile classes were more mobile, and it was to this group that Arlen traced his ancestry.

The Kouyoumdjians' origins lie in the ancient city of Ani on the Armenian plateau. At some point they began a migration westward and southward that took them first to Istanbul, "thwarted kiss of two continents" in Robert Byron's famous description, before they landed in Bulgaria, at the fringes of the Ottoman Empire.[2] This was perhaps the beginning of the nineteenth century, by which point the Armenian population in Bulgaria had grown to 140,000.³ Many were professional men and artisans, working as doctors, pharmacists, jewellers, tailors, masons and builders. There were significant Armenian settlements in Sofia and Varna, but the Kouyoumdjians' business interests seem to have taken them first to Plovdiv (then better known by its Western name of Philippopolis) before they settled finally in the Danube port of Ruse. With its handsome boulevards and ornate buildings, and bridges and ferries over the river to Romania, Ruse was a trading hub and meeting-point of cultures, a suitably cosmopolitan background for a family whose members would later end up in England, the Americas and the Middle East. Already a centre of the Bulgarian national revival, the city became part of the newly independent Bulgarian state in 1878 following the Ottoman defeat in the Russo-Turkish War.

Ruse was the birthplace, in 1859, of Sarkis Kouyoumdjian, who would later prosper as a merchant and philanthropist in the city. He married a local girl, Satinik Aslanian, at the Armenian church in 1883, and they went on to have five children: a daughter, Ahavni, and four sons, Roupen, Tacvor, Krikor and – last of all, on 16 November 1895, Dikran, the future 'Michael Arlen'. Sarkis was in business with his father-in-law Garabed Aslanian, and together they founded a trading company with its head office in Ruse and branches in Varna, Plovdiv and Sofia. It seems to have been an eclectic import-export business, trading in fabrics, hardware, watches, jewellery and a diversity of other products.

Showcase for the family business was an imposing neo-Rococo building on Otets Paisii Street, completed in 1900. Effectively Ruse's first department store, the stone-tiled ground floor was 560 square metres of retail space. On the upper floor, of clinker bricks with embedded stone decorative details, was warehousing. One customer recalled how the big beautiful store sold imported goods like Russian galoshes and baboushkas.[4] The building still stands, its ground floor occupied by the popular 'Chiflika' tavern, the upper storey now the Danube Arts and Crafts Centre.

Dikran was born in the family's spacious house on the corner of Dondukov-Korsakov Street and Panayot Volov. Designed by Spiros Valsamaki in Ruse's historicist style, the building is still there, albeit a little dilapidated, home now to an Armenian cultural centre. The memory preserved within the Aslanian family is that Satinik took a special interest in her youngest son's upbringing. She is remembered by her descendants as a talented piano-player, a speaker of several languages and a passionate reader who encouraged Dikran to explore her library of world classics. The memories on the Kouyoumdjian side are less flattering. Arlen's son, Michael John, who knew her only at the very end of her life, recalls "a dear, small, old lady, seemingly always in black, and lace, and rimless eyeglasses, and with a smell of old flowers" who still struggled to speak English.[5]

Sarkis had two brothers and while the youngest, Vagharshag, joined the business in Ruse as a partner, the other, Manouk, forged international ties by moving to Manchester in 1892. Manouk appears at various addresses in and around the city in the following decade and in 1897 successfully applied for British nationality.[6] Sarkis himself, though he never became a British subject, must have travelled frequently between the two countries in the 1890s; the Manchester Trade Directory for 1894 has a listing for a "Sarkis Kouyoumdjian, shipping merchant" and he was sufficient of a presence in England to be elected to the Manchester Chamber of Commerce in 1897, while continuing to exercise a managerial (and paternal) role in Bulgaria.[7]

By 1900 the British connection was evidently flourishing and Sarkis took the decision to move his entire family to England.[8] The older children must have received elementary education in

Bulgaria – perhaps in part though the Armenian church, since they seem to have had a knowledge of written Armenian not shared by their youngest sibling. Schooling for Dikran, only four at the time, would await him in his new-found land.

Sarkis operated the business from central Manchester, appearing in the records first at Albert Square (1906-7), then in Whitworth Street (from 1908). The family settled initially in south Manchester, at 102 Palatine Road, Withington. This was an area already popular with *émigrés* – the presence of many Jewish immigrants gave rise to its jocular alternative name of 'Palestine Road' – and home by the turn of the century to many Armenians. The young Dikran was enrolled at a private preparatory school in nearby Didsbury.[9]

In 1906 the British business was registered as a limited company under the title of the 'Anglo-Bulgarian Company, Sarkis Kouyoumdjian Ltd'.[10] Sarkis's priorities in his new country, once the business was on a sound footing, were to see his daughter make an advantageous match, preferably within the Armenian community, and to see his school-age sons fashioned by education into English gentlemen.

The first ambition got off to a rocky start. On 4 April 1907 Ahavni walked out of her marital home, Orsett Terrace, Bayswater, accompanied by her father and brother Roupen. In October 1902 she had married Vahan Gulbenkian in a private ceremony at a London townhouse according to Armenian rites. For the eighteen-year-old Ahavni this was an arranged marriage (there was some doubt whether it was even legal under English law) and it was not a happy one, however propitious it might have looked on paper. Her bridegroom belonged to one of the most successful of Armenian immigrant families and was an older brother of the future oil baron and philanthropist Calouste Gulbenkian, or 'Mr Five Per-Cent' as he was popularly known in recognition of his business acumen. It was Ahavni who initiated divorce proceedings against her husband "by reason of the incapacity of the respondent to consummate marriage with the petitioner". He seems to have counter-sued, for, according to court records, following Ahavni's departure her husband petitioned the High Court in July 1907 for "restitution of conjugal rights". Nonetheless, the marriage was declared "null and void" in July 1908. Both parties would go on to make successful second marriages, Vahan defying the aspersions cast on his virility in the court case by fathering three children by his second wife.[11]

In April 1909, aged thirteen, Dikran was sent to join his older brother Krikor as a boarder at Malvern College. Lying at the foot of the Malvern Hills in the heart of England and founded in the 1860s "for the Education of the Sons of gentlemen", this all-boys public school was pre-eminent in sport. Indeed, the county in which it nestled was sometimes referred to as "Fostershire" after the dynasty of cricketers, the seven sons of Rev. Henry Foster and Old Malvernians to a man, who had gone on to play for their county. Since Arlen's name does not appear among the sports stars, it is safe to assume that the cultural life was his escape from the demands of competitive games. He took 'arts' subjects, according to school records, and was an elected member of the essay society later known as the Wheeler Bennett Society. Known as 'Dick', he was appointed a House Prefect in 'House 5', which was quite an honour in those days, but, unlike most apprentice writers, seems not to have sharpened his pen in the pages of the school magazine.[12] C.S. Lewis spent an unhappy year at Malvern, beginning just as Dikran left in 1913. He records at some length in his autobiography the crushing effect of the English public school ethos on a sensitive boy from beyond the Home Counties (Lewis grew up in Northern Ireland.) How much of this weighed likewise on young Dikran is hard to say. Certainly, Lewis's description of the 'Bloods', whose most important qualification was athletic prowess and who ruled at the top of a pyramid of which the 'fags' formed the exploited base, resonates with Arlen. For Lewis, "fagging was with us as impersonal as the labour-market in Victorian England... All boys under a certain seniority constituted a labour pool, the common property of all the Bloods".[13] This was somewhat inaccurate, since only prefects had 'fags', and historians of the school counter that many boys "took the hierarchy in their stride and approved of it even when they were still at the bottom".[14] In his novel '*Piracy*' (1922), Arlen would reduce the relationships to a witty formula, which gives little idea of how he viewed it: "The difference between a College Prefect – Coll Pree – and a House Prefect – House Pree – is that a Coll Pree can do what he likes everywhere, and a House Pree can do what he likes in his House. Inferiors can do what they like in their studies, more or less. Fags can't do what they like anywhere."[15] Entries in the school prefects' minute-books from before World War I show a range of disciplinary offences, from smoking through swearing and lewd talk to "meeting and talking to girls on Sundays", spreading scandal, and "disgusting behaviour".[16]

Several incidents from his time at Malvern found their way into Arlen's fiction. The most celebrated was that of the 'Night Prowler':

> It would have been almost bearable if the night-prowler had prowled only about the grounds, but he prowled into the Houses, he prowled actually into the house-masters' sides of the House; he prowled into their studies, he sat on their chairs, he read their books, he drank their port, he tested their barley water, he smoked their cigars, he left a neat little bit of Greek verse on their desks to thank them for same – and then, as it were for a joke, he bolted the windows from the inside, locked the doors from the outside, and left the keys in such an obvious place that

no one ever found them until new ones had been made. And this went on, once or twice a week, for more than a month!¹⁷

Watch was kept; a detective made a bungled attempt to apprehend the felon. Eventually, the culprit was identified. A search in houses during chapel one Sunday morning led to the discovery of torch, jemmy, and a photograph of the boy in burglar's costume in his locker. In *'Piracy'*, Arlen used this incident as the pretext for his hero Ivor Marlay's expulsion from school. Marlay's real-life original suffered a similar fate.¹⁸

Arlen himself was guilty of no such pranks, but his autobiographical fiction hints at the prejudice he inevitably suffered as a foreigner. The masters ragged him over his curious surname. "'Now tell me, is it pronounced Guimjun or Cowjan?'" one of them demanded to know. (Ironic, really, since this master's name was 'Mugliston', which he insisted on pronouncing 'Muggleston'.)¹⁹ In *The London Venture* a schoolfellow he calls "Marsden", a "dark-haired, sallow-faced youth" accuses young 'Dikran' of being an "Armenian Jew". Arlen, confident that he is not Jewish and suspecting there is no such thing anyway as an Armenian Jew, is riled and, actuated by "a base passion for notoriety", aims a jam pot at his accuser's head, striking him neatly just above the right eye. His punishment is "six cuts from a very supple cane" and the assignment to write a Georgic. This defiance earns Dikran the respect of a contemporary he calls "Louis" who started a term after him; as robustly English as Dikran was visibly alien, Louis moves effortlessly from the dormitories of Malvern to officer training at Sandhurst. Together, later reunited in London, the friends form a "club for Well Mannered People", but Louis is among the earliest to be drafted to the Western Front, only "to die in his first attack with a bullet in his chest".²⁰

Warren Lewis, C.S. Lewis's older brother, was an exact contemporary of Arlen's at Malvern. Preserved among the Lewis family papers are some disobliging remarks that Warren made about his schoolfellow. Arlen, recalled Lewis Sr., in those days "was still an Armenian boy called Kouyoumgjain" [sic]. He made no mark of any kind at school, being one of a trinity of 'dagoes' of whom the other two were also in my house".[21] In his first couple of years at the school, the presence of Arlen's older brother must have been a solace (Krikor left in 1911) at times of adversity.

Many hours were spent playing competitive sport or being compelled to watch other people play it. Boredom is a recurrent plaint in school memoirs of the era. However, for boys of a less athletic turn, there were compensations at Malvern. The well-stocked College Library, known as the Grundy, was a place of sanctuary. Even the most vulnerable pupil was 'unfaggable' once he had gained its doors. C.S. Lewis's turn to the classics and to English literature was much inspired by his Latin master at Malvern, Harry Wakelyn Smith, known to the boys as 'Smugy', a bespectacled, donnish figure who was a friend of Sir Edward Elgar.[22] Forty years later Lewis still recalled the drama, rhythm and sensuality with which this pedagogue recited English poetry, how his pupils were in thrall as "every verse he read turned into music on his lips". There can be little doubt Smugy was among Arlen's teachers also. For Rebecca West, a friend of Arlen's in the Twenties, the best to be said about his schooling was that it sent Arlen out into the world "with such a knowledge of literature that the line 'they flee from me that sometime did me seek' would start him off reciting most of the best of Wyatt, and that with the right rhythms, which are not simple."[23]

Among Arlen's contemporaries at school was the future literary critic Raymond Mortimer. A decade later, after Mortimer had made some generous comments about Arlen in a *New*

Statesman review, the novelist attempted to renew acquaintance. "As I think on the train which you yourself started, my memory goes as far as a House number three cap," Arlen mused. "In spite of your horror of meeting novelists, and your very decent reluctance to biting the hands that feed you... I should still like to meet you because of the pleasure I have had from some of the things you say: and the profit, in a personal way."[24]

Arlen's uncle, Manouk, already well-established in England, had meanwhile moved with his own young family to the seaside town of Southport and this seems to have inspired Sarkis Kouyoumdjian to do the same. For much of the nineteenth century, Southport had been the most popular seaside resort in the north of England. Despite this it never became over-commercialised and much of the town centre retained an elegance that draws admirers to this day. For these successful entrepreneurs, it offered a leafier and healthier retreat than the Manchester suburbs. At the time of the 1911 census Sarkis, listed as a "shipper of manufactured goods", was settled at 2 Cambridge Road, Southport, with his wife, two adult children (the now-divorced Ahavni and Tacvor, a "clerk in the shippers' trade"), a Bulgarian nurse (this 65-year-old widow was evidently a family retainer to whom they owed a continuing loyalty), a Greek housemaid and a Welsh cook. By 1913 they had moved again, to 6 Hesketh Road, the spacious home which would remain in the family's ownership until the early 1980s.[25] When Arlen left school in July 1913, this is the house he returned to. Several years later, he evoked the scene from his bedroom window:

> Looking aimlessly for consolation, I turn to the windows; windows seem, somehow, to be far more commanding in a bedroom than in any other room. It chances that the scene from mine has the tranquillising effect that my ruffled temper is in need of. Over a stretch of golf-

links, with their churchyard mounds and hillocks, their patches of affectedly smooth velvet, I can dimly see tracts of sand, disappearing endlessly into thick curtains of mist; and behind the mist is the sea. Perhaps indoors the wind seems shriller and fiercer than it really is; but if the gale is all it sounds, then the mist is hiding from me just what, above all things, I most want to see; for I love to watch this dirty grey Irish sea being at last roused from its monotonous sulkiness to great heights of anger; wave after wave, great rollers of them, capped with surf as they come near, some weakening and retiring beaten, some leaping too soon and sprawling nearer helplessly till they are over-ridden in a shower of oncoming spray; and some big and strong, battling their way easily and proudly, rearing surf-covered crests, and crashing down with a roar, to come licking venomously at your feet– this is the Irish sea when the wind blows. Yet, I confess, this scene more often serves to foster than to satisfy my longing.[26]

In autumn 1913 Arlen matriculated at Edinburgh University. In his fictionalised account, he was destined for Oxford:

Even now I don't know why I went to Edinburgh and not to Oxford; I had always intended going to Oxford, my family had always intended that I should go to Oxford, up to the last moment I was actually going to Oxford– when, suddenly, with a bowler hat crammed over my left ear and a look of vicious obstinacy, I decided that I would go to Edinburgh instead. Of course it was a silly mistake. The only thing I have gained by not going to Oxford is an utter inability to write poetry and a sort of superior contempt for all pale, interesting-looking young men with dark eyes and spiritual hair who are tremendously concerned about the utter worthlessness of Mr. William Watson's poetry. [...] I, up at Edinburgh, was on the high road to general fecklessness. I only stayed there a few months; jumbled months of elementary medicine, political economy, metaphysics, theosophy – I once handed round programs at an Annie Besant lecture at the Usher Hall – and beer, lots of beer.[27]

It is often assumed from this account that Arlen enrolled as a medical student. In fact, he was in the arts faculty and, since he had not taken sciences at school, was unlikely to have been accepted onto a medical course.[28] One reason for this self-invention may have been the high reputation of the Edinburgh medical faculty, whose distinguished graduates included Arthur Conan Doyle. J.M. Barrie and Robert Louis Stevenson also attended the university, adding to its lustre for an aspiring man of letters. Arlen did not stay long, "a few months". Elsewhere he implies that he had dropped out before Christmas[29] – certainly he stayed for no more than one academic year, as he does not appear on the university roll for a second year – but I think it possible he remained until mid-1914. His reference to Annie Besant, president of the Theosophical Society, may be significant, for she gave only one lecture in Edinburgh at this time, in June 1914,[30] and was out of the country for much of the preceding year. When he applied for British nationality in 1922, he told the authorities that he had left Edinburgh "a few months after the beginning of the War",[31] but this is hard to verify, as is the claim by Compton Mackenzie to have encountered a carefree Arlen on a train in northern France in July 1914: "When I told him we were hurrying home in case war was on its way he smiled indulgently at my overheated fancy".[32] (Maybe, at the time of this last encounter, he was on his way back from Switzerland, where he claimed to have completed his education and "specialised in bridge".[33])

> And then, one night, I emptied my last mug, and with another side-glance at Oxford, came down to London; "to take up a literary career" my biographer will no doubt write of me. I may of course have had a "literary career" at the back of my mind, but as it was I slacked outrageously...'[34]

Arlen's first known address in London was 46 Redcliffe Road, where he lodged from November 1915.[35] If he was in the capital for a year or more previously, where was he living? Nancy Cunard recalled mention of a "miserable room in muddy Whitechapel".[36] One possibility is that he traded on his school's old-boy network to find both a place to live and worthwhile occupation. Since the 1880s, Malvern College had run a Christian mission in the East End of London, its purpose to spread the College's ethos beyond those who could afford to pay for it, "to better the lot of the poor, and cast a ray of sunshine into their dark and gloomy homes, and bring up the little children in the light of Christianity". The Mission flourished in Arlen's day under the headmastership of Sydney Rhodes James, and the resident missioner would report termly to the school assembly and encourage past and present pupils to visit Canning Town to see the social transformation being wrought. A key figure was Reginald Kennedy-Cox, Old Malvernian and sometime playwright, who became a social worker at the Mission in 1908 following a visit to the Old Bailey, where he'd gone in search of material for a play. The sight of a young sailor from the East End sentenced to death for murder fired his conscience and he came away from court determined to bring "beauty", "cleanliness" and "peace" into lives blighted by poverty and ignorance.[37] It's very possible that Arlen, newly arrived in London, made contact with Kennedy-Cox, even offered his services for the cause (albeit with lukewarm commitment if, as he later claimed, he "slacked outrageously" as a newcomer to the capital.) Some such experience must lie behind the strangest of Arlen's earliest fictions, 'Michael Arlen: A Fragment of A Novel'.[38] In this story, the first-person narrator visits the East End Mission run by his old boarding school and, quitting his lodgings in St James's, briefly takes a room in Limehouse with an amiable landlady and a YMCA eating-house next door. There he befriends 'Michael Arlen', a young social worker, "a person of moods and mental digressions", who is wasting away from a "disease of the lungs". Solitary, torn between a "love of beauty" and "an intense inability to express anything of it", bereft of faith "at first in himself, then in everything" and perpetually mourning his dead beloved "Viola", this is "a man whose pent-up, overfastidious aestheticism had no other effect than to make of him a monk without a monastery". By the story's end, 'Michael Arlen' the character has died a "sanitary" death in Poplar, while our narrator has moved back west to settle in Chelsea. As Harry Keyishian observes, "the question arises as to whom Dikran was 'killing off' in this story."[39] Three years after writing it, he would adopt his dead anti-hero's name as his *nom de plume*, and with it launch a bid for celebrity and social status that was anything but monastic.

In July 1915 Arlen's father died suddenly while holidaying with his wife at the Grand Hotel, Llandudno. Arlen, we may assume, hurried home for the funeral on 30 July and interment in the family plot in Manchester's Armenian cemetery.[40] Sarkis had accepted that his youngest son was not destined for the family business and supported his ambitions in London with an allowance (variously, "thirty shillings a week" or "three pounds a week", depending which version of the story Arlen was telling). These were tumultuous times for the Armenian community in exile. What became known as the 'Armenian genocide', the Ottoman Turks' systematic ethnic cleansing of a minority, began on 24 April; reports reached the West by the end of the month.[41]

In November he moved into a top-floor flat in Redcliffe Gardens, South Kensington (at 13s. 6d. a week, bed and breakfast). The historical novelist Margaret Irwin, author of *Young Bess*, lived on the first floor. Allegedly, they never met, but after he moved out a strange thing happened. The flat beneath Arlen's was taken by a Scot with second sight who was disturbed nightly by ghostly pacings on the floor above, followed by "footsteps" rushing to the window whenever a taxicab stopped below. Irwin was to learn later that Arlen had spent hours pacing the floor, waiting for a certain lady.[42] She made this detail the starting-point of a rare excursion (for her) into contemporary fiction. Her novel *Knock Four Times* (1927) concerns an ambitious young foreign-born writer called Dictripoulyos, 'Dicky the Dago', scion of a nation "many centuries older" than the English, who, having refused to go into his father's business, determines to "spurn Kensington beneath his feet and march on Mayfair". He affects a literary style of fantastical metaphor that is "rich and slow-dropping and mellifluous and frequently meaningless". So closely does Irwin's novel replicate details of Arlen's life in the ten years after he left Redcliffe Gardens that we must assume, at very least, that she followed his career closely:

> He spoke with eloquent and candid ardour of the methods he would pursue when he had the chance. The writing, he said, was the least part about it. The thing was to acquire a reputation for knowing what he wrote about. To be seen in with the right people in the right place by the right journalist who will mention it in a chatty column in the right way...[43]

Arlen launched what looks like a retaliatory strike in his 1929 story 'Confessions of a Naturalized Englishman'. In this autobiographical fiction, set on 1 May 1916, 'Dikran' returns to his lodgings to find his flirtatious married friend 'Priscilla' waiting for him, her "long shining slenderness" conveniently "vibrat[ing] through the bedroom":

> "How did you get in?" I asked.
> "A woman – I think it was a woman – let me in. Looking outraged."
> "Miss Lapwing," I said.
> "And who is Miss Lapwing?"
> "She writes novels."
> "Oh dear, she downstairs and you upstairs!"[44]

This location, which Arlen calls 'Monday Road' (for Irwin it's 'Rainbow Road'), was two rooms at the top of a "tall dusty house" off the Fulham Road. Nowadays the area is heavily gentrified and beyond the means of most young renters, but in 1915 it was distinctly *déclassé*. From his "small square window", Arlen's fictionalised self looked over the roofs of South Kensington and Earl's Court: "The night, dripping with starlight, did not cloak their meanness, their grubbiness. What stuffiness, what economies, what futile sacrifices and strivings and unrecognised hard work, those cringing roofs hid!"[45] The milieu was to prove equally dispiriting for John Middleton Murry, who lodged on the same street – at number 47 – from February 1917. Katherine Mansfield joined him there for a few weeks before and after their marriage in 1918, but as he wrote later, their two ground-floor rooms were "gloomy and sunless, quite unsuited for one in Katherine's [tubercular] condition, and my one preoccupation was to get away from them."[46]

However drab his own quarters were, autumn 1915 saw Arlen's

first decided engagement with London literary life, or "literature and its parasites," as he puts it in one of his autobiographical fictions: "teas at Golder's Green and Hampstead, and queerly serious discussions about sub-consciousness; 'rags' at Chelsea, and 'dalliance with grubbiness,' and women".[47]

What brought him to Redcliffe Gardens may have been its proximity to the offices, in nearby Redcliffe Square, of the Armenian United Association of London. As principal representative of the *émigré* community, the Association was at the forefront of promoting the Armenian cause to an English-speaking public. Its journal, *Ararat: A Searchlight on Armenia*, provided an early outlet for Arlen's patriotic writings. He gave his friend Paul Selver the impression that he was the paper's editor, but he certainly was never that, only a contributor.[48] Nonetheless, he was on his way.

NOTES

1. Hovanissian, 20.
2. Michael J. Arlen, *Passage*, 190.
3. Lang, 106. According to the first census in Ruse (1883), Armenians accounted for 3% of the population, compared to 43% ethnic Bulgarians, 39% Turks and 7% Jews (Wikipedia entry, 'Ruse').
4. Keyishian, 'Ararat', 6. Or was this Plovdiv, which also had a store? (The Kouyoumdjians had connections there as well.) My researches into the Bulgarian sources ran into the sand at this point.
5. Michael J. Arlen, *Exiles*, 64. See also Arlen Sr's comments about his mother in the *Haratch* interview discussed in a later chapter.
6. National Archives (hereafter "NA"), HO 144/415/B25073. Manouk was awarded an OBE in 1919.
7. George 91; *Manchester Guardian*, 18 June 1897.
8. The date is usually given as February 1901, following Arlen 'Confessions', 76. However, when Satinik applied for British

nationality in 1923 she stated that she had lived in England with her husband and family since July 1900 (NA, HO 144/2989.)
9 *The Bystander*, 6 Dec 1933. History does not record which school. The 1911 Street Directory for Manchester and Salford listed 564 private schools, of which 15 were in Didsbury.
10 *Manchester Guardian*, 16 Feb 1906. Bulgarian records show a head office in Manchester, with a branch in Ruse managed first by Vagharshag Kouyoumdjian, then by Stepan Papazian (Satinik's nephew).
11 Hewins, xiv; NA, J 77/915/7795.
12 Information courtesy of Syd Hill, Malvernian Society. At the time Malvern school houses were known by the name of their housemaster.
13 Lewis, 1298-9.
14 Blumenau, 75.
15 Arlen, 'Piracy', 20.
16 Blumenau, 71-2. "Disgusting behaviour" may be a euphemism for homosexual relations between boys, although from C.S. Lewis's account of Coll and House 'Tarts' – the pretty, effeminate-looking small boys who serviced their seniors in return for favours – it is unclear how far such behaviour was officially censured (*Surprised by Joy*, 1294-5).
17 Arlen, 'Piracy', 23.
18 Blumenau, 74. In his autobiography, Sydney Rhodes James, Malvern's Headmaster at the time, offered corrections to Arlen's "pardonably inaccurate" version of events (*Seventy Years*, 160-2).
19 Arlen, *Babes*, 24. F.U. Mugliston was the real name of a member of staff, who took over as Housemaster of House 5 in 1915. To the boys he was simply 'Mugs' (Blumenau, 54; Allen, 241).
20 Arlen, *London Venture*, 109, 117.
21 Wilson, 33. Since Warren Lewis was in a different House from Arlen, I assume the other two "dagoes" were in School House with Lewis Sr., not in House 5. Diligent research in the school register might even uncover their names.
22 Lewis, 1307; Wilson, 35.
23 West.
24 Two letters from Arlen, March 1924, held in Princeton University Library; *New Statesman*, review of *These Charming People*, 23 June

1923. It is overall a hostile review, typical of what would crystallise as the 'highbrow' response to Arlen. If he could only "resist the snares of his own facility," Mortimer concluded, he might accomplish something "possibly less popular but certainly better worth while."

25 The entry under 'Michael Arlen' in the *Oxford Literary Companion to the British Isles* gives two additional addresses in Southport: 'Rosslare', Park Road, and 85 Hesketh Road. I have been unable to verify these.
26 Kouyoumdjian, 'Figures in a Room'.
27 Arlen, *London Venture*, 112-13.
28 Edinburgh University records. Private communication to the author.
29 Arlen, 'Confessions', 76, where he suggests he came to London to "seek [his] fortune... at the age of seventeen", i.e. no later than November 1913. A Hollywood gossip columnist in 1926 was given to understand that "when he was sixteen years old he went to London and there became a reporter" (Shearing, 72).
30 Reported the following day in *The Scotsman*, 6 June 1914, p8.
31 NA, HO/144/1760/428994. One would expect that in this official legal declaration, if nowhere else, he was telling the truth.
32 Mackenzie, 220. In his naturalisation application Arlen states he had never left the country before 1920. Since Arlen was totally unknown at the time, it seems unlikely that Mackenzie would have recognised him.
33 Selver, 63. Two of his older brothers, Roupen and Tacvor, received part of their education at the Institut Concordia in Zurich, so there was a family connection to Switzerland (NA, HO 144/19034; HO/144/1724/261637).
34 Arlen, *London Venture*, 113.
35 NA, HO/144/1760/428994.
36 Cunard, 'Memoir', 9.
37 Allen, 161-2.
38 Kouyoumdjian, 'Michael Arlen'.
39 Keyishian, *Michael Arlen*, 22.
40 *Manchester Guardian*, 31 July 1915.
41 E.g. 'Appeal to Turkey to stop massacres', *New York Times*, 28 April 1915, p2.

42 Waugh, 259.
43 Irwin, 37, 11, 45, 79, 146, 129.
44 Arlen, 'Confessions', 66.
45 Ibid.
46 Murry, 481. By then, however, Arlen had moved on: to new lodgings in Shepherd Market, the decidedly more louche milieu he was to celebrate in *The Green Hat*.
47 Arlen, *London Venture*, 9. Over the years Arlen would retell many versions of his early life. Sometimes he was a cub reporter covering 'hatches, matches and dispatches' for the local press in Southport. Sometimes the claim was that he got his start, after writing "two hundred" unpublished stories, by working on an (unnamed) newspaper: "I had, for the sum of £4 a week, to turn out one short story a week. I did that for fifty-two weeks – one year" (qtd. in *Daily Express*, 4 November 1935, p7).
48 Selver, 63.

SUCCESS: NEW YORK, 1925

On 16 January 1925 the place to be was the opening of London's newest social attraction, the Gargoyle Club, a private members' club on the upper floors of 69 Dean Street, Soho. The brainchild of the Hon David Tennant, it raffishly combined old and new. The lower floor was dark blue, lit from silver stars in a sapphire ceiling – a 'moonlight' effect created by electric lights disguised behind coloured silk. The upper floor was a complete contrast: homely, with high-backed settees and a huge brick fireplace on which steaks were spitting. (In later years the décor of the Club's main room would be enhanced further when Henri Matisse suggested covering the walls with a mosaic of mirrored tiles). Arlen, joined by Noël Coward, Compton Mackenzie and the Canadian actress Margaret Bannerman, was among three hundred members and their guests who filtered under the Gargoyle lamp marking the club's entrance on that mild winter's night – a succession, as Tennant's biographer evokes the scene, of "tall hats, white silk scarves, fur coats, long dresses, short skirts".[1]

To be a founder member of this most exclusive of clubs was just one of the advantages Arlen was now discovering as a best-selling author. *The Stage* reported on 5 February that he and Frederick Lonsdale, already a well-established dramatist in lighter vein, were off to the South of France the next day to "knock up a play together". It was to be "a new modern comedy of manners". With plenty to distract them from their labours, this plan seems to have come to nothing. Later in the month, gossip columnists spotted the two playwrights, with time on their hands, watching the tennis among the *beau monde* at the Beaulieu Club on the Riviera, where the champion Suzanne Lenglen was consolidating her status as one of the earliest sporting celebrities.

By early March he was back in England, preparing for his first ocean voyage. Enthused by the transatlantic success of his early books, Arlen was all for an early visit to the United States. George Doran, his American publisher, was less sure, suspecting that his client's relative anonymity was an advantage. "He was no speaker and had no platform presence," Doran wrote later. "Why jeopardize in any degree popularity and fame?" In the event, these fears were misplaced. Arlen's first visit, between March and May, was a public relations triumph. New York society fell over itself to fête the new arrival. As Doran conceded, "Michael came; he saw and was seen; he made conquest where conquering mattered."[2] New York loves success – unabashed, in a way that London cannot match – and Arlen, ever ready with a quip, lapped up the adulation while it lasted.

Thus when RMS *Aquitania* docked at New York harbour on 11 March 1925, she was bringing with her one of Britain's most celebrated exports, a 29-year-old author who was accorded the attention usually reserved for film stars or aviation heroes. Probably the welcoming party on the quayside wasn't quite as crazed as Arlen later described it to Claud Cockburn, with souvenir-hunting fans ripping off his trouser-buttons[3] – the group included, after all, a delegation of Armenian sobersides – but no one doubted a titan was in their midst. He put up at the

SUCCESS: NEW YORK, 1925

A literary lion arrives in New York, 1925 (Alamy).

Ritz-Carlton. He'd not been in town a day before he was forced to shut off his phone and later had to move to another floor of the hotel to avoid the stampede of the curious in hallways. Journalists ushered into his sitting-room by his watchful (male) secretary found themselves rationed to ten minutes of the interviewee's time. From this slender material, many of them obligingly filed copy lauding Arlen as "the most talked-of young man writing today, either here or in London", the "Oscar Wilde of his generation" with "the same sparkling dialogue, the same audacity and brilliance and a like distinction in style."

New York's hostesses competed for the privilege of entertaining him. During Arlen's first two weeks in America, the *New Yorker* drily observed, socialite and interior designer Elsie de Wolfe arranged no fewer than three formal gatherings, "each with the purpose of introducing the author to herself". On March 18, he was the guest of Mr and Mrs Gilbert Miller (the husband was a prominent theatre producer) at the Lido-Venice, where he mingled with silent film starlet Vilma Banky and magazine publisher Condé Nast. Themed parties were then the rage on both sides of the Atlantic. Later in his stay, Arlen would attend a dinner in the Park Lane where Gloria Swanson was the principal guest. Girls in French costumes went from table to table distributing Napoleonic and Marie Louise paper hats to the guests. Soon, even movie mogul Adolph Zukor, Swanson's husband the Marquis de La Coudraye and the visiting novelist were "sporting the headgear".

On March 22 the *New York Times* ran a lengthy interview with the visitor. His clothes, his studiedly English tailoring, especially his "vests" (waistcoats), were as usual commented upon. His features, noted Herman Mankiewicz, were "Slavic, his close-cropped moustache might not get accepted as something really English". In the interview Arlen described his working methods, how he wrote, and repeatedly rewrote, in longhand, how he preferred to write in the mornings, although *The Green Hat* – all 100,00 words of it – was composed in two months by dint of working ten hours a day. Casting himself above all as a storyteller, he confessed admiration for American authors like Sinclair Lewis and Sherwood Anderson. O. Henry (who had died in 1910) he declared to be "the master technician of the short story", going on to praise this virtuoso exponent of the surprise ending in terms that shed light on his own practice:

> So much of the O. Henry language has dated, unfortunately, that many people who should know better think he was nothing but a trickster, for the decline of the language makes the technique stand out in bolder relief. If they'd only stop to look they'd find his real aim is to tell his story and that he tells his story. And, having finished his story, trick ending and all, he has completely convinced his reader of the relentless logic of what he's had to relate.

Two days later, and rather surprisingly, he accepted an invitation to address the Armenian Educational Foundation at the McAlpin. The encounter showed how great was now the gulf between his new assumed identity and those Armenian nationalists who wished to claim him as one of their own. Arlen began by teasing his law-abiding audience about their adherence to Prohibition: "You have given me my first glass of water since landing in America". When other speakers praised him for "admitting his Armenian blood", he grew irritated: "One doesn't admit to these things. I don't 'admit' I'm an Armenian. I merely 'say' I am one. I don't care what nationality a man is. He either does his job well or he doesn't. All the trouble in the world comes from this driving at nationalities – jealousy, ill-will, warfare. Forget about it." Although the American press would often misdescribe him as "Jewish", some of those he met were aware of his true ethnic background and would turn it against him for sport. One night in New York, when he was winning heavily in a poker game, a player in a bored voice inquired, "How about starting a kitty for the Turks?" Irvin Cobb, then the highest-salaried staff reporter in the United States, paid him a backhanded compliment: "I like Mike – he is the only Armenian I have met who has not tried to sell me a rug." One interviewer, better informed than some, asked him whether he thought his background gave him a great advantage in writing. "I do think my foreign origin gives me a fresher eye. I do believe I can more easily understand American conditions than if I were wholly English." Did that mean he was less insular? "Well, perhaps not that, but I am more able to grasp American ideas and points of view than the average Briton, who is excessively conservative."

The following week he was guest at a "gypsy-themed" party given by Mrs William Randolph Hearst at the Ritz-Carlton. (The party was ostensibly to honour an ambassador departing for a foreign posting.) The hotel's famous Crystal Room was transformed into a "gypsy" camp nestled among pine trees, complete with imitation fire. Brightly coloured streamers hung from the trees. A full moon shone from the far end of the forest and, in a gypsy wagon stationed near the entrance to the tent, two palmists told fortunes, while an organ-grinder– with inevitable monkey – wandered among the guests. Arlen was kitted out in "gypsy" ensemble, reportedly one of Rudolph Valentino's old costumes (supplied by an obliging studio head) cut down to fit Arlen's smaller frame.

Arlen's book sales had attracted the attention of film producer Jesse Lasky. In the mid-1920s Lasky was riding high as one of the founders of Famous Players-Lasky Corporation (later to become Paramount Pictures), and he was currently in town to discuss an upcoming movie project with Arlen. In the autumn the author was due to return to America, and on this occasion he would travel on to Hollywood, to provide 'scenarios' for one of the studio's biggest signings. This was Pola Negri: Polish stage and screen actress and the first European star to be invited to Hollywood – on screen a specialist in *femme fatale* roles, off screen celebrated for her love affairs with Chaplin and Valentino among others. On 21 March she was to leave America for an extended visit to her family in Poland and, the night before her departure, Famous Players-Lasky gave a dinner dance at the Ritz-Carlton in her honour. Everyone was curious to meet the "flippant London litterateur" who was to be her new 'scenarist'. Jessie Lasky gave a stirring speech, noting that Arlen was "rightfully considered to be one of the world's foremost writers" and anticipating that this versatile young man "will have a greater vogue on the screen than has been his through the written word." Although the rumour mill would later try to link Arlen romantically to Negri, on that night it was another actress, Bebe Daniels, who monopolised his attention. All efforts to cut in when he was dancing with her – which was most of the time – failed. Some days later Arlen visited the Paramount Long Island studio, ostensibly to "make a study of motion picture technique". But he spent much of his time watching Daniels shoot her latest picture, *The Manicure Girl*, and, as the press coyly reported (complete with an artist's impression of the scene), he "enjoyed the pleasure of having the movie star perform some minor operations on his nails". No print of this film, the tale of a humble beautician who is tempted to desert her electrician boyfriend for a wealthy adulterer, survives.

There was also an invitation to the famous Algonquin Round Table, the self-styled 'Vicious Circle', home to native wits like Dorothy Parker and Robert Benchley. Although Arlen was subjected to what one reporter called "the most trying ordeal I ever saw a guest of honour have to submit to", he gave as good as he got. In an oft-quoted anecdote, Edna Ferber sized up the dashingly dressed young arrival with the words, "Why, Mr Arlen, you look almost like a woman." His reply, "So do you, Miss Ferber", became legendary. For readers unfamiliar with Arlen's jousting partner, the press helpfully explained that "the woman is of a rather decided masculine type, usually wearing mannish clothes, smoking cigarettes and talking in deep tones."

In a busy schedule Arlen seems also to have found time to seek out less high-profile diversions. The cabaret at Mrs Hearst's "gypsy" party had featured W.C. Fields in his early vaudevillian mode (the comedian's film career had yet to take off) and in early May Arlen was spotted by a columnist at a vaudeville matinee in New York. He told an interviewer that he found it "amazing" that American authors had left cabaret and night life, "this most interesting phase of your life", practically untouched. "Why is it they all choose to write about grubby Middle Western life and middle-class people, when this other and more interesting aspect is right at their doors?" He was almost minded, he said, to write an American edition of *These Charming People*. (He never did.) It's also likely that he resumed contact with Alfred Orage, onetime editor of *The New Age* and Arlen's earliest literary patron, who was in town promoting the ideas of G.I. Gurdjieff, the Armenian mystic whose spiritual teaching, or at any rate his alternative healing methods, also held an attraction for Arlen (as they had for Katherine Mansfield in her final days). The eligible bachelor in him was not idle, either. At some point he was romancing the musical comedy star Marilyn Miller – either on this visit when she was playing in *Peter Pan* at Werba's Brooklyn Theatre or his next trip to New York, by which time she'd moved on to a lead role in a new Jerome Kern musical, *Sunny*.

Nonetheless, the social round proved wearying on both sides. It was observed that almost every newspaper man in New York had been introduced to him a dozen times, "only to have the little fellow say once more that he was overjoyed at the privilege". Early in his American visit, Arlen learned a social trick to see him through. On being introduced to any stranger, he'd respond, "Didn't I meet you at tea?" whereupon the gratified stranger, so flattered to be 'remembered', would become a friend for life. According to reports, he even planned to cut short his stay, reserving a cabin on the *Olympic* for its April 18 sailing, but in the event remained until mid-May, by which time his theatrical adaptation of *The Green Hat* would be launched.

With a premiere of his own on the horizon, Arlen was nervously aware of a need to take in as much of New York's theatre scene as possible. In spite of numerous other claims on his time in his first twenty-four hours in the city, he insisted on seeing Bernard Shaw's *Candida* at the Ambassador Theatre. A later evening found him at a revival of J.M. Barrie's *The Little Minister* (despite his telling a reporter that he'd been put off Barrie when he first read him at the age of ten by the "Scotch dialect".) He sat through one entire scene with his face buried in his hands. When the critic and Algonquin regular Alexander Woollcott (later to become a good friend) reminded him that he was under no obligation to stay till the final curtain, he "took his hat and topcoat and fled into the bespangled night".

Candida was worth seeing to the end, though, because the title role was taken by Katharine Cornell, the actress tipped for the lead role in the American stage version of *The Green Hat*. She and her husband, the director Guthrie McClintick, had read the original novel and although McClintick thought it "claptrap", Cornell was intrigued by the possibilities of Iris March as a stage character. Al Woods, her manager, was anxious for her to take the part and, overcoming McClintick's reservations, they went into rehearsal in New York while Cornell was still playing in *Candida*. Whenever she saw Woods she asked, "Are you sure you want me?" "Absolutely," he said, "I think you can do it, don't you?" The actress, evidently still in need of reassurance, retorted, "Let's not decide until Arlen comes". But when Arlen arrived, the team found they must reach their own decisions. He dashed into rehearsal, staying only two or three minutes at a time, declared that the show looked "fine – wonderful" and vanished again. As Cornell wrote in her autobiography, "he was very agreeable; he was pleased with everything: with Guthrie, with me, with the cast, with his own waistcoats, with life" but "he was clever enough to know how difficult the play was" and left the director to do his best.[4]

The New York opening was set for September, when Arlen would return to the States. Before that there was a short try-out tour for the play, with runs in Detroit and Chicago. Casting was finalised, with Leslie Howard, then near the start of a long career playing stiff upper-lipped Englishmen, as the tight-jawed, credulous Napier. It would fall to him to keep a straight face while delivering lines such as "You have a white body that beats at my mind like a whip."[5] Nerves prevented the author from sitting through an entire performance. He saw one act in Detroit and another in Chicago. In Detroit, Cornell, her reserves exhausted from playing and rehearsing at the same time, thought she gave a shocking performance. But the opening went well and the notices were good. Arlen wrote to a family member the next day: "The play opened here last night to an amazing reception. And they have recieved [sic] me here as though I was the Prince of Wales. I can't write as I am fagged out. I am dining tonight with Mr Henry Ford and his son." (For a keen petrolhead like Arlen, this meeting with the automobile pioneer must have been gratifying indeed.) Alexander Woollcott reported from out of state to his New York readers that *The Green Hat* was "a most absorbing play, distinguished by several moments of still and steadfast beauty". All this was but a prelude to the frenzy that would accompany the play's New York opening in September, when Arlen would go head-to-head with another 'coming' man, Noël Coward: *The Green Hat* and *The Vortex* would hit Broadway within twenty-four hours of each other.

McClintick was heartened by the Detroit opening but, still feeling the play needed work, sent out for Arlen's other novels and went through them assiduously cribbing lines to shoehorn into *The Green Hat*. After two weeks in Detroit the company moved on to the Selwyn Theatre in Chicago. Arlen meanwhile returned to New York to continue pressing the flesh before boarding the 20th Century Limited for the luxury express rail journey to Chicago. Here the play really caught on and demand for tickets became so great that the production stayed on through the season for fourteen weeks. In Chicago, Arlen kept a lower profile. According to the local press, he "spent a quiet Saturday to Monday with a few of his Chicago friends, and then hurried back to the east." Sitting in his suite at the Congress, he flattered reporters with praise for American women ("they are pretty, they are well-groomed, they are charming") and American courtesy: "If I ever write a book about America I think I shall call it 'You're Welcome'". He also returned to a favourite trope, the writer as unapologetic jobsworth. "I don't know what a writer means by temperament," he told an interviewer. "But if he means that he waits for inspiration to go to work, I can only ask him if the stockbroker waits for an inspiration before he operates, or if the bookkeeper waits for the divine moment before he begins to do sums."

His departure on the *Mauretania* for the voyage home was set for 15 May, but not before a bizarre story circulated in the media. It was reported that he had signed "the most extraordinary contract known to literary history". *Cosmopolitan*, the Hearst Corporation's flagship magazine, was to pay him $3,500 for every short story that he wrote "during the term of his natural life". This seems to have been a *canard* bruited abroad by his

English press agent, but such was the buzz around Arlen, such the appetite for news of his near-miraculous literary powers, that rival publications, like the fledgling *New Yorker*, were prepared to give it credence. Back in London, he was greeted by the news that advance orders for *May Fair*, his next volume of short stories, due out in June, had already reached 26,000. The man was unstoppable. Or so it seemed.

NOTES

1 Luke, 31. Unless otherwise stated, details in this chapter are taken from syndicated press reports in US newspapers or from *The New Yorker*.
2 Doran, 174.
3 Cockburn, 181.
4 Cornell, 76-77.
5 Mosel/Macy, 197.

ENCOUNTERS

One way to tell Arlen's story would be to tell it through his encounters with people whom posterity has treated more kindly than him, people whose lives are better documented. Here's a possible roll-call. Some would only merit a paragraph, but from among them I've selected half a dozen cases – all encounters with fellow writers – for longer treatment.

Meggie Albanesi; Richard Aldington; Fred and Adele Astaire; Alice Astor;
Tallulah Bankhead; Cecil Beaton; Lord Beaverbrook; Arnold Bennett; E.F. Benson; Louise Brooks;
Barbara Cartland; Viscount and Doris Castlerosse; Henry 'Chips' Channon; Charlie Chaplin; Winston Churchill; Cyril Connolly; Katharine Cornell; Noël Coward; Maud Cunard; Nancy Cunard;
Bebe Daniels; Bette Davis; Maurice de Forest; Norman Douglas; Daphne du Maurier;
T.S. Eliot; Maxine Elliott; Elvire Jan; Audrey Emery;
Ronald Firbank; F. Scott and Zelda Fitzgerald; Ian Fleming; Gilbert Frankau;

Greta Garbo; Martha Gellhorn; William Gerhardie; George Gershwin; Mark Gertler; Lillian Gish; Paulette Goddard; Josef Goebbels; The Gulbenkians;

Nina Hamnett; Ernest Hemingway; A.P. Herbert; Aldous Huxley;

Margaret Irwin;

Grace Kelly;

Hedy Lamarr; D.H. Lawrence; C.S. Lewis; Sinclair Lewis; Wyndham Lewis; Beatrice Lillie; Frederick Lonsdale; Clare Boothe Luce;

Katherine Mansfield; W. Somerset Maugham; Elsa Maxwell; Mercati family; Grace Moore; Ottoline Morrell; Oswald Mosley; John Middleton Murry;

Pola Negri; Beverley Nichols;

Serge Obolensky; A.R. Orage;

Anthony Powell; J.B. Priestley;

George Sanders; William Saroyan; Norma Shearer; Wallis Simpson; The Sitwells; Joseph Stalin; G.B. Stern;

Gore Vidal; Elizabeth von Arnim;

Peter Warlock; Alec Waugh; Evelyn Waugh; H.G. Wells; Rebecca West; Dennis Wheatley; Henry Williamson; P.G. Wodehouse; Thomas Wolfe; Virginia Woolf.

D.H. LAWRENCE

D.H. Lawrence must first have encountered Arlen (then still known by his birth name) in the autumn of 1915. The plan for an ideal, utopian community ("Rananim") was again alive in Lawrence's mind and he was in need of raw recruits willing to uproot and follow him (America, he had decided, was now the Promised Land). Although Arlen claimed in fictionalised versions of his autobiography to have lived in London since the start of the War, if he did, he had no fixed abode. When applying for British citizenship in the early Twenties, he listed his first London address as "Redcliffe Gardens, South Kensington, November 1915".[1] His father had died in the summer, having accepted that his youngest son was not destined for the family business, and Arlen was now provided with a small allowance to support his literary ambitions. The Lawrences had moved to Byron Villas, Hampstead, on 4 August, so the initial meeting (or meetings) between the two writers must have occurred between then and 12 December, when Arlen is first mentioned in Lawrence's letters. The likely intermediary is their mutual acquaintance Philip Heseltine (later to achieve fame as the composer and polemicist "Peter Warlock"). Arlen and Heseltine had almost certainly met at the Café Royal (where regulars like the artist Nina Hamnett came across both of them). We know that Lawrence's first meeting with Heseltine was over dinner on 16 November, where the two men had a "long talk", as Heseltine reported to Frederick Delius (Warlock, II 495). Lawrence spoke of his wish to go to Florida for the winter (though presenting it as a personal desire at this stage, for health reasons, rather than a group migration) and Heseltine came away more than ever convinced that Lawrence was a "marvellous man" and "perhaps the one great literary genius of his generation – at any rate in England". For his part, Lawrence was impressed by the young musician: "I like him *very* much: I think he is one of the men who will count in the future. I must know him more" (*2L* 442). This would suggest that Heseltine visited Byron Villas later in November, perhaps bringing along one or more of his friends, among them the Indian Hasan Shaheed Suhrawardy and the "Armenian" Arlen, all potential recruits for the Florida venture as the idea unfolded.[2]

Lawrence was keen that his new young friends should meet Ottoline Morrell. "She is a big woman, essentially genuine and religious," he told Heseltine, notwithstanding her "outside queernesses" (*2L* 448). On 29 November he and Frieda visited her country home, Garsington Manor, in company with Heseltine and Suhrawardy.[3] Heseltine visited again two weeks later, this time accompanied only by Arlen. Lawrence found it necessary to warn the hostess what to expect (although she had presumably already met the musician, on his earlier visit):

> I hear Heseltine and Kouyoumdjian are coming to you tomorrow. Heseltine is a bit backboneless and needs stiffening up. But I like him very much. Kouyoumdjian seems a bit blatant and pushing: you may be put off him. But that is because he is very foreign, even though he

doesn't know it himself. In English life he is in a strange, alien medium, and he can't adjust himself. But I find the core of him very good. One must be patient with his jarring manner, and listen to the sound decency that is in him. He is not a bit rotten, which most young cultivated Englishmen are (2L 473-4).

The two young men arrived on Monday 13 December and stayed until Thursday 16th. Both succumbed to the charms of the young ladies of the household. Heseltine (already involved with another girl – Minnie Channing, nicknamed "Puma") was soon "drunk with passion" for Juliette Baillot, then governess to Lady Ottoline's daughter (Warlock, II 496-7).[4] Arlen's fancy was taken by Ottoline's niece, Dorothy Warren (of whom more below). While Arlen was absent at Garsington, his uncle Manouk, one of the pillars of the family business, had checked into the Savoy and summoned his nephew to what may have been intended as a serious discussion of his future, perhaps a recall to the family business after his father's death. Returning to London on Thursday evening, Arlen discovered the missed appointment. He wrote excitedly to his mother in Southport: "The last four days I have spent away have certainly been the most peaceful I have spent anywhere in my life and certainly in a quiet talkative way the most enjoyable." Evidently Lawrence's invitation was ruffling feathers back home, as the letter continues: "The decision on Florida seems to have brought out a lot of new truths in one way or other. In fact they only seemed to discover that the business was not going as well as it might be when I said I was leaving England." Later, as "Michael Arlen" the popular novelist with enviable earning power, he would elide the distinction between Art and Commerce, but to the twenty-year-old under Lawrence's spell, these were contrary principles. He craved his mother's understanding:

> Let us throw away all that is indefinite and be logical. [...] Let us throw up the arts and become as the masses – just to live and eat and smell. And then where will we be? Better or worse, the gutter of money or of ambition? The world says better. I say worse. And the God we worship being the God of self, I am right.[5]

Meanwhile, Arlen had left no favourable impression with his hostess back in Garsington. Lady Ottoline confided to her diary:

> What strange creatures Lawrence and Frieda attract to themselves. He is enthusiastic about both Heseltine and Kouzoumdjian [sic], but I don't feel attracted to them, indeed quite the reverse. Heseltine is tall and blond, soft and so degenerate that he seems somehow corrupt. Kouzoumdjian is a fat dark-blooded tight-skinned Armenian Jew, and though Lawrence believes that he will be a great writer, I find it hard to believe. Obviously he has a certain vulgar sexual force, but he is very coarse-grained and conceited. I cannot sit in the room with them for long. He and Heseltine seem to pollute the atmosphere, and stifle me, and I have to escape from their presence – also I get very tired of the continual boasting of what they are going to do. They flatter Frieda and pay her more attention than they do Lawrence, so naturally they are both great geniuses in her eyes, and she is enthusiastic about them.[6] (*Ottoline at Garsington* 77)

The anti-semitism on show here – inaccurately targeted as well as insulting, since Arlen was not Jewish – is untypical of the hostess, and in retrospect she conceded that she had got him wrong: "Much as I felt repelled by him at that time, I expect he is a kind man. I have always heard that when Lawrence was ill and poor he pressed financial help upon him – which Lawrence refused." Although she never met Arlen again, she continued to wear a yellow shawl he sent her as a thank you gift, "as he remarked that I was fond of yellow". In 1928, when the Morrells were seeking to sell Garsington, Philip Morrell wrote to the now affluent author renewing acquaintance and offering to sell him the Manor. Arlen, by now preferring the balmier climes of the South of France, declined, but he was pleased to hear Ottoline still had his gift because he "felt it was such bad luck for her to have a strange young man thrust into her house by the exalted and wolfish tactlessness of our friend Lawrence."[7]

On 10 December 1915, Aldous Huxley, then an Oxford undergraduate, came to tea at Byron Villas. Lawrence at once invited him to join the Florida project. Afterwards Huxley wrote to Ottoline Morrell, who had suggested the meeting, that he found it "questionable" whether he could "immure" himself with "one Armenian, one German wife, and, problematically, one or two other young people" (Huxley 21). A few days later, on 18 December, John Middleton Murry wrote to Katherine Mansfield describing an awkward lunch date he had endured in London that day with Frieda Lawrence. Lawrence himself had cried off ("in bed with a bad cold") but Frieda arrived with Monica Saleeby, the poet Anna Wickham and

> an Armenian called Kewyewmjun (that's how it was pronounced) – a vile experience. The Armenian was another Willie Macqueen – at present he is the L's darling – but that will only last a day or two – he is just a low swindler of a peculiarly hateful kind. Hair brushed back, semi-Oxford manner, probably makes his living in Leicester Square.[8] (Murray, *Letters* 73)

"I think your lunch sounded quite *too horrid*," Mansfield responded from Bandol on 23 December (Mansfield 214).

At the end of 1915 the Lawrences left London for the village of Porthcothan in north Cornwall, "the first move to Florida" in Lawrence's view, at least geographically (*2L* 491). Their new friends Heseltine and Arlen were invited to stay shortly afterwards. Heseltine was first to arrive, on New Year's Day, with Arlen following on 10 January. "I hope we shall like him," Lawrence wrote on the eve of the Armenian's arrival. "He is at any rate more living than poor Philip who really seems as if he were not yet born, as if he consisted only of echoes from the past" (*2L* 501). In the event, while he found both his guests "trying" and "antagonistic", Arlen was the more so, bringing with him "the atmosphere of London, most disturbing." "I think he is in love with Dorothy Warren, and not at all sure that she will reciprocate. So he is a little more self-assertive than ever, and tiresome." Lawrence could not understand why these young men were "always either tacitly or noisily asserting themselves", noisily and offensively in Arlen's case. "They spend their time in automatic reaction from everything," he complained to Lady Ottoline (*2L* 504). "It is a wee bit painful," he wrote on the same day to Bertrand Russell, "these young individualists are so disintegrated" (*2L* 505).

By the following week, while Heseltine was still in favour, Arlen had outstayed his welcome. Lawrence was again in poor health ("my old wintry sickness and inflammation") and hit on the stratagem of inviting Lady Ottoline to stay and telling Arlen they needed his room for their esteemed guest. Evidently Ottoline had conveyed to Lawrence the low opinion she recorded in her diary: "You were right about Kouyoumdjian," Lawrence wrote, "I don't care for him. I shall ask him to go away" (*2L* 507).[9] In the meantime the party beguiled their evenings by writing a play, "which is rather fun" (*2L* 508). This was presumably the "comedy for stage, about Heseltine and his Puma and so on" that Lawrence announced in high spirits on 9 January (*2L* 501). No record of this collective effort survives, although some of the material may have found its way into *Women in Love*. Among Arlen's papers there is a single page of a play that he dispatched from Cornwall on 18 January for typing, but it does not appear to correspond to Lawrence's description.[10] Arlen finally left on 22 January, having apparently alienated not only Lawrence but also his erstwhile companion, Heseltine. The latter stayed on in Porthcothan and wrote to a friend: "As for the Armenian who was here, I had to expel him by violence, he proved so intolerable to all of us and so impervious to all our hints of displeasure at his presence!" (Warlock, III 14).

In later life Arlen, who was well known for colourful hyperbole in telling stories about his life, would exaggerate Lawrence's part in his life. For example, he told his son how "he used to go down to the country to visit Lawrence", implying there were multiple visits rather than this one, less than happy, episode (*Exiles* 52). The fog of memory may have descended on others, too. In 1925, when the Lawrences were living in New Mexico, they were tracked down by an American journalist, Kyle Crichton, for an interview. In an account written a quarter-century later, Crichton recalled that he had asked Lawrence about Arlen, then riding high on the success of *The Green Hat*, and received this reply:

> "The pride of Mayfair, and when we first knew him he hadn't even *seen* an aristocrat. He was a nice young fellow, who was making a literary living on odds and ends, but when we next saw him he came to our house in Poland [sic] in riding togs. I'm sure he had never ridden a horse in his life, but there he was in riding breeches with loud black and white checks and a pointed hat with a feather – like an old time chevalier." (Nehls, II 413-14)

Crichton is an unreliable commentator. Neither Lawrence nor Arlen ever visited Poland, but if we read "Porthcothan" for "Poland", the story becomes plausible. Invited to the country, Arlen, ever the dandy so far as funds would permit, tricked himself out in what he supposed to be the country attire of an English gentleman.[11] Likewise, in his own dandified prose in the pages of *The New Age*, Arlen would go on to turn his two-week sojourn amid the Cornish landscape into a storm-tossed melodrama:

> …And how depressing I found North Cornwall one month of January! I could find neither rest nor hope in the stark greyness of coast and sea and rocks; all held sternly aloof as though to warn me that man must not measure himself with Nature. The eye tried to turn away, but could not; it was held fixed, yet repelled, and the earth would have as little of me as the rocks and the sea; till, at last, I was driven back like a baffled lover, and, like him, since I could attain nothing, was made angry and contemptuous of what I had striven for. It seemed to me that the whole land was furious and bitter as though it had some grudge against the world and men… [etc.] (Kouyoumdjian, "Figures').

Heseltine was also to fall out with Lawrence, principally over the author's interference in his love life. It cannot have helped relations that, following their visits to Garsington, he and Arlen had reportedly confirmed Frieda's suspicions that Lady Ottoline, however much she esteemed Lawrence, had no great regard for his German wife (*2L* 512). Heseltine wrote to Delius in April 1916 that "Lawrence is a fine artist" but "personal relationship with him is impossible" (Warlock, III 31). Arlen may have reached the same conclusion, but he was still to enjoy one or two kindnesses at Lawrence's hand. During his stay, Arlen must have told Lawrence he was in need of a typist for his manuscripts; Lawrence put him on to Douglas Clayton, a nephew of Constance Garnett who ran a typewriting service in Croydon, and Arlen continued to use Clayton's services until December 1921.[12] The Lawrences were also sporadic matchmakers on their friends' behalf, and after Arlen's departure Lawrence wrote to Dollie Radford asking her to invite Arlen to tea in London: "And I think he would like to bring Dorothy Warren with him. She is beautiful" (*2L* 516). The Florida project was on hold by this stage, Lawrence having discovered he would be unable to leave the country in wartime, but it was always his intention that, "like the denizens of the Ark", his pilgrims should travel in pairs. According to Catherine Carswell, Lawrence caused "much amusement" with the suggestion that Arlen might marry Dorothy Warren (27).[13]

Lawrence "has practically no friends left," Heseltine crowed in April 1916. "The last one to drop off before me was an Armenian who published in the 'New Age' directly after the quarrel a most scathing and amusing satire on a 'brilliant young author, whose work was too good to be published' discovering his subconscious self in the middle of the night!!" (Warlock, III 31). The reference is to a piece that appeared in the issue of 2 March 1916 (Arlen's first known publication, indeed, albeit cloaked behind the *nom-de-plume* of "S. Dik-Cunningham"). It is an obscure satire set in an "A.B.C. tea-shop in Hackney" concerning an argument between an "Ancient Mariner" and an "Eminent Chiropodist" which is interrupted by the intervention of a "Brilliant Author with a Red Beard and Spiritual Eyes". The Chiropodist gains the upper hand over the Mariner by explaining that the "Sub-Conscious Self was the same thing as Letting Yourself Go" but then the Mariner, made to look small, "beat[s] back the Brilliant Author in confusion by asking him what was the difference in Effect between finding his Sub-Conscious Self and Getting Drunk." At this, the Brilliant Author retires, "thinking of the Gross Indecency of Quite Material People, and wondering whether he should confute all Ancient Mariners in his Great Philosophy (which was too Good to be Published)". The red-bearded Author is clearly Lawrence; the "Philosophy" is Lawrence's unpublished (and now lost) essay 'Goats and Compasses', a treatise that dealt with homosexuality, which was among the creative work Lawrence did in Cornwall (Harrison 40). Whether the Chiropodist and the Mariner can be identified with Heseltine and Arlen, and what else to make of this rambling farrago – these are near-unanswerable questions a century later. A.R. Orage, editor of *The New Age*, who delighted in stirring controversy and was one of Arlen's earliest supporters in London, must have found value in his contribution and expected it to hit home. Perhaps it did. After Lawrence fell out with Heseltine, he requested the musician return to him the loaned manuscript of 'Goats and Compasses' and refrain from talking about him in London. "The whole business is so shamefully fit for a Kouyoumdjian sketch," Lawrence reflected (*2L* 598, *ante* 22 April 1916).

Later in 1916 there was an incident in the Café Royal, which occasioned exchanges of letters among those who were there – and those who were not. In fictionalised form, it even found its way into *Women in Love*.[14] Briefly, Katherine Mansfield was dining with Lawrence's friends, the Russian-born translator Samuel Koteliansky and the British painter Mark Gertler. The café was packed and they had had to share a table with an "Indian", who was soon joined by another man of colour and "a long thin white herring of a woman with a terrific high bunch of crimson hair". In Gertler's embarrassingly racist account, the "red headed piece of dried dung produced a volume of Lawrence's poems [the recently published *Amores*] and commenced to discuss Lawrence with the other, in this perfect English and carefully picked, long words." Their ensuing banter was too much for Mansfield, who asked to see the book, and still holding onto it, rose from the table and marched out of the café, followed "most calmly" by Koteliansky and Gertler (qtd. in Alpers 216). In his biography of Mansfield, Antony Alpers assumes that the red-headed woman was a prostitute, although given the café's bohemian clientele, she may have been an artist's model or one the many exotics of artistic bent who floated through London society at the time. By his own admission, the "Indian" was Suhrawardy (Huxley 34); the identity of the other "University Black" (in Gertler's ugly phrase) is unknown. In the game of Chinese whispers that followed, the impression arose that the other mockers at the table were Heseltine and/or Arlen. Murry, in his *Reminiscences of D.H. Lawrence*, claimed that the culprits were "a handful of people who used to visit Lawrence at Byron Villas," one of whom "has since become an immensely popular writer" (95). When Richard Aldington was researching his biography of Lawrence in the late 1940s, he approached survivors for help with identification. Frieda Lawrence supplied a garbled version of the incident which placed Heseltine at the scene, despite evidence to the contrary (*Frieda* 89).[15] He then asked Murry, who told him to contact Arlen for the details. Arlen, reluctant for once to place himself at the centre of a story although he claimed to have been "sitting at Heseltine's table", replied to Aldington:

> It was Heseltine, most mockingly, but alas with malice more than mockery, who read from D.H's Amores. In 1915-16 Lawrence thought – I was too young to know for certain – very highly of Heseltine. But Philip later, despising himself, decided to goad Lawrence into despising him, Heseltine, too. You must remember

Heseltine's background – son of fairly rich parents, misunderstood chap. (qtd. in Aldington 186)

What is going on here? The likelihood is that those who relied on hearsay accounts of the incident, like Frieda and Murry, knew one thing for sure – that the figure of Halliday in *Women in Love* was modelled on Heseltine – since Lawrence had confirmed as much in 1916, even if, when faced with a threat of libel action in 1921, he denied there was any "shadow of a resemblance" (*2L* 36; *4L* 116). It therefore made sense for them to 'retrofit' actions attributed to Halliday in the novel to the real-life Heseltine, regardless of Lawrence's licence as a novelist to *invent*. (One notes how Frieda in 1948 assumed it was a "letter" that Mansfield snatched from hostile hands in the Café, rather than a book; the *letter* derives from Lawrence's fictionalisation of the incident.) Since Arlen was a known associate of Heseltine during the War, he thus became prime suspect for Heseltine's partner-in-crime.[16] That he colluded in this flattering fiction shows his capacity for self-invention. As a middle-aged author "in retirement" in New York, Arlen regaled his coterie at the St Regis with tales of the literary lions he had known in his youth. If his listeners were a little confused between T.E. and D.H. Lawrence, he would "sketch Lawrence in five sentences for the benefit of a cosmetics account executive." But, his son observed, it was as if these experiences had happened to somebody else, "as if it had been somebody else all along" (*Exiles* 152).

"S. Dik-Cunningham" was a one-off. For his subsequent contributions to *The New Age* Arlen used his birth name. A review in November 1916 of Gilbert Cannan's *Mendel* (a *roman à clef* based on the life of painter Mark Gertler, a participant as we have seen in the Café Royal incident) afforded an opportunity for Arlen to rate Lawrence against his contemporaries. He takes off from Walter Pater's definition of artistic greatness as a "strange interfusion of sweetness and strength":

> Mr D.H. Lawrence, for instance, has strength, immense strength, but no sweetness; and he is great enough to make many of his contemporaries, good in their way, and expressive enough of their generation, as Compton Mackenzie, Hugh Walpole, and Gilbert Cannan, seem like hacks beside him. ('Clever Mr Cannan!')

From 1918 Arlen began to publish in *The New Age* his semi-autobiographical 'London Papers', which would later be collected to form his first book, *The London Venture*. In the first paper he recalls "teas at Golder's Green and Hampstead, and queerly serious discussions about sub-consciousness" before introducing the reader to that "strange and great man" D.H. Lawrence. He finds in him "a bitterness so concisely and philosophically articulate, that, under the guise of 'truth' it will penetrate into the receptive mind". This is a man who "seems to lack humility definitely, as a man would lack bread to eat, and a note of arrogance, as splendid as it is shameless, runs through his written words... as though to impregnate each with his own egotism". Over several pages of gushing oxymorons, the young Arlen struggles to articulate the combination of awe and unease he felt when faced with such a "mass of passionate strength, that of an angry man straining with his nerves because he despises his hands."

However strong the memories of 1915-16 were for Arlen, there is no evidence of further contact between the two writers until the late 1920s. In the meantime, while Lawrence's literary fortunes fluctuated, Arlen's prospered. He settled on his new anglophone *nom de plume*, thereby, he hoped, "robb[ing] my readers of their last excuse for my obscurity" (*London Venture*,

'Apologia pro nomine meo'). His breakthrough commercial success came with *The Green Hat* (1924). In the novel's opening scene, the hat-wearing *femme fatale* Iris March rummages through the narrator's book collection. She expresses admiration for a variety of writers – Ford Madox Ford, Compton Mackenzie, Romer Wilson – and indifference to Joyce's *Ulysses*, which she looks at "vaguely" and drops "absently" on the floor. "Hers was that random, uninformed but severely discriminating taste which maddens you," we are told. The narrator elaborates:

> She used some words as though she had never heard anyone else use them. "Nice," for instance, she used in a calmly immense sense. […] D.H. Lawrence was "nice". "Nice?" I said. "Well, wonderful," she said, with wide eyes, so that I was made to seem slow and stupid. (33-4)

Reading this passage one senses that by 1924 Arlen, having now found his own niche in what would later become known as the 'middlebrow', was situating himself and his characters in a literary landscape where Lawrence, albeit *primus inter pares*, is viewed from a distance. For his part, Lawrence could not escape the publicity surrounding *The Green Hat*. Like everyone else, he read the book but, as David Ellis observed, "it must have been just the kind of would-be *avant-garde* production he most despised" (*DG* 386). In April 1925 Arlen was on a triumphant visit to the United States, where the stage adaptation of the novel had just opened in Chicago. Lawrence, meanwhile, having arrived back in Taos, was catching up on his unopened correspondence, a time-consuming process he described in the essay 'Accumulated Mail'. The bulk of the essay is a lively riposte to a piece on Lawrence by Edwin Muir that appeared in the New York *Nation* in February (*DG* 248). Muir had praised Lawrence for bringing "a new mode of seeing into literature, a new beauty". Lawrence responds with tongue firmly in cheek: "Easy, of course, as re-trimming an old hat. Michael Arlen does it better! Looks more modish, the old hat" (*RDP* 243). In June Lawrence completed another essay, 'The Novel', and once again he demonstrated his antipathy to Arlen's novel (*DG* 250). He argues that all too many novels are disfigured by a conflict between a didactic "purpose" and the novelist's "passional inspiration". This is wrapped up in a familiar Lawrentian invective against the "absolutes" of Christianity which undermine the truer perception that "everything is relative". Tolstoy's instinct, Lawrence writes, urged him to endorse the relationship between Vronsky and Anna Karenina, but his conventional social being prompted him to condemn it (cf. *DG* 251). Whether it is Conrad or Joyce, Arlen or Margaret Kennedy (author of *The Constant Nymph*), novelists have the same "snivelling purpose", to prove their own "Jesus qualifications":

> And there is a heroine who is always "pure," usually, nowadays on the muck-heap! Like the Green Hatted Woman. She is all the time at the feet of Jesus, though her behaviour there may be misleading. Heaven knows what the Saviour really makes of it: whether she's a Green Hat or a Constant Nymph (eighteen months of constancy, and her heart failed), or any of the rest of 'em. (*STH* 182)

The Green Hat purports to tell the story of a racy, short-skirted heroine, possessed of "a pagan body and a Chislehurst mind" (58). Arlen evokes her versatile love life with titillating glee, only to reposition her at the end of the book under the voluminous skirts of Victorian morality. On their wedding night her first husband, the idealized 'Boy' Fenwick, throws himself to his death from their hotel window – we are led to believe following the discovery of his bride's colourful past. In fact, as we learn in the protracted dénouement, Boy was suffering from syphilis and mortified with shame. To preserve his spotless reputation among his peers, the selfless heroine has allowed the misconception to persist that the wrong was hers: Boy died "for Purity" (110). She takes his "sin" on herself and, once the truth is out, in a final act of pseudo-atonement, crashes her Hispano-Suiza into an old oak tree. Her actions sound, in Lawrence's phrase, distinctly "Jesusy":

> What's the good of pretending that the lives of a set of tuppeny Green Hats and Constant Nymphs is Life-as-it-is, when the novel itself proves that all it amounts to is life as it isn't life, but a sort of everlasting and intricate and boring habit of Jesus peccant and Jesusa peccante. (*STH* 182)

Lawrence's complaint is that, while Arlen's heroine may be adorned with the trappings of modernity, including a fashionable disregard for the conventions of polite society, her life-story is ultimately patterned on a contrived template of comforting, familiar Christian dogma. In consequence, her creator, and other writers like him, can never rise to the challenge of Realism – the representation of lived reality.

The year 1927 was an eventful one for Arlen. In May he had to cut short a visit to South America following what may have been a recurrence of tuberculosis. In June he was said to be "very ill" and convalescing in Sussex; the *New York Times* reported in early September that he was to "undergo an operation in London". At some point, perhaps October, he was taking the cure in Davos (*6L* 220-1). But he also managed a trip to Venice in September to attend the Schneider Cup races for seaplanes which proved happier, for there he first met the Greek aristocrat Atalanta Mercati whom he would marry the following year in a lavish ceremony in Cannes. Her father and stepmother lived in Florence and it must have been his ardent pursuit of this young beauty that took him to Florence, where he rented a flat in early November. There was parental opposition to overcome and a reputation to live down. Her father, a former Lord Chamberlain to the King of Greece, thought Arlen an unsuitable match and Alice Astor, who had the task of chaperoning Atalanta in Venice, worried that "old Michael had a reputation for being a very naughty boy" (qtd. in Obolensky 313). With his usual jauntiness, Arlen wrote to his mother early in the new year announcing the *fait accompli* of his engagement: "[Her] family are terrified of me. They have heard I have had affairs with every woman in Europe. I have told them they are quite right, and in America too."[17]

However, it was a less self-confident Arlen that Lawrence encountered by chance on the Lungarno on 17 November. He was "thinner, perhaps sadder" than at their last meeting eleven years earlier, "otherwise much the same". Lawrence's sympathies were aroused. Just as at their first meeting, he recognised a fellow outsider:

> There's something about him I rather like – something sort of outcast, dog that people throw stones at by instinct, and who doesn't feel pious and Jesusy on the strength of it, like Cournos [another writer friend], but wants to bite 'em – which is good. He's one of the few people I don't mind making their pile – just to spite 'em (*6L* 220-1).

Although Arlen was still "trying to be rakish", he now looked "diminished", Lawrence thought, and "lonely" (*6L* 223, 224). In three different letters he refers to Arlen as a "sad dog" (223, 225, 236). The embattled Arlen was invited to the Villa Mirenda, where the Lawrences were staying, on 19 November, a visit that made such an impression on Lawrence that he recorded it at unusual length in his 'Memoranda'. This time his visitor put Lawrence in mind of "a sad *lost* dog". Arlen confided to Lawrence the nature of the mysterious "operation" mentioned in the press in September – it was for removal of a tubercular testicle. They discussed Arlen's hopes of marriage – "he wants a Greek or Georgian wife, something Oriental" – but it is unclear whether Arlen told Lawrence he was courting someone in particular. The US tour of *The Green Hat* had netted him $5,650 in a single week and he was on his way to becoming a millionaire. Arlen's frankness about his earnings prompted Lawrence to speak of his own poverty, something he regretted the next day when he had a "horrible reaction, & felt sort of pariah". The encounter only increased Lawrence's hatred of "the whole money-making world" and underlined the truism that money does not bring happiness (*6L* 225). Lawrence also noted that "the Florence snobs cut him dead". Again, we do not know how far, if at all, Arlen confided his specific circumstances and the opposition he was facing from the Mercatis. Lawrence's interpretation is that the whole "Mayfair set" who had so praised him at first was now turning on him, having been "taken in by him" (*6L* 227). However, there is little evidence that Arlen was being "cut" more generally in society. Although he rarely lived in London after 1926, doors remained open to him and his vigorous social life continued.

Arlen met Lawrence at least once more during his stay in Florence.[18] This was at a lunch party with Norman Douglas, then resident in Florence, and others on 29 November. Douglas was not looking forward to it, writing to a friend: "What ho! Both of them are pretty damned ill" (qtd. in *DG* 688). However, Frieda reported that it was a "nice lunch" where "nobody said anything nasty about anyone else" (*6L* 253). Around 8 December Arlen left for St Moritz. Lawrence seemed unsure whether it was for the "snow" or for his "lungs" (6L 236, 239). There was certainly pleasure to be had: a rendezvous in the Alpine resort with an old friend, Noël Coward, is recorded in a charming photograph of Arlen and Coward in a two-man toboggan. But, in fact, the Mercatis' removal to St Moritz for the Christmas season may have been the primary incentive.

Lawrence was not sorry to see Arlen go – "my God, these writers, they are *dismal!*" (6L 239) – but his reappearance had had a lasting effect on the older man. In late November Lawrence began his third, and final, rewriting of *Lady Chatterley's Lover*. Arlen inspired the introduction of an entirely new character, Michaelis – Connie Chatterley's first extramarital lover, an Irish playwright who although commercially successful is held in contempt by the very 'society' figures he depicts. The similarities between fictional character and his real-life prototype are many. Michaelis is "caddish and bounderish" (*LCL* 20); Arlen's reputation likewise preceded him.[19] Both have (or had, in Arlen's case) apartments in Mayfair (21). Michaelis is a "hopeless outsider" who had his greatest success in America; like Arlen he conspicuously "wasn't an Englishman" but still "pined to be where he didn't belong... among the English upper classes" (22). Michaelis, we are told, is thirty years old (21) – very nearly Arlen's age when Lawrence met him again (in fact, Arlen would celebrate his thirty-second birthday in Florence.) The Irishman has an income of $50,000 "from America alone" (23).[20] Like Arlen, Michaelis is on the marriage market: Arlen's Greek *inamorata*, if she was ever spoken of, has become "a Turk or something... something nearer to the Oriental" (23). Both Michaelis and Arlen belong to an "old race that is hardly here in our present day" (25) (Armenian, in the latter's case, a heritage he was far from disowning).[21]

The most striking carry-over from the letters is how

Michaelis is repeatedly compared to a dog: he is a "mongrel", "much kicked, so that he had a slightly tail-between-the-legs look" (22), a "stray dog" (25), a "sad dog" (28), an "ownerless dog" (28), a "lone dog" (31). Broadening out, Lawrence declares both Michaelis and Clifford to be "alien dogs" (24), both of them "sensually a bit doggy and humiliating" (248). Michaelis also has a speech which sounds suspiciously like Arlen in self-justifying mode. "I may be a good writer or I may be a bad one," the Irishman tells Connie, "but a writer and a writer of plays is what I am, and I've got to be" (22). Compare Arlen in his autobiographical fiction of the late 1920s:

> Bad or good writer, I'm a born writer. It's as natural for me to make a living out of writing as it is for a plumber out of plumbing. And a born writer, a man like me, writes anything that comes to his hand. ('Confessions' 42)

As David Ellis has identified, with this new character Lawrence was able to focus several of his emergent themes (*DG* 388-90). There is a new emphasis on how commercial motivation in art enjoins worship of the "bitch goddess, Success" – a phrase that Lawrence derived from William James, uses repeatedly in the novel (*LCL* 62, 63, 72, 107) and applies specifically to Michaelis (51). Clifford is recast as a literary intellectual with a healthy income of £1,200 a year who does not scruple to use the "new channels of publicity" to "build himself a monument of a reputation quickly" (21). Infantilism, a besetting fault of Clifford's, is first flagged up via the emotionally immature Michaelis, who is described as "forlorn like a child" (23), an "infant crying in the night" (25), with a "child's soul" contained in a "curiously child-like body" (28-9). Moreover, Lawrence uses Michaelis to highlight what Ellis calls "the struggle for power within sexual relations". Whatever public success Michaelis enjoys in the world of men, in the bedroom he suffers from chronic sexual inadequacy; Connie complains of his "pathetic, two-second spasms" (71). "Like so many modern men, he was finished almost before he had begun" (54). Eventually, Michaelis wilfully crashes their relationship with his complaints about his lover's delayed clitoral orgasm, thus "bring[ing] down the whole show with a smash" (54).

In chapter 5 of *Lady Chatterley* we learn that Michaelis has put Clifford centre-stage in a play, and Clifford looks forward to being displayed "to advantage" (51). This, from an author, Lawrence, who courted controversy by fictionalising his friends, feels like a final tongue-in-cheek allusion to the Michaelis-Arlen relationship. Michaelis has put Clifford on stage, just as Lawrence has put Arlen "on stage". And Arlen, like Clifford, was rather gratified. The Paris-based publisher Edward Titus, who spent time with Arlen and his new wife in 1929, reported to Lawrence that "Mike is a tremendous admirer of you and he feels greatly elated at having served as one of the characters in Lady Chatterly [*sic*]. He keeps you on a pedestal…" (*7L* 476). Ellis comments that "one would have liked confirmation of this from Arlen himself", since Lawrence's characterisation of Michaelis, although by no means unsympathetic, shows a man who under-performs in the bedroom – hardly flattering to the real-life prototype (*DG* 390). No such confirmation exists, but his son's impression was that it was flattery enough for Arlen that he had been "to some degree friends with these titans he so much admired, the serious literary men, the Lawrences and Wellses and so on" (*Exiles* 52).[22]

The re-encounter with Arlen in November 1927 may have influenced *Lady Chatterley* in a further, material sense. Lawrence recorded Arlen's earnings in particular detail and without apparent envy, noting for example how he had put his American earnings into a trust which in future would yield "perhaps £100,000 a year" (surely a hugely exaggerated figure). In a letter to Koteliansky on 22 November we then find Lawrence announcing plans for private publication of his own novel and shrewdly calculating his profits on a print run of 700 copies (*6L* 225). It seems that this brief exposure to a writer as commercially-minded as Arlen concentrated Lawrence's thoughts on how there might be a way to bring to market even a book that no mainstream publisher would handle.

In late May 1928, while he was correcting the proofs of *Lady Chatterley*, Lawrence's thoughts may have turned again to Arlen. He wrote a terse short story, 'Mother and Daughter', about a domineering mother (Rachel Bodoin) and the stifling effect she has on her daughter Virginia's marriage prospects. After Rachel has frightened off her daughter's previous lover, Virginia finds salvation in the form of a 60-year-old Armenian widower, Arnault. Jeffrey Meyers makes a persuasive case that the story is an "allegory of Katherine Mansfield's seduction by the mysticism of Gurdjieff" but concedes that Arnault may also be drawn "with a few hints from the Armenian Michael Arlen" (444, 448). The hints are certainly there, albeit projected onto a much older man. Like Kouyoumdjian, the suitor has an unpronounceable surname "which seemed to have a lot of bouyoums in it". He is of the merchant class, with family in Bulgaria. A former millionaire, he has been "terribly humiliated" but retains "a certain dogged conceit" and is now "doggedly" rising up again. He is an "outsider", scion of a "defeated race" and "physically lonely", in need of a cicerone who will help him to "understand the English", with whom he must do business (*VG* 115-17). And perhaps it is no accident that the Armenian's frenchified forename, "Arnault", is a homophone of "Arno", the river that flows through Florence?

"You have a great friend in Arlen," Titus assured Lawrence

following a conversation he had in October 1929 with Arlen and representatives of Heinemann and Nelson Doubleday; they all agreed that Lawrence could strike a better publishing deal in America than his current arrangements (*7L* 520, 534). Lawrence responded the next day: "My affection to Michael Arlen – I always stick up for him, too – in Germany, battles" (523). The allusion to Germany is obscure. The Lawrences had stayed in Frieda's native country from July to September 1929, so Lawrence may be referring to some argument that broke out during their stay. Alternatively, he may be recalling the autobiographical piece 'Getting On', which he wrote in early 1927 for the German publishing house Insel-Verlag, although it never appeared in his lifetime. In it he reflects how his late mother would have been "chagrined" by his lack of "real" success, disappointed "that I am not *really* popular, like Michael Arlen" (*LEA* 32). In April 1928 Dorothy Warren, on behalf of a German publisher friend, wrote to Lawrence about securing German rights for the translation of *Lady Chatterley*. She remarks in passing that other German agents seemed only interested in boosting Galsworthy and Arlen (Nehls, 3 201). However, this reference, like that in 'Getting On', is hardly "sticking up" for Arlen.

In January 1930 the Arlens, who had yet to settle permanently in the south of France, were staying at the Villa Fiorentina in Cannes, the home of Atalanta's grandmother. When Arlen returned to Paris in February, he learned from Titus that Lawrence had moved to the Ad Astra sanatorium in Vence. Titus informed the patient of a visit missed (or thankfully avoided?) "Arlen was in to see me the other day. He was just back from the south, and he was very sorry that he didn't know your address; he would have visited you if he had had it" (*7L* 648-9). On the eve of Lawrence's move to the sanatorium, Frieda wrote to Titus asking him to solicit Arlen's opinion of Laurence Pollinger, the young agent at the Curtis Brown office in London who handled

Lawrence's books (*Frieda* 1). Pollinger had recently stayed for five days in Bandol (*DG* 524), but a fair deal for Lawrence's US rights was still to be resolved. Arlen was represented by the same agency and, a few days later, Frieda renewed her pleading with Titus: "Rich, the Curtis Brown man in New York, hates Lawr's [*sic*] work. Michael Arlen knows Pollinger; perhaps he would talk to him in London – You see a bit of friendliness goes such a long way with Lawrence" (*Frieda* 3).

January 1933 saw the publication of Arlen's most ambitious novel. "I'm through with women in love. My new novel is about politics," he told an interviewer. "People seem to forget I'm *really* a serious writer" (qtd. in Keyishian 101). Clearly indebted to H.G. Wells and Aldous Huxley, *Man's Mortality* is a science fiction fantasy, written purportedly in 2060 AD and looking back to the events of 1987, when an autocratic international combine is overthrown in a world war, ushering in the formation of a world state which is predicted to be "something between a workhouse, a sanatorium and an asylum" (347-8). The principal advocate in the novel of such a state is Julian Craddock, "President of England". In discussion with another character (provocatively named "Hemingway"), Craddock asks: "Do you ever read that fellow Lawrence, who was the god of the 'fifties? [i.e. the 1950s] The young chaps now are belittling him as no more than a sentimental philosopher, but he says things in that *Apocalypse* of his..." (350). Craddock then quotes in juxtaposition two sentiments from the final page of Lawrence's work (*A* 149). The first is cited approvingly: "For man the vast marvel is to be alive. For man, as for flower and beast and bird, the supreme triumph is to be most vividly, most perfectly alive". The second is dismissed as a "hedonistic howler": "The dead may look after the afterwards". For Craddock, living in the moment should not exclude thoughts of our posterity: "As though there wasn't contained in the 'vast marvel of being alive' the fact that we are also part of the dead and the afterwards". In a novel that proved to be his single, misfiring attempt to reinvent himself as a "serious" writer, Arlen here engages once more with the most "serious" writer he can think of – his putative mentor D.H. Lawrence.

Whether or not Arlen was ever able to use his good offices with agents on Lawrence's behalf, Frieda remained well-disposed towards Arlen after her husband's death, and the two dined together in London in January 1931 (*Frieda* 28). On that occasion, an inevitable topic of conversation must have been the arrival of Arlen's firstborn, named Michael John, on 9 December. The son grew up to be a distinguished journalist, a staff writer on *The New Yorker*, and author of a memoir of his own early life, *Exiles*. The latter contains the vestiges of what Arlen told his son about Lawrence. The boldest claim in the book is that, at the time of their first acquaintance, Arlen would bring Lawrence stories he was working on and read them aloud to the older man, who would offer advice. Arlen's earliest model, we learn, was Arnold Bennett.[23] "One weekend", Arlen showed Lawrence a new effort in different vein, "a romantic, highly stylized fable about a girl (which later became one of the sketches in *The London Venture*)". Lawrence, "with all his didactic authority", told the young author that he should stop trying to imitate Bennett and write "fantasies" instead. Arlen, his son recalls, "was always pleased to say that it was Lawrence who turned him towards his particular style" (*Exiles* 52).[24] Impossible without corroboration to verify this anecdote – it surely suffers from the hyperinflationary effect of being retold at a hundred dinner parties – but if the claim *were* true it would be a striking example of disinterested advice from Lawrence that enabled the apprentice to far outdo his master in earnings potential.[25]

Given their different approaches to fiction, the friendship between Arlen and Lawrence might seem unlikely. Why were these two men drawn to one another? It began, on Arlen's side, with literary careerism: for a young aspirant on the rise, the patronage of an established writer was opportune. At the time Lawrence, as so often, was in search of disciples. If the friendship did not mature, it was because Lawrence was disappointed by his new follower, as he so often was by would-be acolytes. When happenstance brought the two together again, the roles were reversed. By 1927 Arlen was an 'established' writer. In the intervening years he had developed a critical distance from the older man's work, but he never stopped thinking of Lawrence as someone to learn from (or, less creditably, as a name to drop when there were listeners to impress). And perhaps now he might use his new-won influence to improve Lawrence's financial situation?

Examining Lawrence and Arlen in tandem raises interesting questions about the relationship between commercial success and high art. All his life Lawrence was barely able to make a living from his writing, but the path he chose was of his own choosing. As he wrote in a late essay, the fact "that I have not got a thousand friends, and a place in England among the esteemed, is entirely my own fault" (*LEA* 38). He recognised that he could never compete with 'professionals' like Compton Mackenzie or Arnold Bennett, whose royalties sustained handsome lifestyles and who could rely on substantial advances against future publications. For a challenging modernist like Lawrence, the 'highbrow' end of the publishing market was a precarious place. But he was writing what he wanted, and needed, to write. Arlen, by contrast, must have seemed to him a worshipper of the "bitch goddess Success", exactly the sort of professional writer that Lawrence refused to be and was incapable of becoming. By catering to popular taste, Arlen had earned himself a sizeable income, celebrity status (he was even featured on the cover of *Time* magazine in May 1927) and an *entrée* to fashionable society:

all reasons for Lawrence to despise him. Yet when the two met again in Florence Lawrence felt once again, at a personal level, the sense of identification that stirred at their first encounter in 1915. Lawrence could not begrudge Arlen his success, seeing in him a fellow outsider, a "sad dog" whose own "place among the esteemed" would never be secure from prejudice. "Never trust the artist. Trust the tale," Lawrence famously wrote (*SCAL* 14). In Arlen's case, Lawrence could sympathise with the artist even while finding little merit in his tales.

NOTES

1 His application is preserved in the National Archives (HO/144/1760/428994). As a Bulgarian national he was an "enemy alien" after Britain declared war on Bulgaria in October 1915 and required to report regularly to the police. Nancy Cunard recalled hearing that his first London digs was a "miserable room in muddy Whitechapel" (unpublished memoir, Harry Ransom Center, University of Texas [hereafter "HRC, Texas"]).

2 On 27 January 1916 Lawrence reminded Dollie Radford that she saw Arlen "at our house" (*2L* 516). Arlen's son implies that Lawrence and Arlen met at the Café Royal (*Exiles* 152) but this seems less plausible. Lawrence "had never himself been an *habitué* nor did he approve of its bohemian atmosphere" (*DG* 149; cf. *2L* 221, 499, 649).

3 Due to miscaptioning in Ottoline Morrell's original album, in reproductions of a photograph taken on that day the figure of Suhrawardy has sometimes been mistakenly identified as "Michael Arlen" (e.g. Smith plate 17). Cf. the confusion over the identity of the Café Royal diners (discussed below). To complicate matters further, Hasan Shaheed Suhrawardy has sometimes been mistaken by scholars for his better-known brother, Huseyn Shaheed Suhrawardy, a future Prime Minister of Pakistan!

4 Juliette, who would later marry the biologist Julian Huxley, tells the story of her relationship with this "unusual young man" in her

memoir (*Leaves* 48-9).

5   Letter dated "Thursday" [15 December 1915]. (Private collection.) Michael J. Arlen recalls that his grandmother could "barely speak English" (*Exiles* 51). She must have struggled with the adolescent posturing in Arlen's letters home.

6   This entry, dated "December 3rd, 1915", implies that Arlen was part of the earlier party, although all other evidence points to his making his first (and only) visit to Garsington in mid-December. Cf *2L* 476.

7   Arlen to Philip Morrell, May 14 [1928] in reply to Morrell's letter, which does not survive (HRC, Texas).

8   For Willie MacQueen, who stayed with the Lawrences in April 1915, see *2L* 319, 323. He was also one of the party at Garsington on 29 November (452 n. 2).

9   Lawrence delivered the identical judgment on Arlen ("I don't care for him") in letters to John Middleton Murry and Katherine Mansfield and to Mark Gertler (*2L* 508). Evidently he was now *persona non grata* for any group migration. However impractical under wartime restrictions, the "Rananim" dream was still alive at the start of 1916. "There are several young people very anxious to come," Lawrence told Bertrand Russell on 29 December, "we shall be six or seven" (490). Anticipating Arlen's arrival in Cornwall the following week, Lawrence wrote to Barbara Low on 5 January: "We are trying to think of a plan of getting out of the country on a ship" (496).

10 It is the opening of a one-act social comedy, *A Wisp of Straw*, in which an indolent young man, Candidus, "good looking in a conventionally refined way, but now livid and dissipated looking", is served breakfast by a stereotype Cockney charwoman, Mrs Harris. (HRC, Texas).

11 There was no mention of Arlen in the interview originally published in *The World* (New York), 11 October 1925, section 3, p.4. (I am grateful to Andrew Harrison for his comments on Crichton's reliability as witness.) Another somewhat far-fetched version of the Porthcothan trip came from Arlen's sometime friend Rebecca West. In a late interview, she reminisced about how Arlen "had read of some of Lawrence's early works and then went down to Cornwall where Lawrence was living and enlisted himself as a

disciple, was a general dogsbody there, cooked and cleaned the house and bought the stamps and licked the stamps until one day Lawrence said, 'Oh, you're a dreadful young man. Frightful bore.' And threw him out" (Gerard 190).

12 The Arlen-Clayton correspondence, which is preserved in HRC, Texas, begins with Arlen writing from Cornwall on 18 January 1916 "on Mr Lawrence's recommendation". On Clayton, see *TE* 89, and Baldwin 71. Lawrence declared him an "excellent typist and perfect in reliability" (*2L* 446).

13 The Lawrences had already tried to pair off Miss Warren, as another candidate for Florida, with either Heseltine or his friend Robert Nichols (Smith 78, Gray 89-90).

14 Chapter XXVIII, 'Gudrun in the Pompadour'. For a detailed discussion of this incident, see Jobson.

15 Cecil Gray, Heseltine's first biographer, sought out Koteliansky, who assured him "quite definitely" that Heseltine was not one of the offenders (225). Paul Delany accepted this but decided that Suhrawardy's companion was "almost certainly... Arlen, who could have passed for a 'coloured man' to Gertler's jaundiced and no doubt drunken eye" (248). Alpers bluntly accuses Arlen of "lying" (439).

16 This 'retrofitting' process may continue into the present. The editors of *Women in Love* and the *First 'Women in Love'* in the Standard Edition suggest that the "young man with a thick, pale, jeering face" who accosts Pussum in chapter VI of the novel is based on Arlen (*FWL* 60, 465; *WL* 70, 538). It is unclear to me where the resemblance lies. Lawrence tells us only that the character is Jewish and cowardly and has an "influence" over Halliday.

17 Undated letter, "Palace Hotel, St Moritz" [January 1928]. (Private collection.) The reference to Arlen as "a very naughty boy", which appears in the 1958 US edition of Obolensky's memoirs, was cut from the 1960 UK edition. Obolensky's implication that he and his wife acted as inadvertent matchmakers is contradicted by Elsa Maxwell, who claimed in a 1941 article to have invited Arlen to "a certain dinner, in Venice, and planted for his eyes the stunning... Atalanta". Atalanta's parents were divorced and both had remarried by 1927: her father lived in Florence, her mother in Geneva. Arlen himself told Vincent Sheean yet another yarn:

that he had first spotted Atalanta at a corner table at Harry's Bar in Venice and determined then and there to marry her (letter, Sheean to Keyishian, 28 October 1970); this bar didn't open until May 1931, three years after Arlen's marriage.

18 A scheduled visit on 23 November had to be cancelled because Frieda had a cold and Arlen was "terrified" of catching it (*6L* 224). Lawrence told Ada Clarke on 8 December that Arlen was at the Villa "a few times" (236). Orrick Johns remembered seeing Lawrence lunching with Arlen at Doney's, "the fashionable place for tea on the Tornabuoni". However, he places this anecdote in *summer* 1927, which casts doubt on its credibility (Nehls, 3 149).

19 Although many of his lady friends found him "charming", a young Barbara Cartland once had to flee his clutches when he propositioned her in a hotel bedroom (Heald 47).

20 Revised downwards in the manuscript from $100,000 (*LCL* 344). The higher sum corresponds to Arlen's expected earnings from his American trust (*6L* 225).

21 Further tentative comparisons are possible between fiction and real life. Michaelis's reappearance in Venice in Chapter 17 (*LCL* 259) may have been suggested by Arlen's initial courtship of Atalanta in that city, supposing Arlen had taken Lawrence into his confidence. Connie credits Michaelis with "a certain sort of generosity" (27), reminding us that a newly affluent Arlen gave cash subventions to Noël Coward and Alfred Orage among others and, according to Ottoline Morrell, offered Lawrence financial help.

22 The only extant letter from Arlen to Titus suggests the two men were on less friendly terms than Titus implied to Lawrence. Dated September 14 [1929], it begins "Dear Mr Titus" and politely declines an invitation to contribute to a periodical – presumably *This Quarter*, which Titus edited (HRC, Texas).

23 There is a surprising affinity of interest here with Lawrence, who while working on his first three novels (1908-1913) was deeply immersed in works by Bennett as well as those of Galsworthy and Forster. Lawrence's early reading is explored in an article by Miller.

24 Alec Waugh, one of the few *literati* whom Arlen could call a friend, gained a rather different impression: "D.H. Lawrence shrugged when Arlen asked him for advice. 'I am a realist,' he said, 'you are a

romanticist. You have your own way to make. I cannot guide you'" (260).

25 Paradoxically, the one example we have of Kouyoumdjian's earlier, grittier manner, the story 'Michael Arlen: A Fragment of A Novel' (*The New Age*, XXI/15, 9 August 1917, 330-2), provided Arlen with the pseudonym he would later adopt for his new persona. Alfred Orage, editor of *The New Age*, has also been credited with steering Arlen towards a more artificial and decorative style (Keyishian 21).

KATHERINE MANSFIELD

Some of Arlen's literary connections merit little more than a digressive footnote. Such are his contacts with the New Zealand-born short story writer Katherine Mansfield. As a candidate for 'Rananim', Arlen was one of the group of "Lawrence's Bing Boys" that Mansfield refers to in a letter of 12 September 1916, confessing herself "a little hazy" about another member of the group, Hasan Shaheed Suhrawardy.[1] (*The Bing Boys Are Here* was a popular musical running in London at the time. The Boys of the title were provincials who yearned for a more extensive view of life through travel.)

As we've seen, by January 1916 the Lawrences had decamped to Cornwall and Lawrence invited two of his young *protégés* – Arlen and the composer Philip Heseltine (aka 'Peter Warlock') – to stay at the rented cottage. The hosts quickly grew tired of their boisterous guests; Arlen, in particular, was encouraged to leave after a week. Mansfield, who was receiving gossip about these events from her friends, wrote to Ottoline Morrell on 26 February: "Thank you for letting us see Frieda's letter... I am thankful that the Armenian is gone but I wish he had taken Haseltine [sic] with him."[2]

Like Mansfield, Arlen enjoyed the patronage of editor A.R.

Orage, and some of Arlen's earliest publications were in the pages of *The New Age*. On a couple of occasions in 1917, work by the two writers appeared in the same issue: 3 May ('Two Tuppenny Ones, Please') alongside Arlen's 'A Defence of Tailors', and 14 June ('Mr Reginald Peacock's Day') alongside Arlen's 'Tigranes the Slave'. Interestingly, in the story 'Michael Arlen: Fragment of a Novel', which appeared in the issue of 9 August 1917 and is the site where Arlen first tried out what would later become his *nom de plume*, the hero is described as "a monk without a monastery" – the same phrase that Mansfield applied to Murry, her partner.[3]

None of these coincidences and concatenations tell us whether Mansfield and Arlen ever met or whether she joined up the dots between "hazy" references to "Armenians" to surmise that they pointed to one and the same person. As Mansfield scholar Gerri Kimber commented to me, "some of her notebooks have a lot of pages physically cut out of them. Who knows what she was writing on those pages, or about whom?" Mansfield's failure to use Arlen's given name, if indeed she recognised it, is no surprise. English-speakers struggled to remember it or to pronounce it correctly.

In August 1923 the American writer Sinclair Lewis and his first wife, Grace, took a lease on Le Val-Changis, a country house at Avon, Seine-et-Marne. Although Lewis was suspicious of Gurdjieff as a man who "runs the latest thing in phoney High Thought colonies,"[4] the couple couldn't resist checking out the nearby Institute for the Harmonious Development of Man; so when Arlen arrived for a ten-day stay with the Lewises, his host squired him on a visit. (Arlen was perhaps intrigued by the involvement of his old mentor Orage in this venture, or by Gurdjieff's Armenian ancestry?) Grace Lewis takes up the story in a letter to a friend:

[Sinclair] and Michael Arlen have gone to the soirée of

the Russian colony almost next door, the colony where the writer Katherine Mansfield died. I have been to two of these vaudeville shows and never again. There you work with your hands for twenty hours, sleep four hours, eat little, or fast, dance à la Jacques Dalcroze, think, think, think, but speak little, regard your soul at all hours, and try to burst from your caterpillar state into that of a butterfly like – Well, perhaps like Gudjieff [sic] the head, a shaven-headed Tartar monster who cracks the whip every time he speaks. All rather interesting, but I wonder! All sorts of well-known people have stayed there, but I have not seen any of them since their passing through the fire.[5]

In early 1926 the literary journalist John Shand offered a satirical piece on Arlen to T.S. Eliot, editor of *The Criterion*. Eliot loftily rejected it on the grounds that the subject matter was "not of sufficient importance to justify *The Criterion* in recognising the existence of Mr Michael Arlen." John Middleton Murry had already offered to publish it in *The Adelphi* and Eliot advised Shand to go with his offer, since no other quarterly would rush to print it "owing to the unimportance of Mr Arlen".[6] It duly appeared in the March issue of *The Adelphi*. Did Murry realise that the subject of the article was that same "low swindler" he had met on a London street ten years before and described in such unforgiving terms to Mansfield?[7] I think he must have done.

NOTES

1   *The Collected Letters of Katherine Mansfield, Vol 1: 1903-1917*, ed. Vincent O'Sullivan and Margaret Scott (Oxford: OUP, 1984), p. 280.

2   Ibid., p. 247.
3   As reported in John Middleton Murry, *Between Two Worlds: An Autobiography* (London: Cape, 1935), p. 344.
4   Sinclair Lewis to E.J. Lewis, 31 July 1923, qtd. in Richard Lingeman, *Sinclair Lewis: Rebel from Main Street* (New York: Random House, 2002), p. 231.
5   Grace Lewis to Stella Wood, 12 August 1923. Unpublished (Harry Ransom Center, University of Texas).
6   18 January 1926. *The Letters of T.S. Eliot, Volume 3: 1926-1927*, ed. Valerie Eliot and John Haffenden (London: Faber, 2012), p. 34. This view of Arlen's unimportance was not shared by the author Frances Melville Perry. In the same year she published a how-to manual for "readers concerned with forming taste" and writers seeking "to develop practical ability in story-writing" in which she classed Arlen alongside Mansfield among the "Masters of Expressionism and Latter-Day Classicism" (F.M. Perry, *The Art of Story-Writing* [London: G. Bell, 1926]).
7   See Murry's letter of 18 December 1915 quoted in the Lawrence chapter above.

ERNEST HEMINGWAY

In a memoir of his early life, Michael J. Arlen, son of the novelist, recalls a chance encounter with Ernest Hemingway in New York in the early 1950s. Father and son, the latter just down from college, dropped into the 21 Club (a celebrated bar on West 52nd Street) for a drink. They were on their way out when

> suddenly, a voice boomed out: "Michael!" My father stopped. The room seemed quite dark. Over in a corner sat Hemingway. Unmistakable. The beard. The face. I walked on over, following my father. "Good to see you, Michael," he said with evident feeling. (*Exiles* 156)

Hemingway, it seemed, was being interviewed by newspapermen, and Arlen Sr. was reluctant at first to gatecrash the party. But his old friend was insistent that father and son join him; the journalists' presence was swiftly forgotten. Arlen Jr. continues:

> I guess I should remember what they said, what who said to whom, but it wasn't like that at all. Mostly I remember

a kindness that seemed to exist between the two men, in the resonance of the voices, in the eyes, in the echoes that moved back and forth across the tablecloth.

As the writers reminisced about "old friends in Paris and London", the son was struck by "a very real warmth" between the two:

> I remember Hemingway pleased, my father easeful, a kind of ease I'd rarely seen in him, none of that wit, that dapperness, that St Regis amusingness. ... Briefly I think that for a few moments in the dark of that room, he must have felt himself on hard ground again, known.

Finally they parted, with "lots of handclasping, shoulder clasping" (157).

Having told us that he cannot remember what was said, Michael J. Arlen proceeds nonetheless to reconstruct the conversation.[1] Hemingway complained about the bad reviews he had recently received for *Across the River and into the Trees*. He spoke of his son, Patrick, who was "in Africa" and of his hopes to get out to his cabin in Idaho. According to the chronology established a few pages earlier, this encounter took place in March of the son's senior year at Harvard, i.e. March 1952 (154). This cannot be right. Hemingway was not in New York at this time; indeed, he spent the whole of 1952 in Cuba. A far more plausible date is March 1950, when Hemingway was staying at the Sherry-Netherlands Hotel in New York City from March 27 to April 6, socialising freely and talking to reporters (Chamberlin 277; Baker 482-3). One further detail in the son's anecdote seems to confirm this dating, and it is the sort of personal observation that would lodge in the memory. He describes how Hemingway was recovering from a skin disease: "He kept rubbing the side of his face with the flat of his hand. 'Those damned doctors,' he said. 'All that money to fix one's hide'" (157). Hemingway had indeed developed a skin infection. While still in Europe in February 1950 he had been shooting with a new automatic shotgun with a fast and simple blowback. His doctors decided that his face must be allergic to gunpowder and put him on a dose of penicillin, supplemented by aureomycin and ichthyol ointment (Baker 481-2).

However, if the anecdote is backdated to March 1950, then the "conversation" as reported cannot have taken place. The bad notices for Hemingway's novel followed its publication in book form in September 1950. Patrick Hemingway was still a student at Harvard in spring 1950. He visited his father in the New York hotel suite to announce his engagement, but it was only after his marriage later that year that the newly-weds moved to Africa. What seems to have happened is that Arlen Jr., unable to recall the conversation, has substituted information about Hemingway he picked up at a later date. In summer 1952, the younger Arlen, just graduated from Harvard himself, obtained his first job in journalism, working for *Life* magazine. That summer, *Life* was in the process of publishing Hemingway's *The Old Man and the Sea*. The new recruit was privileged, he tells us, to be allowed to bring the galley proofs home with him: "an indication, which I hoped everyone would find reassuring, of how far I had proceeded into the professional world" (84). The likelihood is that there was talk in the magazine's office of the rough critical reception meted out to Hemingway's previous novel, and someone doubtless mentioned young Arlen's fellow Harvard alumnus, Patrick Hemingway, who was by then in Africa.

All of this would be so much nit-picking if we accept the *spirit* of Arlen Jr.'s anecdote: that he witnessed the heart-warming reunion of two old friends. But did he? What do we know about the relationship between Ernest Hemingway and Michael Arlen?

In May 1925, a couple of weeks after Hemingway's first meeting with Scott Fitzgerald in Paris, Fitzgerald invited Hemingway to join him on a road trip to south-east France. Fitzgerald needed to retrieve a Renault that he and Zelda had temporarily abandoned in a garage there. The two men took the train down to Lyon and drove the roadster back. According to the colourful account that Hemingway gave decades later in *A Moveable Feast*, Fitzgerald spent much of the return journey recounting the plots of "each and every one of Michael Arlen's books". Hemingway, already nettled by Fitzgerald's earlier behaviour during the trip, was not impressed:

> Michael Arlen, he said, was the man you had to watch and he and I could both learn much from him. I said I could not read the books. He said I didn't have to. He would tell me the plots and describe the characters. He gave me a sort of oral Ph.D. thesis on Michael Arlen. (158)

On his return to Paris, Hadley asked her husband if he had "learn[ed]" anything on his trip. "I learned about Michael Arlen, if I would have listened," he replied (159). Although Hemingway's later retelling of events is to be treated with caution, some such conversation undoubtedly took place. In a letter of December 1926, Hemingway told his publisher Maxwell Perkins that "my contact with Arlen was through Scott's talking about him and his stuff when we once drove Scott's car from Lyons to Paris" (*Letters* vol. 3 178). Writing to Fitzgerald in April 1931, Hemingway confesses that he has not kept up with "Arland (sic) or any other of the boys" and invites Fitzgerald to give him a "cultured synopsis of what the lads have been doing" (*Letters* vol. 4, 489), a probable reference back to the "oral Ph.D. thesis" to which he had been subjected in 1925.

In early June 1926, after Hemingway had submitted *The Sun Also Rises* to Scribners, he invited Fitzgerald to read the typescript. Fitzgerald's response was a ten-page report which did not pull any punches. He found parts of the book "careless + ineffectual" and jibbed at superfluous stylistic flourishes, especially in the opening chapter (a section which Hemingway would eventually cut). "And to preserve these perverse and wilful non-essentials," Fitzgerald complained, "you've done a lot of writing that honestly reminded me of Michael Arlen" (qtd. in Bruccoli 249-50). What did he mean by this? It is hard to think of two writers with more sharply contrasted styles than the economical Hemingway and the verbose Arlen. Hemingway's first published volume of stories, *In Our Time*, already shows him on the way to developing the stripped-down manner for which he is known, and Fitzgerald's comments may be intended to spur him further in that direction. Yet, to the critical reader in 1926, what Fitzgerald calls "condescending *casualness*" (250) when detected in another writer might well have suggested the affected "fine writing" of Arlen, then riding high in popularity. As originally written, Hemingway's novel began: "This is a novel about a lady. Her name is Lady Ashley and when the story begins she is living in Paris and it is spring" (Bloom 5). Compare the openings of two consecutive Arlen stories from his 1923 collection *These Charming People*. "This is quite a simple story, but it is about a lord" (148) is how one begins. And the next: "This is a story about my friend George Tarlyon, who is a brave man and no bigger liar than most" (156). Fitzgerald also found fault with the "snobbish" treatment of Brett Ashley's aristocratic connections in Hemingway's original version. It was "shopworn", he argued, unless accompanied by "the realisation that that ground has already raised its wheat + weeds" (qtd. in

Bruccoli 250). In the mid-Twenties no writer had striven harder to market London 'society' types to a lay audience than Michael Arlen.

We can be confident that one topic covered in Fitzgerald's "oral Ph.D. thesis" on Arlen would have been the latter's most recent novel, *The Green Hat*. Despite the markedly different plots of the two books, many early reviews of Hemingway's novel detected a connection between Brett Ashley and Iris March. "The heroine of *The Sun Also Rises* is another lady of *The Green Hat*, except that she is a little more outspoken and a little heavier drinker," noted the *Chicago Tribune* (qtd. in Leff 52). The *Kansas City Star* observed that "Ernest Hemingway seems to have borrowed the Green Hat of Michael Arlen, knocked it out of shape, kicked it across the room once or twice, and then gone off to a bullfight wearing the remains pulled pugnaciously down over one eye" (qtd. in Tyler 58). In the *Saturday Review of Literature*, William Rose Benet commented: "Brett, Lady Ashley, came as something of a shock. She had strayed out of 'The Green Hat'. We couldn't see what she was doing in Hemingway's novel" (qtd. in *Letters* vol. 3 147). Similar points were made by Allen Tate in the Nation, Edwin Muir in the *Nation and Athenaeum* and Burton Rascoe in the *New York Sun* (Tyler 56).

Hemingway was never comfortable with admitting his possible influences, and his letters of the time show had badly he took these insinuations. He wrote to Maxwell Perkins: "I see that Mr. Bill Benet is very disappointed to find me lifting a character from Michael Arland (sic) and that is rather funny as I have never read a word of Arland. ..." He goes on to say that he is "afraid" to read Arlen, lest there actually is some similarity between the characters (*Letters* vol. 3 146-7). A couple of weeks later he wrote to Scott Fitzgerald about the novel's reception:

Reviews have been good although the boys seem

> divided as to who or whom I copied the most from you or Michael Arlen so I am very grateful to both of you – and especially you, Scott, because I like you and I don't know Arland (sic) and have besides heard that he is an Armenian and it would seem a little premature to be grateful to any Armenian. (164)

He told Louis and Mary Bromfield that he was "discouraged" by the reviewers' imputation of borrowing and teasingly asked his correspondents if they could lend him a copy of *The Green Hat*: "I'd like to read it. Maybe I could get some more characters without having to ruin my liver drinking with them" (174).

What Hemingway sought to convey in these letters was that he could not have been *influenced* by *The Green Hat* since *he had never read it*. His knowledge of Arlen was limited – at a literary level – to the plot summaries Fitzgerald had provided on their car journey the year before and – at a personal level – to what he had heard through the grapevine. The word on the boulevards, so he informed Maxwell Perkins, was that Arlen (or "Arland", as Hemingway persistently calls him) was an ambitious parvenu who consorted, after the War, with Lady Duff Twysden, Nancy Cunard, Marie Beerbohm and Iris Tree. These well-connected women took him up "as a deserving Armenian youth and let him in on a few things and then dropped him as soon as he became annoyingly Armenian and less deserving – but not before he had gotten a little way behind the scenes into various people's lives" (*Letters* vol. 3 146). Recycled in December 1926, this was the same inaccurate, second-hand information that Hemingway had apparently conveyed to Fitzgerald during their road trip of 1925: "I remember telling Scott who the people were who had taken Arlen up – and even getting quite irritated about Arlen" (178). Likewise, his knowledge of Arlen's novel was pure hearsay: "I took it for granted that the Green Hat must be a cheap book when I *heard* that the heroine killed herself – because the one very essential fact about all those people that Arlen knew was that none of them had the guts to kill themselves" (178, emphasis added). Perkins agreed with him: Arlen's heroine was no more than a "saccharine lady... all smeared over with fake 'glamour'" (qtd. in Leff 52).

There *are* similarities between Brett and Iris, but is it right to speak of "influence"? In her discussion of *The Sun Also Rises*, Lisa Tyler devotes an entire section to a "Source Study" tracing correspondences between Hemingway's novel and Arlen's (56-8). For example, Iris, like Brett, is presented as a bewitching Circe-like figure, threatening men with "a pit of dark enchantment" (*Green Hat* 232). And, like Brett, Arlen's heroine defies conventional gender expectations. She has a "boyish look" in her eyes (330). "You always chose the man's part," the narrator tells her, struck by that "queer, unconscious way she had of always meeting men on their own ground" (141, 305). However, these similarities could, with equal plausibility, be explained as coincidences arising from a commonality of subject-matter between the two authors. The uncontested 'source' for the character of Brett is the real-life figure of Lady Duff Twysden.[2] In the same letter to Perkins in which he rails against the critics for misunderstanding him, Hemingway insists that his character was drawn from life, not from literary precedent:

> So now it is pretty amusing to have known a girl and drawn her so close to life that it makes me feel very badly – except that I don't imagine she would ever read anything – and watch her go to hell completely – and assist at the depart – and then feeling pretty damn badly about it all learn that you had with boyish enthusiasm lifted a character from the un-read writings of some

little Armenian sucker after London names. (*Letters* vol. 3 147)

It is feasible that any similarities between the two literary characters might arise because Hemingway's real-life prototype, Duff Twysden, was familiar with Arlen's character and took inspiration from her. This seems to have been in Fitzgerald's mind when, in another part of his pre-publication critique of *The Sun Also Rises*, he turned his attention to Hemingway's female protagonist: "My theory always was that she [i.e. Duff/Brett] dramatised herself in terms of Arlen's dramatisation of somebody's dramatising of Stephen McKenna's dramatisation of Diana Manners's dramatization of the last girl in Wells's *Tono Bungay*..." (qtd. in Bruccoli 251). Duff may not have read Arlen's novel – Hemingway tells us she was no great reader – but its tropes had gained sufficiently widespread currency in the mid-Twenties as to be inescapable; in particular, the eponymous hat became a fashion 'must-have'. The hat worn by Katharine Cornell in the US stage version of *The Green Hat* was a design by Caroline Reboux, the sought-after Parisian milliner. Thousands of copies were sold commercially in the USA (Marcus 114). When the play opened in London in September 1925, its star Tallulah Bankhead took to wearing green offstage as well as on, a style aped by the actress's fanatical female fanbase (Mosel 200). In Arlen's novel Iris sports a green felt hat, "bravely worn" (*Green Hat* 16); Brett's is a "man's felt hat" (*Sun* 24). When Duff visited Edward Fisher in his Paris apartment, the hat was green (Sarason 250). Malcolm Cowley also remembered Duff's "floppy-brimmed" felt hat as being green, although given that he left Paris in 1923, his testimony is less reliable than Fisher's (Sarason 101, 250). In *The Green Hat* the narrator comments that Iris was "the first Englishwoman I ever saw with 'shingled' hair. This was in 1922" (53). Hemingway's narrator tells us that

Brett's hair "was brushed back like a boy's. She started all that" (*Sun* 19). Whether or not Duff drew inspiration from Arlen's novel, it was natural for those she met and who were familiar with *The Green Hat* to view her through this lens. Donald Ogden Stewart, another of the American *literati* in Paris, recalled that she was "right out of the gay brave hell of Michael Arlen", while her companion Pat Guthrie was "another *Green Hat* character from the overdrafts of Mayfair" (143).

An alternative possibility is that Duff was Arlen's model for Iris March. Rumours circulated in Paris to that effect. Harold Loeb, her sometime lover who appears in *The Sun Also Rises* in the unflattering guise of "Robert Cohn", believed that she was, at least "in part", despite Duff assuring Loeb that she was not (Sarason 101). Loeb's notion can be swiftly dismissed. It is generally accepted that Arlen's principal inspiration for his character was the poet and social activist Nancy Cunard, with whom Arlen was romantically involved between spring 1920 and summer 1921 (Chisholm 61-73). There is no evidence that Arlen even knew Duff Twysden, although their social paths may have crossed in London in the early Twenties.[3] And here we come to the most startling claim in Michael J. Arlen's recollections of the meeting with Hemingway in the 1950s, which he reserves for the final paragraph of his memoir. As the two old comrades part, Hemingway says conspiratorially to his friend: "I still owe you, Michael". Once they have left the restaurant, son inquires of father what Hemingway meant by this parting shot. "An old private joke," Arlen Sr. explains: "'One autumn in Paris I introduced Ernest to a girl I was with... Duff Twysden. Ernest later made that book around her. You know: Lady Brett... At some time or other everybody was in love with Duff Twysden'" (*Exiles* 158). Again, this claim is not supported by any other evidence: there are more convincing candidates for the role of intermediary. Arlen Sr. rarely missed an opportunity to place himself at the centre of a story, even if he was miles away at the time. In spring 1924, when Duff is known to have entered Hemingway's life, it was probably as a friend of Harold Loeb, who had conceived a passion for the Englishwoman (Baker 144-5). An alternative claimant is Robert McAlmon, one of Hemingway's first publishers in Paris, whom he had known since February 1923. McAlmon recalled many years later: "I did introduce Hemingway to Lady Duff, and the title seemed to electrify him, and for weeks he was up with her in Montmartre, actually paying drink bills for her and Pat Guthrie" (qtd. in Sarason 227).[4] Arlen was briefly in Paris in March 1924 – we have a letter to the critic Raymond Mortimer written from "Hôtel Westminster, Rue de la Paix" on 24 March[5] – but, as previously shown, Hemingway was emphatic that he did not know Arlen personally at this time.

Mark Spilka has suggested that another Arlen heroine may have contributed to the characterisation of Brett Ashley. If so, could this be another of the plots that Fitzgerald recounted to his reluctant listener during the eventful car trip of 1924? 'The Romantic Lady' was the title story of Arlen's 1921 collection. It is a confection with a "twist in the tale" typical of its author. At the theatre one night the narrator spies an attractive woman alone in a theatre box. He designs, in the most gentlemanly of ways, to pick her up. She accepts his invitation and he is taken home by her only to find a dinner table already set for two. It is *she* who has picked *him* up. On parting she commands him that when leaving he must not look to see the number of the house or the name of the street, thus ensuring that he will never see her again. It later emerges that the lady has done this before – and if her lover of one night makes the mistake of returning next day hoping to pursue the romance, as the narrator duly does, she insists that he marry her. Spilka suggests a number of parallels between Arlen's story and Hemingway's novel (206-8).

However, here again, there can be no certainty that both writers are not simply reaching into the same repository of received tropes: the *'femme fatale'* as seen through male eyes.

More intriguing is a suggestion Spilka relegates to a single sentence in an endnote (351 n.12). *The Torrents of Spring*, dashed off in ten days in November 1925, is Hemingway's bad-tempered satire on certain writers of his time – principally Sherwood Anderson, who had done much to encourage the young author, although it also takes swipes at Gertrude Stein and Scott Fitzgerald by name (and possibly Arlen, by implication). In chapter 14, Yogi Johnson, a war veteran closeted inside the "Beanery" with a number of "Indians", offers a lurid refashioning of Arlen's "romantic" anecdote, framed in the retelling as "something that happened to me in Paris". A "beautiful woman" leans out of a passing car, randomly picks him up and takes him to a mansion in a distant part of the city, where a "very beautiful thing" happens to him. Afterwards she tells him that "she would never, that she could never" see him again. On leaving, he tries to get the number of the mansion but is unable to do so. Thereafter he seeks to find her again; once, he thinks he has spotted her in the theatre. Finally, a city guide takes him to a "mansion", where military men are voyeuristically peering through slits in the wall. On looking through a slit himself, Yogi recognises the beautiful woman of his search about to give herself to a "young British officer". Disillusioned with women and with "the decay of morality in general", Yogi declares that the "beautiful thing" turned out to be the "ugliest thing" that ever happened to him (95-7).

The likeliest time for a first meeting between Hemingway and Arlen is 1926, either in the spring when Arlen was staying at hotels (usually the Grosvenor or the Ritz) or in the autumn, when he rented a flat in the rue Fourcroy.[6] That said, there is only one documented meeting between the two writers during

Hemingway's Paris period. In 1929 the Paris-based publisher Edward Titus was engaged in trying to secure a better publishing deal for D.H. Lawrence in the United States. He wrote to Lawrence on 9 October:

> After I wrote my last letter to you [c. October 3] it so happened that I had a visit from Mr. Reeves, one of the big men at Heinemann's in London. He, Nelson Doubleday, the head of the big publishing house in America, and Michael Arlen called together. They came again two days later and we had an afternoon together at Ernest Hemingway's. (Lawrence 520)

By October 15, when Titus wrote to Lawrence again, the "business" of the latter's financial affairs was looking promising: "Let it for the present remain a little secret between you, Doubleday, Heinemann's and myself. Arlen knows about it and Ernest Hemingway also, as the matter was touched upon at his place when we were all of us calling on him" (534). What other matters were touched upon at this meeting, on or around October 5, we can only speculate. On October 3 Hemingway was seething over the cover design of *A Farewell to Arms* and berating Perkins in an incoherent letter. On the 8th he and Pauline Pfeiffer attended a party given by James and Nora Joyce. On the 10th Hemingway's son Patrick was diagnosed as having a severe case of tuberculosis (Chamberlin 97-8).

By October 15 of that year Arlen was back in London for the publication of his new volume of four short stories, *Babes in the Wood*. This has a curious connection with Hemingway. One story, already published in a magazine earlier in 1929 under the title 'Riviera', now reappeared in slightly expanded form as 'The "Lost Generation"'. Arlen's central character is called "Hemingway". This Hemingway is not a pugnacious young writer but rather a forty-year-old mining engineer, "one of those men whom you don't associate with romance, and even less with sentimentality" (181). Uncharacteristically, he falls in love with the very unsuitable Beulah Ley, whose usual social group comprises "artists, intellectuals, and poets, being something of the kind herself" (183). With her "aristocratic contempt for manners", she proves "heady stuff for a simple man" (184-5). His hopelessly idealised view of her is undermined when he realises that she is "no more than a light woman", "an English lady – behaving like an obscene nymph" (188-9). In a distasteful climax, set during a house party in the south of France, Hemingway attacks Beulah in her bedroom as she prepares for an assignation with another male guest (218). On the train journey south to this final meeting, Hemingway's reflections elevate Beulah from individual to representative:

> Yes, she was one of the "lost generation", born thirty or so years ago, the children of a decaying continent. Well, wasn't Europe decaying while you looked at it? And did those clever young people, the "lost generation", do anything for it? On the contrary, their spiritual word was "departure" – a restless flitting from one thing to another. … Yes, Beulah was a poor devil, really. And her friends too, those clever young puppies, those pale young men, inclined to prance as they walked. One had to be sorry for them – the poor brainy filleted bright young people – *castrated and damned*. (194, emphasis added)

As Michael Soto observes, Arlen here "engages the rhetoric behind the Lost Generation myth", using none-too-subtle references to the work of Hemingway (the writer) and Fitzgerald (41-2). Like Jake Barnes in *The Sun Also Rises*, emasculated by a war wound, these young men are "castrated"; like Fitzgerald's couple in *The Beautiful and Damned* their hedonism condemns them to fall from grace and suffer.

In his futuristic fantasy *Man's Mortality* (1933), Arlen once again introduces a character called "Hemingway". The mild-mannered Rt. Hon. James McNeill Hemingway is a director of International Aircraft and Airways, Inc., the global corporation which has ruled for fifty years before being overthrown by rebels within its own ranks. This pusillanimous figure is unable to function in the absence of his fellow director, Marie-Therese Abazar (another of Arlen's long line of man-eating *femmes fatales*). As he faces arrest, he presents a sorry spectacle:

> There was something really touching in the tender smile of this lean, worn, weak man who, having been thrust into high and dangerous places by the contemptuous affections of a woman of genius, now at last found himself lost, deserted, despised, a minnow in a whirlpool which his own pitiful little tail had helped to create. (338)

Why is this character a "Hemingway"? So far removed is he from the womanizing, hard-drinking pugilist of the Ernest Hemingway myth that one might suppose some satirical intent – point-scoring, a case of "getting even" for some now unrecorded slight. Yet Arlen was not someone to bear grudges. The ill-treatment he had received at the hands of English snobs and the literary intelligentsia left him pathetically grateful for the companionship of any "men of letters" who would have him. *Man's Mortality* shows an undoubted affinity with Aldous Huxley's *Brave New World*, published in February 1932 while Arlen was at work on his novel, and it is possible Arlen had simply learned from Huxley's practice with names. In Huxley's future, the world of "Bernard Marx" and "Lenina Crowne", names like Marx and Lenin have long since lost any historical resonance, rather as in the present day we name our sons "Matthew", "Mark", "Luke" or "John" without intending any reference to the Gospel writers who bore those names. Arlen's choice of name, mangling James McNeill Whistler with Ernest Hemingway, might simply conform to this pattern.

For his part, Hemingway found occasions in the 1930s to fire broadsides at Arlen. In autumn 1937, at the time of his burgeoning relationship with Martha Gellhorn, he was in Madrid at work on a play, *The Fifth Column*. His talents did not lie naturally in this direction and the resultant work has never found success on stage. His principal characters, Philip Rawlings, a war correspondent and secret agent for the Spanish Republic with "big shoulders" and a "walk like a gorilla", and Dorothy Bridges, a fellow journalist boasting "the longest, smoothest, straightest legs in the world", are little but cardboard versions of himself and Gellhorn (62, 41). At one point, Dorothy suggests the two of them get away from the war; Philip runs bitterly through all the attractive locations they might visit, which leads to this exchange:

> DOROTHY. And we'll do all that and Saint Moritz, too?
> PHILIP. Saint Moritz? Don't be vulgar. Kitzbühel you mean. You meet people like Michael Arlen at Saint Moritz.
> DOROTHY. But you wouldn't have to meet him, darling. You could cut him. ... (89)

In 1934 the American-Armenian writer William Saroyan published his first volume of short stories, *The Daring Young Man on the Flying Trapeze*. In one story, 'Seventy Thousand Assyrians', he spoke of "a great philosophical work on tennis, something on the order of *Death in the Afternoon*", which he called a "pretty fine piece of prose", adding that even when

Hemingway was a fool, he was "at least an accurate fool" (34). This, and Saroyan's *ad hominem* jibes at other established authors, provoked Hemingway to one of his intemperate outbursts. In an article for *Esquire*, Hemingway took aim at Saroyan's supposed bumptiousness:

> Which brings us to ta-ta-ta-ta (music) William Saroyan, who tells the boys in his stories how he can write like, or better than, other people if he wanted to try. Whoopee! What's his name? William Saroyan is his name and we don't charge him a nickel for this.
> The answer is: there was another bright young Armenian and he turned out to be Michael Arlen. ... You want to watch yourself, Mr. S., that you don't get so bright that you don't learn. And you don't want to forget the old fellow countryman, Mr. Arlen. He was as bright as you and brighter and look what happened. ('Notes on Life and Letters')[7]

What *did* happen? The side-swipe at Arlen, and the casual racism directed at those of Armenian heritage, is of a piece with Hemingway's private dismissal of Arlen in his correspondence. What happened to writers, in Hemingway's world-view, was that they either betrayed their talent, like Sherwood Anderson, or they became competitors who threatened to equal or even surpass his own achievements, like Scott Fitzgerald. Furthermore, they stirred in Hemingway the 'anxiety of influence': what if he owed some debt to another writer, or at any rate what if the critics *thought* he owed a debt to another writer? And these considerations, far from being isolated in some literary silo, spilled over into Hemingway's personal relations, so that by the 1930s he would turn upon erstwhile friends like Fitzgerald or Dos Passos with undisguised contempt. Some or all of these processes may have been at work in his relations with Arlen. The encounter in a New York restaurant in the early 1950s suggests the renewal of a once-warm friendship. Neither Hemingway nor Arlen – nor indeed Arlen's son – is a reliable narrator of his own life, which makes it especially challenging to reconstruct the relationship between these disparate figures. Yet a relationship of diverse kinds, on both personal and literary levels, there undoubtedly was.

NOTES

1   One topic of conversation – concerning Lady Duff Twysden – will be discussed later in this chapter.
2   Lady Duff, born Mary Duff Stirling Smurthwaite in Yorkshire in 1892, had a chequered past. She had married twice, her title deriving from her second marriage in January 1917 to a baronet, Sir Roger Twysden, from whom she separated in 1924. In the mid-Twenties, according to a later hearing for bankruptcy, "she spent most of her time in Paris, where she earned £50 or £60 a year as an artist" and was receiving an allowance from Twysden of £300 a year until she was again divorced in November 1926 (*Times Law Report*). When Hemingway met her she was living with Pat Guthrie, an alcoholic Scot represented in *The Sun Also Rises* as "Mike Campbell".
3   Prior to moving to Paris, Duff is conspicuous by her absence from the social and gossip columns of the London press. The only references I have found are her attendance "dressed as a Futurist" at the 'Artists' Revel' at the Royal Opera House, Covent Garden in March 1914 where she was squired by Luttrell Byrom, shortly to become her first husband, and an appearance at Royal Ascot in June 1922, where she was accompanied by a Mrs Pope (*Tatler*). Both stories carried photographs. By the mid-Twenties, when the 'Bright Young People' were in the ascendancy, she had left London.
4   In 1954 Hemingway told the credulous Aaron Hotchner that he had met Duff through Scott Fitzgerald (28). Chronology makes

this most unlikely; in any case, Fitzgerald disliked her (Bruccoli 252).
5 Unpublished. Princeton University Library, Special Collections.
6 As discussed in the next chapter, Scott Fitzgerald first encountered Arlen in person in Paris in late June 1926. On that occasion Arlen made the mistake of criticising Hemingway's *In Our Time*. According to Sara Mayfield, who was present, Arlen viewed Hemingway as "a struggling journalist, clumsy on the tennis court, boorish in his manner, and something of a roughneck. His criticisms of Scott's current hero nettled Fitzgerald, who retorted that Arlen was 'a finished second-rater that's jealous of a coming first-rater'" (108-9). If this testimony is reliable, it suggests that Arlen and Hemingway had met by June 1926, perhaps even faced each other on the tennis court (Arlen was a keen player). This calls into question Hemingway's insistence, as late as December 1926, that his knowledge of Arlen was all at second-hand.
7 In his reminiscences of Arlen published much later, Saroyan suggests that 'The "Lost Generation"' was some sort of wake-up call for Hemingway: "Everybody knows Hemingway wanted all writers to admire him and was very sensitive about anybody not doing so noticeably. Michael Arlen's story must have provoked him into a firmer hold on his talent at the work-table" (Saroyan, 'The Armenian' 5). However, he bases this unlikely claim on the assumption that the story was written and published in the mid-Twenties "before Hemingway had broken through". In fact, its first known appearance was in May 1929.

F. SCOTT FITZGERALD

When the actress Joan Collins published her autobiography in 1978, she attempted to embellish her 'showbiz' anecdotes with a little high culture. At one point in the memoir she tells us how "I had just read F. Scott Fitzgerald's *The Girl in the Green Hat*" (Collins [1978] 103). It was Ms. Collins's misfortune to be reviewed by Angela Carter in the pages of *New Society* magazine. The acid-tongued Carter seized on this line as confirmation of the publisher's proud boast that the actress had penned the book herself, for "no competent ghost would have let through a cultural reference such as [that]" (112). Sure enough, in subsequent editions, Collins's error was silently corrected and the actress's bedside reading now became simply "*The Green Hat*," author uncredited (Collins [1985] 106).

It is a striking blunder. Few people nowadays would confuse Scott Fitzgerald with Michael Arlen, author of *The Green Hat* – the former still read, respected and taught in schools, the latter all but forgotten – but evidently something of Arlen's tattered glory survived even into the lifetime of Joan Collins (born in 1933). And in the 1920s, as this chapter will demonstrate, these authors could be spoken of in the same breath, their careers developing in parallel, with one responding to the other.

The Fitzgeralds, as is well known, sailed for Europe in mid-April 1924. The first reference to Arlen in Fitzgerald's correspondence occurs in September of that year, when Maxwell Perkins, his editor at Scribner's, brought him up to speed – not always accurately – with the publishing scene back in New York:

> The somewhat conservative and substantial book readers talk a great deal about a book by E. M Foster [sic] called "The Passage to India" [sic], but I have only read about a third of it. "These Charming People" is very popular among people you would be likely to see here, and word has come to those who have been on the other side, about another novel of his called, "The Green Hat." (Kuehl and Bryer 77-78)

Notable here is that Perkins refers to two of Arlen's publications without naming the author – perhaps guessing that Fitzgerald does not need to be told. He mistakenly assumes that *These Charming People* (UK edition 1923, US 1924) is a novel; in fact, it is a short-story collection. The US edition of *The Green Hat* appeared with George Doran in September 1924, the month of Perkins's letter, which may explain his offhand allusion to what would prove a highly lucrative property for a rival publisher.

Following the success of *The Green Hat* on both sides of the Atlantic, Arlen was invited to America. He arrived in New York on 10 March 1925 and stayed for two months, where he was royally feted by socialites and his activities (as well as his trend-setting waistcoats) were the subject of slavish coverage in the press. The ostensible purpose of the visit was to supervise the production of his dramatisation of the novel, but although he travelled to Detroit in March and Chicago in April for the out-of-town try-outs and returned in September for the Broadway opening, he took little interest in the details of casting or staging (Keyishian 68-70; Mosel 196-7). Fitzgerald's friend, the columnist and short-story writer Ring Lardner, observed this visit with a humorist's eye. Fitzgerald had already done Lardner a service by introducing him to Perkins and suggesting a title for Lardner's first volume to appear under the Scribner's imprint (Bruccoli 178-79). On 24 March 1925, Lardner reported to Fitzgerald on Arlen's New York debut:

> Michael Arlen, who is here to watch the staging of The Green Hat, said he thought How To Write Short Stories was a great title for my book and when I told him it was your title, he said he had heard a great deal about you and was sorry to miss you. He also said he had heard that Mrs. Fitzgerald was very attractive, but I told him he must be thinking of someone else. Mike is being entertained high and low. He was guest of honor at a luncheon given by Ray Long. Irv Cobb and George Doran sat on either side of him and told one dirty story after another. Last Sunday night he was at a party at Condé Nast's, but who wasn't? (Bruccoli and Duggan 154)

Lardner had more gossip for Fitzgerald in a later letter. Arlen's itinerary also included an invitation to the famous Algonquin Round Table, the self-styled 'Vicious Circle,' home to native wits like Dorothy Parker and Robert Benchley. Although Arlen was subjected to what one observer called "the most trying ordeal I ever saw a guest of honor have to submit to" (Rascoe 45), he gave as good as he got:

> Here is some more "low down": Some of the Algonquin bunch was sort of riding Michael Arlen, I don't know why. Anyway, when Edna Ferber was introduced to

him, she said: "Why, Mr. Arlen, you look almost like a woman!" "So do you, Miss Ferber," was Michael's reply. (qtd. in Yardley 259)

Versions of this anecdote circulated widely in the press at the time and it is unclear whether Lardner had it at first hand or is simply repeating to Fitzgerald what he had read. Arlen's jousting partner was not named in published reports, which confined themselves to noting that "the woman is of a rather decided masculine type, usually wearing mannish clothes, smoking cigarettes and talking in deep tones" (Dean 4).

In May 1925, around the time of his first meeting with Ernest Hemingway in Paris, Fitzgerald wrote to Perkins: "A profound bow to my successor, Arlen – when I read *The London Venture* I knew he was a comer and was going to tell you but I saw the next day that Doran had already published '*Piracy*'. That was just before I left New York" (*Letters* 182). The letter confirms that he was already familiar with Arlen's work by 1924, having read the latter's first book, *The London Venture,* published in the US by Doran in 1920. It is fair to assume that by the time he met Hemingway he had read most or all of Arlen's other publications up to that point: in addition to *The Green Hat*, the short story collection *The Romantic Lady* (1921, UK and US) and very possibly '*Piracy*' (UK 1922, US 1923; the quotation marks are part of the original title), which he mentions in the letter.[1]

A couple of weeks after that first meeting with Hemingway, Fitzgerald invited Hemingway to join him on a road trip to southeast France. This was the occasion, as described in the previous chapter, when Fitzgerald subjected Hemingway to "a sort of oral Ph.D. thesis on Michael Arlen". Writing to Fitzgerald in April 1931, Hemingway confessed that he has not kept up with "Arland [*sic*] or any other of the boys" and invited Fitzgerald to give him a "cultured synopsis of what the lads have been doing" (*Selected Letters* 339), a probable reference back to the unwelcome "oral Ph.D. thesis" of 1925.

In November 1925 the Fitzgeralds visited London and saw Tallulah Bankhead star in the stage version of *The Green Hat*. As Zelda joked later to their daughter, Scottie: "We went to London to see a fog and saw Tallulah Bankhead, which was, perhaps about the same effect." Her husband's opinion of the play is not recorded but Zelda was clearly underwhelmed. On their return to Paris, she wrote peevishly to her friend Madeline Boyd: "Just got back from bloody England, where the Michael Arlens grow – hardy annuals it says in the seed catalogues" (qtd. in Cline 184). Adapting successful novels for the stage was a fashion of the day. In February 1926 it was the turn of *The Great Gatsby*. The *New York Times* critic was impressed by the results, taking aim at Arlen in the process:

> Of the several attempts to portray on the stage these restless moderns, whose cynicisms and infidelities keep the calamity-howlers hoarse, none has been more able or moving than 'The Great Gatsby,' mounted last evening at the Ambassador. After the several counterfeits by Michael Arlen and his school of bogus sociologists this approach to the whirling, baffled folk who cherish no loyalties, none even to themselves, becomes conspicuous at once for its perspective and sincerity. (Atkinson)

In early June 1926, after Hemingway had submitted *The Sun Also Rises* to Scribner's, he invited Fitzgerald to read the typescript. As discussed in the previous chapter, Fitzgerald's response was a ten-page report which did not pull any punches. To the critical reader in 1926, what Fitzgerald there calls "condescending *casualness*" when detected in another writer might well have suggested the affected "fine writing" of Arlen, then riding high in popularity. Fitzgerald sensed in Hemingway, as in himself, a tendency to "embalm in mere wordiness" a favourite anecdote or joke. He recognized the dangers inherent in a reluctance to let go of such "fine writing" (*Life in Letters* 142).[2] (Such is the "anxiety of influence" that Harold Bloom identified as troubling for so many writers.) It is conceivable that the popularity of *The Green Hat*, narrated by a minor character who reconstructs events, may even have influenced Fitzgerald's narration of *The Great Gatsby* by a peripheral observer. Both novels climax with a terrible car crash. Both novels raise questions about whether it is better to have illusions, false though they are, or try to survive without them.[3]

Sara Mayfield, Zelda's Montgomery friend, was witness to what was probably the first face-to-face meeting between Arlen and Fitzgerald. This was in the ladies' bar of the Paris Ritz one afternoon in late June 1926. Mayfield was having cocktails with René Herrera, son of the Spanish ambassador. Herrera had brought along Michael Arlen, "an elegant young man with a British accent and a Mayfair manner." Fitzgerald then arrived in the company of "two Westport girls and half a dozen Princeton boys" (108). Fitzgerald recognised Arlen and left his companions to join Mayfield's party. Aware that *The Green Hat* was currently outselling *The Great Gatsby*, Fitzgerald told Arlen that he would probably be Fitzgerald's successor as the most popular fiction writer of the day. Mayfield continues: "Arlen winced at the backhanded compliment, but expressed his appreciation of Scott's talent – if in measured terms. Although Arlen was polite about *The Great Gatsby*, he was patently not enthusiastic about it or about Ernest Hemingway's *In Our Time*." The conversation, we are told, was "amiable" until Fitzgerald felt the need to leap to Hemingway's defence. To Arlen, "Hemingway was a struggling journalist, clumsy on the tennis court, boorish in his manner, and something of a roughneck." Such criticisms of Fitzgerald's current hero provoked the American into lashing out verbally and he told Arlen that he was "a finished second-rater that's jealous of a coming first-rater" (109). The confrontation was defused when Fitzgerald suggested that Mayfield leave her party and go with him to visit Zelda, who was in the American hospital at Neuilly recovering from appendicitis (or from an abortion – accounts differ [Cline 191]). This she did.

There is scant evidence for contact between Fitzgerald and Arlen in the later 1920s, although two claims have surfaced in biographies. In the early 1920s, Arlen was romantically involved with the poet and social rebel Nancy Cunard, and she is known to be the primary model for the character of Iris March in *The Green Hat*, an honor she found less than welcome (Chisholm 70). Fitzgerald reportedly encountered Cunard in Paris and had ambivalent feelings about her. Intending to give Cunard a signed copy of *The Great Gatsby*, he later crossed out her name and substituted that of Sylvia Beach (Taylor 163). In her study of the Fitzgeralds' marriage, Kendall Taylor suggests that "the Fitzgeralds were brought into Cunard's circle by Michael Arlen" (163). She does not offer any evidence for this claim. It is true that Arlen and Cunard were both living in Paris between July 1926 and early 1927 and one might expect their social paths to have crossed (although Cunard was by then involved with the Surrealist Louis Aragon and forging new alliances). However, according to Cunard's unpublished memoir of Arlen, after their romance ended in summer 1921, she saw him on only two more occasions, once in London (in the late Twenties) and once, with Norman Douglas, in Nice (in 1938); she makes no mention of any encounters in Paris in mid-decade.[4]

One of the few biographical sources for Arlen's life is the memoir published by his son, Michael J. Arlen, himself an accomplished and garlanded writer. It is an immensely readable book full of anecdotes which are vivid and detailed but often impossible to substantiate. Arlen Jr.'s chronology is not always clear but the following is an incident, seemingly tied specifically to time and place after his parents' marriage:

> Scott Fitzgerald came by one evening, hours late for dinner, striped blazer, white flannels, full of booze from one of Gerald Murphy's parties, embarrassed, garrulous, then silent, leaned his head down on the table top (hair half-way in the soup). "This is how I want to live… this is how I want to live," he said. And fell asleep. (*Exiles* 57)

The setting is (apparently) Cannes, the year (apparently) 1928. The Arlens were indeed in Cannes in summer 1928 – but the Fitzgeralds were not; they remained in Paris all summer, where Zelda began her ballet training with Lubov Egorova, before the couple returned to America in September (Bruccoli xxix). The incident sounds more plausible if moved to the following year, when the Fitzgeralds rented the Villa Fleur des Bois in Cannes from June to October 1929. However, it is unlikely that the two men's paths crossed that summer either, since, by reconstructing his movements from letters and press reports, we see that Arlen was in London and Southport in June, in St. Moritz in July and August, and from September occupying a rented flat in Paris.

In 1929 the magazine *McCall's* commissioned Fitzgerald to write an article about "the present day status of the Flapper." Editor Otis Wiese rejected the submission as too serious (Bruccoli and Atkinson 156). Fitzgerald was all for suing the magazine but his agent, Harold Ober, persuaded him instead to take it elsewhere, and it appeared in *Liberty* in February 1930. 'Girls Believe in Girls' begins with a sort of genealogy of the 'flapper' phenomenon. Fitzgerald traces it back to the Castles, the husband-and-wife dancing team, famous as the originators of the one-step and the turkey trot, who, he suggests, as early as 1912 made modern dancing "respectable." A decade later, according to Fitzgerald, the emancipatory energies unleashed by the War had been so successfully absorbed that "youth had been thoroughly converted" and the "flapper movement" was over: "the whole thing was [now] drippy with sentimentality." But had the flapper's sense of liberation ever been unsentimental, he asks. Literature had long provided examples of sexually adventurous young women:

> ...the young girl making a present of herself to a swain stuck pretty close to the fictional pattern. She was Thackeray's Beatrix Esmond who, in 1912, turned up again in Wells' 'Tono-Bungay' under the name Beatrice Normandy and was passionately emulated by a very select and daring crop of London debutantes. The fascinating Beatrice begot the ladies of Michael Arlen and of almost everyone else who dealt in heroic English girls... (*MLC* 100)

One notices the same succession of authors invoked as in Fitzgerald's Hemingway critique of 1926. Once again, Iris March is simply the last etiolated expression of a character-type running through English literature from the Victorians to the present.

Although it is unclear how much contact there was between Arlen and Fitzgerald in the late Twenties, they were certainly on social terms in April 1930 when there is an account of the two men drinking together at the Fitzgeralds' home. Zelda burst into the flat, in distress. She felt that her husband preferred Arlen's company to hers. When she excused her behaviour to Arlen by telling him she had been ill, the visitor suggested she try a clinic (Cline 258-9). She entered the Malmaison clinic voluntarily on 23 April 1930. Writing to Fitzgerald in summer 1930 from another clinic, this one in Switzerland, Zelda recapitulated her history of recent months. She complained that despite urging her husband to "manifest some interest" in what she was doing, he "never saw fit to either guide or enlighten" her. She continued: "To me, it is not astonishing that I should look on you with unfriendly eyes. You could have saved me all this trouble if you had not been so proud of Michael Arlen the day I went to Malmaison...." (Bryer and Barks 85). Zelda seems to have condensed several events here. Given that she consulted her ballet teacher, Madame Egorova, about the choice of Parisian clinic in April (Mayfield 149), the encounter with Arlen may well have occurred a day or two before she checked into the ominously named Malmaison.

At the time of Zelda's collapse Fitzgerald was still struggling with the novel that would become *Tender is the Night* (1934). Given the long gap since his last book publication (the short stories collected as *All the Sad Young Men*, 1926), Harold Ober was urging him to give the public something, perhaps the Basil Lee stories in book form (*BJG* 3-184); but Fitzgerald resisted publishing before he was ready. He wrote to Perkins around 1 May 1930:

> ...I know too well by whom reputations are made and broken to ruin myself completely by such a move – I've seen Tom Boyd, Michael Arlen, and too many others fall though the eternal trapdoor of trying to cheat the public, no matter what their public is, with substitutes – better to let four years go by. (*Letters* 221)

He replied to Ober himself a few days later:

> I could have published four lousy, half-baked books in the last five years and people would have thought I was at least a worthy young man not drinking himself to

pieces in the south seas – but I'd be as dead as Michael Arlen, Bromfield, Tom Boyd, Callaghan and others who think they can trick the world with the hurried and the second-rate. (*Letters* 395)

It is noteworthy that while socialising convivially with Arlen in Paris – and preferring the latter's company to his wife's, if we are to believe Zelda – he was privately dismissing Arlen as a busted flush.

The *New York Times* review of Arlen's novel *Lily Christine* (1928) had described its author as "an English F. Scott Fitzgerald who has still to achieve his *The Great Gatsby*" ('Mr. Arlen's Syrup'). In his next novel, *Men Dislike Women* (1931), Arlen seems to have taken on the challenge. At the centre of the convoluted plot is Charlie Macrae, an American racketeer, a Gatsby-like figure except that this ideal is not in the past but in his imagination. He idealises an Englishwoman, Sheila Hepburn, but being an idealist, cannot tolerate the truth about her when it emerges, that she has "led a sloppy, silly life, seeking happiness in trifling love affairs" (163). Macrae throws lavish parties at his mansion in Great Neck and Arlen borrows from Fitzgerald the device of using the Queensboro Bridge that links Manhattan and Long Island as a symbolic link between two ways of life. Despite these and many other superficial similarities between the two novels, one is compelled to agree with Harry Keyishian that the differences are more striking:

> Unlike Fitzgerald's profoundly obsessed character, who "invents" himself, as Nick Carraway puts it, in the confused aftermath of World War I, Macrae remains one-dimensional; he is a caricatured naïve American who is created to take part in a romance which turns into a melodrama. (97)

Fitzgerald saw himself as the principal chronicler of the Jazz Age. "I claim credit for naming it," he wrote to Perkins, declaring that it spanned the decade from the May Day Riots of 1919 to the Wall Street Crash in 1929 (Kuehl and Bryer 171). He allowed himself this reflection in 1931, the year in which he published a retrospective essay, 'Echoes of the Jazz Age' (*MLC* 130-38). In the essay he tabulates a dozen literary works "written for various types of mentality during the decade" which came as "revelations" to anyone aged over twenty-five. The list includes, predictably, *Ulysses, Lady Chatterley's Lover* and *The Well of Loneliness*, but also *The Green Hat*, which is commended for demonstrating "that glamorous English ladies are often promiscuous" (*MLC* 133).

Fitzgerald once again uses Arlen as a cultural reference point in the short story, 'Crazy Sunday,' written in January 1932 and first published in *The American Mercury* in October of that year. Joel Coles, the central character, writes 'continuity' for a Hollywood studio. He is invited to a party at the home of a respected director. In the hope of impressing the director's wife, to whom Joel feels strongly attracted, he performs a song of his own composition – and makes a fool of himself in the process. The song is a burlesque on the "cultural limitations" of an independent producer known to all the party. Joel mimics how the producer would "build up" a flimsy scenario and a lead character within it as he dictates a "treatment" to his secretary: "'If we make him a Menjou type, then we get a sort of Michael Arlen only with a Honolulu atmosphere'" (*TAR* 9). The reference is to the American actor Adolphe Menjou (1890-1963). A starring role in Chaplin's *A Woman of Paris* (1923) had established Menjou's image as a well-dressed man-about-town, and with his carefully trimmed moustache and dapper, somewhat "Mediterranean" appearance, he was often likened to Arlen in the Twenties. Furthermore, he had starred in *The Ace of*

Cads, a film version released in 1926 of a story from Arlen's 1925 collection *May Fair* (59-94). It is possible that Fitzgerald saw the movie, although Menjou himself assured George Bernard Shaw that it was "a very bad film" and no copy survives today – suggesting that it was not widely distributed ('Mr. Shaw').

Fitzgerald's final references to Arlen occur in *Tender Is the Night*, which after a long gestation finally appeared in 1934. The novel centres on Dick and Nicole Diver, a glamorous American couple who rent a villa in the South of France. In book 2 chapter 21 Nicole's sister, Baby Warren, recommends that Dick and Nicole take a house in London. "The English are the best-balanced race in the world," she ventures. Dick disputes this:

> "I've been reading a book by Michael Arlen and if that's–"
> She ruined Michael Arlen with a wave of her salad spoon.
> "He only writes about degenerates. I mean the worthwhile English."
> (*TITN* 244)

In a later scene (book 3 chapter 5), when Dick and Nicole attend a party on Golding's yacht, Dick's thoughts turn again to Arlen. Fitzgerald introduces a new character, Lady Caroline Sibly-Biers, an Englishwoman with a reputation as "the wickedest woman in London." Apparently based on Bijou O'Conor, with whom Fitzgerald had an affair in autumn 1930 (and whom he had already parodied in the 1931 short story 'The Hotel Child' [*TAR* 288-309]), she also bears some resemblance to Lady Duff Twysden (in her abrupt speech-patterns and use of colloquialisms like "cheerio," "chap" and "chum"). Dick is seated next to her at dinner and talks to her in a "dogmatic voice." Nicole can only hear snatches of his drunken rant, but what she hears strikes home: "'... It's all right for you English, you're doing a dance of death... Sepoys in the ruined fort, I mean Sepoys at the gate and gaiety in the fort and all that. The green hat, the crushed hat, no future'" (*TITN* 304; ellipses in original). Voiced through his character, Fitzgerald is conflating the demise of Empire (the reference is to the Indian Mutiny of 1857) with the affected 'decadence' of the post-war era epitomized by *The Green Hat*. By now Arlen's name and work had become Fitzgerald's convenient shorthand for referring to the 'Jazz Age' in its short-lived British manifestation.

The Green Hat was the fifth bestselling novel of 1925 in the United States. *The Great Gatsby*, published in April of that year and now recorded as the most studied novel in American high schools, did not make the 1925 bestseller list at all. Quoting these facts, John Sutherland reflects that "Fitzgerald was running a longer literary race" (12). Indeed he was. We have seen that Fitzgerald had high expectations of Arlen at the outset of the Armenian's literary career, even seeing him in some degree as a successor to himself, but became disillusioned with his output by the end of the decade. On a personal level the two men seem to have enjoyed friendly relations throughout the 1920s, despite falling into argument at their (likely) first meeting. Almost none of Arlen's incoming mail survives, which makes it difficult to reconstruct any of his relationships in detail. More information may yet emerge – for example, none of the scholarship on Nancy Cunard to date has dealt adequately with her contacts with the expatriate literary community in Paris – but it is time for the author of "*The Girl in the Green Hat*" to emerge from under the shadow of his greater contemporary.

NOTES

1   In *The Torrents of Spring*, the satirical squib that Hemingway dashed off in ten days in November 1925, Yogi Johnson tells a lurid version of Arlen's story 'The Romantic Lady' in which a beautiful

woman uses him for voyeuristic purposes (79-81). See the earlier chapter on Hemingway.

2   Arlen was routinely castigated on similar grounds: for example, Alec Waugh said of him that "he did not so much tell a story as embroider one" (Waugh 260).

3   Although one can find Arlen's and Fitzgerald's names mentioned on the same literary pages of newspapers throughout 1925 (albeit not always the same exact column), I have not so far discovered any contemporary reviews of *The Great Gatsby* that specifically compare it to *The Green Hat*.

4   Unpublished typescript, Nancy Cunard Archive, Harry Ransom Center, University of Texas. In fact, there was at least one more meeting in Paris, probably in 1926, an awkward dinner party bringing together Cunard with Arlen and Aragon, her past and present lovers. Aragon thought Arlen looked like "un garçon-coiffeur" [a hairdresser's assistant] and complained that he talked incessantly the whole evening (De Courcy 186; Duhamel 249).

ALDOUS HUXLEY

In 1925 Louise Brooks was performing in the 'beauty chorus' of the Ziegfeld Follies. Her elevation to film stardom as the heroine of German Expressionist classics like *Pandora's Box* and *Diary of a Lost Girl* lay several years in the future.[1] Brooks did not endear herself to the other dancers in the chorus, who thought she had pretensions beyond her station. As she later recalled, "I was reading things like Aldous Huxley's *Crome Yellow*. The other girls were reading the *Police Gazette*. They would look at me and say, 'Who is this Kansas bitch? How dare she?'"[2] Brooks's shared dressing-room became, in her words, "the cultural drop-in of such clowning gentlemen as Walter Wanger, Herman Mankiewicz, Michael Arlen, Charlie Chaplin." In a later interview she spun the anecdote in a different direction:

> "…Because it was Herman Mankiewicz who used to bring me all these books. Of course, they really wanted to get into the Follies dressing room because I dressed with Dorothy Knapp, and she was always posing practically naked in front of her mirror. But the gag was that they were coming up to hear me review the latest Huxley book or something like that."[3]

Whatever their motives in paying her attention, the "clowning gentlemen" were all influential figures in the entertainment world of the 1920s. Apart from the globally successful Chaplin, her visitors included Paramount producer Walter Wanger, screenwriter Herman Mankiewicz – and author Michael Arlen. Arlen, for reasons to be explored in this chapter, may have been more interested in discussing Huxley than the others, for by 1925 the two writers' paths had already crossed and re-crossed several times.[4]

We cannot be sure when Arlen and Huxley first met. Their lives first overlapped in late 1915, when both were potential recruits for the utopian colony which D.H. Lawrence proposed to found in Florida.[5] Arlen first met Lawrence, probably, in late November 1915: at Lawrence's request he received an invitation from Lady Ottoline Morrell to stay at her Garsington Manor home from 13 to 16 December. The visit was not a success. Huxley's first meeting with Lawrence, an invitation to tea at the Lawrences' Hampstead home, came a little later – probably 17 December.[6] By this time, Arlen was on board, as Huxley reported to his brother: "[Lawrence] proposes, how unwisely soever it may appear, to go to the deserts of Florida there, with one Armenian, one German wife and, problematically, one young woman called Dorothy Warren, to found a sort of unanimist colony" (*Letters*, 88). He wrote in similarly sceptical terms to Lady Ottoline on 19 December: "Are you going to hustle on the Spring by going to Florida to immure yourself with one Armenian, one German wife, and, problematically, one or two other young people?"[7] Again, the "Armenian" is not identified but the reference is undoubtedly to Kouyoumdjian, then still going by his birth name. It is probable that, like most of his contemporaries, Huxley could neither pronounce nor remember the name, although Lawrence, whose relations with Arlen were good at this point, may well have told him it.

Lawrence's Florida plans came to nothing. It proved impossible for Lawrence to leave Britain during wartime, and married as he was to an "enemy alien," his activities were kept under scrutiny by the security services. Lawrence's writings, in this case his poetry, provide the next point of possible intersection between Huxley and Arlen. On 30 August 1916 Katherine Mansfield was in the Café Royal with her friends the painter Mark Gertler and translator Samuel Koteliansky. According to the account Gertler gave to Mary Hutchinson, the café was packed but they secured a table next to "a long thin white woman with an immensely high bush of crimson hair" who was discussing literature intently with two young "Indians". Mansfield's party took an instant dislike to them, which only intensified when they produced a copy of Lawrence's recently published *Amores*, reading aloud from it and criticising it. "With a sweet imploring look" Mansfield asked to see the book. They politely handed it over, whereupon she confiscated it and swept out of the café with book in hand, beckoning her party to follow her – which they did, exulting over this "best possible revenge."[8] We know, by his own admission, that one of the "Indians" was Hasan Shahid Suhrawardy, Bengali poet and critic, because he met Huxley the following day and told him of the incident. Huxley promptly reported this amusing gossip to Ottoline Morrell, no doubt hoping that she could fill in further details from her circle of contacts (*Selected Letters*, 34). It is clear from Huxley's letter that Suhrawardy recognized Gertler but not Mansfield or Koteliansky. As to the identity of Suhrawardy's companions, an urban myth developed that he had been with one or more of Lawrence's former *protégés*, Michael Arlen and Philip Heseltine (*aka* the composer Peter Warlock). When Richard Aldington was researching his biography of Lawrence in the 1940s he approached Huxley for help with this incident. Huxley, his memory perhaps failing him here, replied: "I know nothing of the episode in the Café Royal and never heard either Lawrence or Heseltine talk about it. Perhaps Arlen could throw some light?" (*Selected Letters*, 398). Arlen obliged by placing both himself and Heseltine at the scene of the crime, despite fervent denials from Heseltine's biographer that the musician was anywhere near the scene.[9]

In the early 1920s, both Arlen and Huxley became romantically involved with the same woman, the poet and society rebel Nancy Cunard. Chronology argues against their being in any sense "rivals" for her affection. Arlen's relationship began in spring 1920 and fizzled out in summer 1921, so far as can be established from fragmentary surviving evidence ("three to four enormous piles" of Arlen's letters to Cunard were destroyed when her home in France was ransacked during the War.)[10] Huxley's affair with Cunard ran (probably) from late 1922 to May or June 1923, although, since the sole sources are oral, dating must remain conjectural (Murray, 145). Its intensity, on Huxley's side, may be gauged from Cunard's appearance in fictionalised form as the driven socialite Myra Viveash in *Antic Hay* (1923), as well as other fainter avatars in later novels.[11] Sybille Bedford blamed Huxley's infatuation with Cunard as the reason for the Huxleys' hasty retreat to Italy in June 1923.[12] However, the picture may be more complicated, since around the same time – late 1922, early 1923 – Huxley seems to have started a relationship with Mary Hutchinson, an affair of much longer duration and one into which the bisexual Maria Huxley would later be drawn also (Murray 143).[13]

In April 1923 Huxley published a story in H.L. Mencken's journal *The Smart Set*. Although it reappeared in *The Smart Set Anthology* in 1934, Huxley himself did not carry it over into his own short story collections, perhaps for good reason.[14] 'Over the Telephone' is a slight piece: yet another rehearsal of a kind of primal scene that recurs in Huxley's early fiction. Walter, a young man of literary bent, develops an infatuation for an unsuitable – and, in this case, unavailable – woman. Her taste in men is deplorable: "She had never, so far as he knew, liked anyone who wasn't perfectly awful, anyone who wasn't in some way or other a monster." She is a "Renaissance princess" who can be taken in by "any clown or any adventurer" (44). As James Sexton has observed, the heroine, Hermione Burges, has aspects of both Nancy Cunard and Mary Hutchinson but more closely resembles the latter (31). The pain that Huxley assuages in re-enacting such moments of rejection through fiction may originate with Cunard, however. Walter recites Hermione's romantic history. It begins with a brief marriage to the "blackguard" Burges, from whom she is separated (just as Cunard was separated from her husband Sydney Fairbairn):

> And then she got entangled with Diamantopoulos, the nimble Greek. If only she had read the Aeneid, she'd have known that it is wise to fear Greeks, even when they bring presents. Not that Diamantopoulos, according to all accounts, had brought many presents; he had more often borrowed twenty pounds. And then, after seeing through the Greek, she had been able to find no better successor than fat old Bob Rumbelow, the journalist… (45)

This may well be a veiled allusion to the Armenian Arlen, as Sexton suggests (45). The dandified Arlen was known for his love of jewellery, which Huxley references in his choice of surname. At Arlen's first encounter with Cunard, she was wearing a large diamond brooch set in platinum with a reconstructed ruby in the centre. When the jewellery accidentally fell to the floor of a taxi they were sharing, Arlen, ever the gentleman, hastened to retrieve it for her (qtd. in Chisholm, 63). On the other hand,

Arlen, unlike Diamantopoulos, was no scrounger; rather, he was known for expansive acts of generosity, as when he bankrolled the London production of *The Vortex*, Noël Coward's first critical success as dramatist in 1924, thereby launching a literary career that would prove more enduring than his own (Keyishian, 75).

Thus, like most novelists, in creating his fictional cast Huxley appears to resist one-on-one identifications, preferring instead a mode of composite characterisation in which he takes one feature from a person of his acquaintance or combines features from a number of real individuals. We see this again in *Those Barren Leaves* (1925). In the fragments of "autobiography" which form Part II of the novel, Francis Chelifer, a struggling poet, recounts how he fell in love with a girl called Barbara. She, like Myra Viveash, delights in toying with men's affections. Hitherto she had "counted few literary men among her slaves," and so, Chelifer surmises, she was "flattered" to have him "abjectly gambolling round her."[15] He was painfully aware, however, that there were rivals for her affections, one in particular, of Syrian nationality, "a stoutish and flabby young man, very black-haired, very dark-skinned, with a large fleshy nose and a nostril curved in an opulent oriental volute." He sports a silver monocle in his left eye and "grains of poudre de riz" glitter in the stubble of his chin (*TBL*, 139). Although the physical description is only partially applicable to Arlen, the "Syrian" has the self-conscious man-about-town image cultivated by the young Armenian. Cunard recalled Arlen's naïve delight in luxuries: "The good things of life – caviar, plovers' eggs, champagne – it seemed to me it was all as if he had never heard of them, but had discovered them all by himself" (qtd. in Chisholm, 73).

Later in the narrative, Chelifer's jealousy mounts. He cannot understand why Barbara

> was equally gratified by the attentions of another literary

man, the swarthy Syrian with the blue jowl and the silver monocle. Even more gratified, I think; for he wrote poems which were frequently published in the monthly magazines (mine, alas, were not) and, what was more, he never lost an opportunity of telling people that he was a poet; he was for ever discussing the inconveniences and compensating advantages of possessing an artistic temperament. (*TBL*, 147-8)

As Cunard's biographer comments, it seems likely that Huxley here is thinking of Arlen, the successful author, substituting Syrian for Armenian and poetry for novels (Chisholm, 79). Chelifer's hopeless obsession climaxes when he spends a miserable night waiting outside Barbara's house, just as Huxley had once waited outside Cunard's (Chisholm, 78). Eventually, a taxi pulls up. Two people alight, a man and a woman. By the dim light Chelifer catches sight of the "glitter of a monocle." He walks away, dejectedly repeating to himself "every injurious and abusive word that can be applied to a woman" (*TBL*, 151). It is interesting to speculate whether, when Huxley was at work on *Those Barren Leaves* in 1924, he was aware of the appearance of *The Green Hat* in June of that year.[16] In characterising his heroine, Iris March, Arlen had drawn quite shamelessly on details of Nancy Cunard's life, including the gynaecological illness that confined her to a Paris clinic in winter 1920.

By 1927 the cult of *The Green Hat* was beginning to wane. Theatre adaptations in the West End and on Broadway had come and gone. Copies of the eponymous headgear as sported on stage had been marketed through department stores. At least three novel-length parodies appeared in the two years following its publication. In fact, as the *New York Times* gleefully observed, the publication of Arlen's next novel, *Young Men in Love*, might prove to be "no event at all. For *The Green Hat* is now an old hat, and no longer is it fashionable or discerning to speak of Michael Arlen in the same breath with Aldous Huxley, Norman Douglas, and other writers who more permanently add to the gaiety of sophisticated nations."[17]

December 1927 found the Huxleys once more in Forte dei Marmi, their favoured home in Tuscany. The essay collection *Proper Studies* had just been published and Aldous was continuing to struggle with a new novel, *Point Counter Point* (Murray, 201). On Monday 5 December he wrote to his brother Julian: "Maria has gone to Florence for a few days and returns tomorrow, bringing no less a person than Michael Arlen for lunch. It rains incessantly, but it is warm. I work away" (*Selected Letters*, 201). A letter of the same date to Mary Hutchinson is in similarly sarcastic vein: "Maria has gone to Florence for some days and threatens to return with Reggie Turner, Orioli and Michael Arlen for lunch on Tuesday. It might be quite amusing" (*Selected Letters*, 204).[18] Arlen was in Florence at this time, apparently in romantic pursuit of his future bride, Atalanta Mercati, whose parents lived in the city. While there he had bumped into D.H. Lawrence on the Lungarno; the two men had renewed an old friendship, and together socialized with other expatriates, including Norman Douglas.[19] Maria Huxley, meanwhile, was staying at Torre di Bellosguardo, the villa overlooking Florence bought in 1913 by Baroness Marion Hornstein, who had married into the Franchetti family, long-time friends of the Huxleys in Italy. "Marion treats me as if I were a princess," Maria wrote excitedly to Mary Hutchinson from the villa on 2 December, before outlining her plans for the day: "To tea today with Orioli and Turner and possibly Michael Arlen who longs to meet Aldous apparently. I will tell you all about it. I shall also go to Lawrence but how I wish you were here to accompany me."[20] The encounter with Arlen in Florence explains Maria's return invitation to Forte dei Marmi the following week, which was clearly less than welcome to her overworked husband.[21]

Aldous Huxley's opinion of Arlen had not improved by 1931, when the latter was the target of a scathing reference in *Music at Night*. In the essay "'And Wanton Optics Roll the Melting Eye,'" Huxley reflects on how six centuries of scientific progress have rendered Dante's cosmology – the underpinning of *The Divine Comedy* – obsolete and his language obscure. Nowadays his poetry is the province only of a "a diminishing band of culture-fans and erudition-snobs." This group, Huxley, observes, "feel as triumphantly superior in their exclusive learning as would the social snob if, alone of all his acquaintance, he had met the Prince of Wales, or could speak of Mr. Michael Arlen by his pet name."[22] One assumes the "pet name" he has in mind is "The Baron", the nickname conferred on Arlen by Nancy Cunard – the result of her misunderstanding of the Armenian word "Bahr-rohn", which simply means "Mister" (Chisholm, 64). In the memoir of Arlen she composed towards the end of her life, Cunard suggests that the nickname stuck after she was in heated argument with St. John Hutchinson, who could not understand her liking for someone he regarded as a "ghastly oriental rug-merchant". Refusing to grapple with the interloper's Armenian name, Hutchinson called him "Krumjy-Jumjy". Cunard considered this "a fine example of xenophobic barrister mentality." Eventually they compromised on "The Baron". "He was 'The Baron' subsequently to a great, great many of us in the earliest Twenties," she concludes (qtd. in Chisholm, 63-4). Evidently, the connections back to Nancy Cunard (and to Mary Hutchinson's husband) still resonated with Huxley, ten years later, as he reached for an analogy.

"I'm through with women in love. My new novel is about politics," Arlen told an interviewer while sitting in the Miramar Bar in Cannes in 1932. "People seem to forget I'm *really* a serious writer."[23] This revelation might have come as a surprise to a writer of patently serious intentions like Huxley. But *Man's Mortality*, the "new novel" referred to, is nothing if not ambitious. The idea of an international air force such as Arlen envisaged in his book was current in the early 1930s. Several governments, including those of France and Spain, submitted plans for such a force or for the internationalisation of civil aviation to Disarmament Conferences in 1932 and 1933. Although it is unlikely that Huxley read Arlen's novel, is worth noting in passing that the concept of an international air force is one that Huxley mocked later in the decade. "In the world of today," Huxley wrote, "it is inconceivable that French and Germans, Russians and Italians, Americans and Japanese would unite together to man such a force... The proposal is not only undesirable but utterly impracticable".[24] *Brave New World* was published in February 1932 while Arlen was at work on his novel, and it seems likely that Arlen had learned from Huxley's example, not only in the macroscopic design of using an imagined future to critique the present, but also at the microscopic level of titles and character names. For the sole occasion in his career, Arlen follows Huxley's preferred practice of deriving his novel's title from a literary quotation: the phrase "man's mortality" is found in a passage from Wordsworth's 'Intimations of Immortality' quoted as an epigraph. As mentioned earlier, at the centre of his convoluted narrative, Arlen places the mild-mannered "Rt. Hon. James McNeill Hemingway" as director of International Aircraft and Airways, Inc. In Huxley's future, the world of "Bernard Marx" and "Lenina Crowne", names like Marx and Lenin have long since lost any historical resonance. Arlen's choice of name, mangling James McNeill Whistler with Ernest Hemingway, seems to conform to this pattern.

Huxley's name was invoked in a number of reviews of *Man's Mortality*. The *Canadian Forum* declared the book "a pompous but empty blend of Mr Wells' *War in the Air* and Mr Huxley's *Brave New World*, with a dash of *The Green Hat* added lest ancient admirers lose heart."[25] Arlen's argument, as *The Bookman* understood it, was that no changes in environment can change the essentials of human nature. But, the reviewer countered,

> the only interest to be had from speculations on probable changes in environment is in their probably effect on human consciousness and behaviour. Failing to realise this, Mr. Arlen, unlike Mr. Aldous Huxley, does not invent people conditioned by the environment he invents.[26]

The *Saturday Review of Literature* was more favourable, finding in the book

> a saving sanity that was wanting in the tone of Aldous Huxley's caustically imagined Utopia, 'Brave New World.' But the two are alike in one thing. Both envisage, as a last resort for intelligent folk, some sort of an asylum. Huxley names Iceland. Arlen does not specify, but hints that his island of sanity will be a nucleus for some far distant world order.[27]

P.G. Wodehouse, another of the expatriate community on the Riviera, was witness to the origins of Arlen's novel and was not enamoured of the genre Arlen hoped to enrich:

> I bought Aldous Huxley's Brave New World thing, but simply can't read it. What a bore these stories of the future are. The whole point of Huxley is that he can write better about modern life than anybody else, so of course he goes and writes about the future, blast him. Michael

Arlen is down here, writing a novel the scene of which is laid in the future. It's a ruddy epidemic.[28]

Man's Mortality was published in January 1933. Later in that year we have another glimpse of Arlen genuflecting before Huxley, a gesture that was most unlikely to be reciprocated. The event was Arlen's sole encounter with Virginia Woolf. Mary Hutchinson, a mutual friend of Woolf and Arlen, had organised a dinner party with the mischievous intent of bringing these two literary lions together.[29] Given Woolf's disdain for 'middlebrow' fiction, this was never going to end well.[30] Still, Woolf made an effort; she wore her "velvet dress." The next day she committed the experience to her diary:

> I had – oh voluminously – all M.A.'s confession, as I expected. He made £50,000 out of The Green Hat, which money he has perpetually to atone for – as by talking of D.H.L. & how he escaped his influence, how he made his own life, how he married his own wife, a dumb Greek called Atalanta – silent, he said, but a perfect lady – & has 2 children & can keep them all, with drains, games, servants – all this is protest & justification. Now he is writing an intelligent novel, from real experience, lacking to highbrows. *Yet oh Mrs Woolf, how I envy Aldous Huxley his background – his education.* I was at a 3rd rate public school, & lived in Earls Court. His father died of a broken heart when Rumania [sic] came into the war. A little scraping dingy porous clammy monkey faced man. My wife the Contessa Atalanta… always still justifying, but I didn't feel that need myself.[31] (Emphasis added)

The unpleasantness was still in her mind several days later when she wrote to her nephew Quentin Bell, telling him that she had only gone to the party for a bet: "M.A. is a rubber faced little sweaty Armenian monkey, full of protestations, as if I'd just whipped him on the behind for writing The Green Hat… He is not a perfect gentleman. But then he has made fifty thousand pounds, and is now going to write a book for highbrows."[32]

Unusually, we have Arlen's side of the story for once. The day after the party he wrote a courteous thank-you letter to his hostess, which survives among Mary Hutchinson's papers. This is the passage about his fellow guest:

> I'd like to go on at length – indeed, next time I see you I shall go on at length – about Mrs Woolf. I've never been able to think that books, any books, no matter how good, are very important, but what is important – since we're all really eager to admire the best materials – is to be given a glimpse of a beautiful human being.[33]

Did Arlen know that the very people he sought to cultivate – respected writers like Huxley and Woolf – held him in contempt?[34]

There is only one documented encounter between Huxley and Arlen and it occurred two years after this uncomfortable dinner party. In November 1935 the Huxleys were in London. A prime concern of theirs at the time was to prevent their German-Jewish friend Sybille von Schoenebeck from having to return to Nazi Germany when her passport came up for renewal. To this end they arranged a marriage of convenience with Walter Bedford, a doorman at a gentleman's club in Westminster (Murray 285). On the eve of the wedding, which was set for 15 November, they were still mobilising support for their friend, a campaign that Huxley described in a letter to Mary Hutchinson:

> A most extraordinary performance – rather like a novel by Kafka – ending off very suitably last night in Mr. Selfridge's party on the top floor of his shop, where lions roared at every step, including Michael Arlen with an astrakhan collar on his great coat, too beautifully in the part to be quite true. (*Selected Letters*, 334-35)[35]

In her memoir *Quicksands,* Sybille Bedford recalls with gratitude how the Huxleys fought her corner at "a large election do on the top of Selfridge's... going from table to table, asking for support."[36] This confirms that the event was the last of Gordon Selfridge's famous election night parties – Arlen was a regular attender – on 14 November 1935. Whether Huxley managed to avoid conversational nuisance with Arlen, indeed whether Arlen offered his support to the cause, we do not know, but the Armenian was clearly playing up to his image. An oft-repeated anecdote told of an American reporter who had once asked Arlen, "What do you think of yourself as an artist?" "*Per ardua ad astrakhan*," came the suave and well-rehearsed reply (*Exiles*, 56). Literary efforts brought material rewards; Arlen might have agreed with Samuel Johnson that "no man but a blockhead ever wrote except for money."[37]

Arlen published nothing but journalism after his last novel, *The Flying Dutchman*, appeared in 1939. His moment had passed, and he recognised it. Interviewed by the *New Yorker* a few years before his death, he summarised his career: "I was a flash in the pan in my twenties. I had a hell of a good time being flashy and there was, by the grace of God, a good deal of gold dust in the pan."[38] But his contemporaries did not forget him or the impact he had once made. He makes an unlikely appearance, alongside Huxley, in the final volume of Evelyn Waugh's *Sword of Honour* trilogy, published in 1961. Waugh's anti-heroine Virginia, wife of protagonist Guy Crouchback, is, we are told, "the last of twenty years' succession of heroines": a younger sister to those "fast" young women who thrilled readers in the 1920s. After she is killed in an air raid in 1945, magazine editor Everard Spruce tries to explain to two young secretaries in his office what was special about her. He reads the passage from *Antic Hay* describing Mrs Viveash's elegant, floating walk, then challenges them: "'I bet neither of you know who wrote that. You'll say Michael Arlen.'" One girl replies that she has never heard of Michael Arlen. Incredulous at her ignorance, Spruce presses on:

> "Anyway, the passage I read, believe it or not, is Aldous Huxley 1922. Mrs Viveash. Hemingway coarsened the image with his Brett, but the type persisted – in books and in life. Virginia was the last of them – the exquisite, the doomed and the damning, with expiring voices – a whole generation younger. We shall never see anyone like her again in literature or in life and I'm very glad to have known her."[39]

Both Huxley and Arlen chose to make the South of France their home in the 1930s. The road journey from the Huxleys in Sanary-sur-Mer to Cannes, where the Arlens lived, is something over 80 miles – no great distance, especially for a notoriously fast driver like Maria. Yet the distance separating these households was more than a physical one, and no meeting of minds was ever likely. Huxley's references to Arlen imply suspicion, even highbrow disdain. Arlen viewed Huxley with envious admiration for his background and education. Like many another 'popular' novelist, Arlen longed to be taken seriously, even as he joked that his goal was simply to make his pile and then retire. Like many another immigrant to Britain he never found total acceptance by the host community. And he would never earn the respect or the friendship of Aldous Huxley.

NOTES

1. On Brooks see my essay 'Louise Brooks' in *Instead of a Critic: Essays Written and Unwritten* (Cambridge: Minos Press, 2022), 120-26.
2. Quoted in Barry Paris, *Louise Brooks* (London: Hamish Hamilton, 1990), 89.
3. Quoted in Donald McNamara, 'Lulu in Rochester: Self-Portrait of an Anti-Star,' *The Missouri Review*, 6.3 (Summer 1983), 63-82 (p. 72).
4. When Kenneth Tynan's famous profile of Brooks appeared in the *New Yorker* in 1979, Brooks was surprised to find that Arlen's name had been removed from the list of visitors to the Follies. She asked the editor, William Shawn, why, and was told that "his son might mind." The son, Michael J. Arlen, was the magazine's TV critic at the time (McNamara, 71-2).
5. John Worthen, *D.H. Lawrence: The Life of an Outsider* (Harmondsworth: Penguin, 2006), 165; Harry Keyishian, *Michael Arlen*, [Twayne's English Authors Series] (Boston: G.K. Hall, 1975), 16.
6. Nicholas Murray dates it to the previous Friday, 10 December (*Aldous Huxley: An English Intellectual* [London: Abacus, 2003], 58). However, Lawrence does not mention Huxley until he writes to Ottoline on 22 December, and it was she who urged the two writers to meet (*The Letters of D.H. Lawrence*, Vol. II, ed. George J. Zytaruk and James T. Boulton [Cambridge: CUP, 1981], 483). Huxley did not come down from Oxford until the 15th (*Letters of Aldous Huxley*, ed. Grover Smith [London: Chatto & Windus, 1969], 87, 88; hereafter *Letters*).
7. Aldous Huxley, *Selected Letters*, ed. James Sexton (Chicago: Ivan R. Dee, 2007), 21. Hereafter *Selected Letters*.
8. Quoted in Sarah MacDougall, *Mark Gertler* (London: John Murray, 2002), 137-8.
9. See the earlier Lawrence chapter for a more detailed examination of this episode, with further sources. Arguing over the identity of the participants might seem futile, were it not that the incident, in whatever form it reached Lawrence's ears, found its way into

Women in Love (chapter XXVIII, 'Gudrun in the Pompadour').

10 Anne Chisholm, *Nancy Cunard* (London: Sidgwick & Jackson, 1979), 277. Chisholm's chapters on her subject's relationships with Arlen (59-73) and Huxley (74-82) remain the fullest examination to date.

11 Edward Marsh, editor and polymath, delivered his verdict on *Antic Hay* in a letter to Robert Nichols: "I must say the first six chapters or so amused me quite enormously, but it tails off into a rather nauseating caricature of X and her surroundings which I think he might have left to Michael Arlen" (qtd. in Christopher Hassall, *Edward Marsh: Patron of the Arts* [London: Longmans, 1959], 515-16). For "X" we may safely read Nancy Cunard, who was still alive when this letter was published.

12 Sybille Bedford, *Aldous Huxley: A Biography, Vol 1 1894-1939* (London: Chatto & Windus, 1973), 137-8.

13 Mary Hutchinson's name will appear frequently in this chapter as an epistolary confidante of both Huxleys. Her extensive correspondence is deposited in the Harry Ransom Humanities Research Center, University of Texas at Austin (hereafter HRHRC). Living on the fringes of the Bloomsbury circle and acquainted with many writers of the day, she married the barrister St. John ('Jack') Hutchinson in 1910. Theirs was, by all accounts, an 'open' marriage. Mary was the long-term mistress of Clive Bell. Her husband was "one of the most devoted" of Nancy Cunard's friends, according to Cunard's biographer (Chisholm, 43).

14 James Sexton, 'The Problems of Love: Three Little Known Stories by Aldous Huxley – "Over the Telephone" – "Nine A.M." – "Consider the Lilies,"' *Aldous Huxley Annual* 8 (2008), 31-48.

15 Aldous Huxley, *Those Barren Leaves* (London, 1925), 147. Hereafter TBL.

16 He certainly shows awareness of it a decade later. In a characteristically wide-ranging passage in *Beyond the Mexique Bay*, he moves from the Mayan preoccupation with the "emblems of mortality" to consider periods in European history where "a good death-appeal was as sure a key to popularity as a good sex-appeal is at the present time." He then compares the international success of *Night-Thoughts*, Edward Young's poetic musings on death published in the 1740s, to that of *The Green Hat* in his own

day (Aldous Huxley, *Beyond the Mexique Bay* [London: Chatto & Windus, 1934], 60).
17   Louis Kronenberger, 'Mr. Arlen's Green Hat Grows Dusty,' *New York Times Book Review* (May 1, 1927), 9. Quoted in Keyishian, 78.
18   The novelist Reggie Turner was part of the English expatriate colony in Florence. Lawrence portrays him in *Aaron's Rod* and *Kangaroo*. Giuseppe Orioli was the Italian publisher of *Lady Chatterley's Lover*.
19   See the earlier chapter on Lawrence. Following several meetings with Arlen in Florence, Lawrence began the third and final version of *Lady Chatterley's Lover*, introducing an entirely new character, Michaelis, who is demonstrably based on Arlen.
20   Unpublished letter, HRHRC.
21   Despite Maria's promise to tell Mary Hutchinson "all about it", I have found no further reference to these meetings in Aldous's published letters or in the unpublished correspondence.
22   Aldous Huxley, *Music at Night and Other Essays* (London: Chatto & Windus, 1931), 38.
23   Derek Patmore, 'Conversations in the South,' *The Bookman*, 82 (August 1932), 370. Quoted in Keyishian, 101.
24   *An Encyclopaedia of Pacifism*, ed. Aldous Huxley (London: Chatto & Windus, 1937), 60. Cf. Brett Holman, *The Next War in the Air: Britain's Fear of the Bomber, 1908-1941* (Farnham: Ashgate, 2014), 155, 161. H.G. Wells certainly read Arlen's novel: he refers to it in *The Shape of Things To Come* (1933) as "an amusing fantasy". Elizabeth von Arnim was shocked that, after reading *Man's Mortality* in manuscript (then titled *The Red Bridge*), Wells had told Arlen to rewrite the second half of it (Leslie de Charms, *Elizabeth of the German Garden: A Biography* [London: Heinemann, 1958], 340.)
25   Gilbert Norwood, *Canadian Forum*, 13 (July 1933), 394.
26   Wynyard Browne, 'Sheep and Goats,' *The Bookman*, 83 (March 1933), 502.
27   Henry Tracy, 'The New Michael Arlen,' *Saturday Review of Literature*, IX (April 8, 1933), 525.
28   Letter dated March 6, 1932, in P.G. Wodehouse, *Performing Flea: A Self-Portrait in Letters*, with an introduction and additional

notes by W. Townend (London: Herbert Jenkins, 1953), 63.
29 In an article entitled 'Fireworks', Mary Hutchinson had written: "No one gives a party who is not tempted by a curious sort of hope – that when two or three are gathered together something very extraordinary must happen" (reprinted in her collection *Fugitive Pieces* [London: Hogarth Press, 1927], 147).
30 See Virginia Woolf, 'Middlebrow' in *The Death of the Moth* (London: Hogarth Press, 1947 [1942]), 115. In this piece, which was originally drafted as a letter to the *New Statesman* in 1932 but never sent, Woolf complains that the "middlebrow" pursues "no single object, neither art itself nor life itself, but both mixed indistinguishably, and rather nastily, with money, fame, power, or prestige."
31 *The Diary of Virginia Woolf: Volume IV, 1931-1935*, ed. Anne Olivier Bell (London: Hogarth Press, 1982), 189.
32 *The Sickle Side of the Moon – The Letters of Virginia Woolf: Volume V, 1932-1935*, ed. Nigel Nicolson (London: Hogarth Press, 1979), 253. When Woolf boasted to Vita Sackville-West about her US sales of *To the Lighthouse*, the latter responded: "you are a purely mercenary writer, like Michael Arlen, and think of nothing but your returns" (*The Letters of Vita Sackville-West to Virginia Woolf*, ed. Louise A. DeSalvo and Mitchell A. Leaska [New York: Morrow, 1985], 237; letter of 25 July 1927). In *Orlando*, the novel she began in October 1927, Woolf confers on Orlando's husband the name 'Shelmerdine', which is suspiciously close to 'Shelmerdene', the name of the "delightful adventuress" whom Arlen introduced in *The London Venture* and revived in *These Charming People* and *May Fair*.
33 Letter dated November 23 [1933] (unpublished, HRHRC).
34 At a later dinner party at the Hutchinsons' Arlen's name came up (in his absence). Woolf noted: "Talk frivolous at first. Jack's jokes with Mary for being in love with Arlen. He sends her books. I do not altogether like Jack's jokes with Mary: her lovers &c" (Woolf, *Diary*, ed. cit., 230 [entry for 24 July 1934]).
35 The letter is dated "ca 6 April 1937" in *Selected Letters*. However, internal evidence makes a date of 15 November 1935 more probable. Around the same time Huxley was writing to Dick Sheppard about "the menace suspended over the head of our young

German friend" (*Selected Letters*, 311). A postcard from Maria to Mary Hutchinson, postmarked 9:15 AM on 15 November, reads simply "Sybille is saved" (unpublished, HRHRC).

36 Sybille Bedford, *Quicksands: A Memoir* (London: Hamish Hamilton, 2005), 335.
37 James Boswell, *Life of Samuel Johnson*, 5 April 1776.
38 [Geoffrey Hellman], 'Loller,' *New Yorker*, XXV (April 9, 1949), 25. Quoted in Keyishian, 13.
39 Evelyn Waugh, *Unconditional Surrender* (London: Chapman & Hall, 1961), 258-9. The reference here is to Brett Ashley, a character in Hemingway's *The Sun Also Rises* (1926). For the confused nexus linking Brett with Lady Duff Twysden, Cunard, Arlen and Hemingway, see my earlier chapter on Hemingway. Arlen was a minor satirical obsession of Evelyn Waugh's. He alludes to him also in *Decline and Fall* ("All Mayfair seemed to throb with the heart of Mr Arlen"); in *Black Mischief* where, for the forward-looking Emperor of Azania, Arlen represents the triumph of Progress over Barbarism; and indirectly in *Vile Bodies*, when the hero, drudging as a bored gossip-columnist, invents a fashion for green bowler hats.

REBECCA WEST

"Every other inch a gentleman": the books will tell you that this was Rebecca West's verdict on Michael Arlen.[1] This *bon mot* has been attributed to others – and Arlen liked it so much he started applying it to himself – but, provenance aside, what lies behind it?

Some years ago, I had an exchange of letters with Arlen's son, in the course of which he alluded to his father's romances prior to his marriage in 1928. "I have long supposed that there were indeed many women," wrote Arlen Jr, "a young Rebecca West certainly..."[2] After a century, such an assertion may prove hard to confirm. The evidence is fragmentary...

For a start, we don't know how they met. One possible intermediary is Eliza Aria, a journalist and *salonnière* who patronised both West and Arlen.[3] She was the aunt of the writer Gilbert Frankau, and the latter's name appears in West's first known reference to Arlen. In the middle of a newsy letter to Louis Golding dating from early autumn 1922, she writes:

> Gilbert Frankau has set up a stately home in Lancaster Gate. 'I have been hunting in the shires,' he told Michael Arlen and me when we met him. 'Ah Ah!' said Michael

Arlen. 'But I've been paying a round of country house visits. So we're quits.'[4]

Shortly afterwards West reviewed '*Piracy*', Arlen's first full-length novel, for the *New Statesman*. It is, overall, a generous review of a writer whom the literary intelligentsia would later castigate as a social gadfly. She is wary of Arlen's concern with documenting fashionable society (allying him with what she calls the "White Spats School of Fiction") but considers his interest in such lives to be "soundly artistic and not social". It is unfortunate, in her view, that "he banks too heavily on his wit, for he is too much amused to be reliably witty". Despite occasional lapses into "rococo romanticism", however, his "strong cards are his subtlety and profundity of feeling".[5]

By the following year West was seeking to extricate herself from her romantic involvement with H.G. Wells. In October 1923 she took the opportunity of a lecture tour in the United States to put distance between herself and her long-term (married) lover. Wells was disgruntled and vented his resentment at her desire for marriage:

> I don't see why you should always tuck in your sense of humour when you are dealing with me and why Jane [Wells's wife] should be dragged in forever in our little differences. You would have gone to California if we had been ten times married and you would have jazzed, bored me with your Arlen and Aumonier and such like and done everything you suddenly wanted to do just as you do now.[6]

In early July 1924, West ("radiant in scarlet with artistic shawl") and Arlen were both guests at a PEN Club dinner. The *Daily Mirror* reported:

Miss Rebecca West, fresh from her success in America, made a grand late entry which set all the guests asking their hosts: 'Who is she?' After the dinner she had a long conversation with Michael Arlen, who kissed her hand very gallantly when they parted.[7]

Later that month, the American movie starlet Blanche Sweet and her director husband Marshall Neilan were in Britain. The ostensible purpose of the visit was to set up a film version of West's novel *The Return of the Soldier*. They met West to discuss their plans. There are various accounts of the meeting and it's unclear whether they refer to one and the same event. There was certainly a dinner with Wells, West and Arlen. On the agenda was not only a film of West's novel but also another proposal: to film *The Green Hat*. Neither project would come to fruition at the time. Decades later Sweet recalled to the film historian Kevin Brownlow:

> One night we had dinner at Rebecca's place, and Wells was there, and a Russian woman (but that's another story) and Michael Arlen [who] was a protégé of Rebecca's.[8]

(The "Russian woman" is indeed "another story". She may have been Eliena Eastman, the wife of the writer and political activist Max Eastman, a friend of Trotsky's. The pair were in London at the time; in his autobiography Eastman recounts visiting Wells while in England.[9]) On 28 July Arlen wrote to the US publisher and editor Eugene Saxton:

> Our friend Rebecca West gave a party the other night – for the purpose of christening a new refrigerator 'Michael Arlen'! Cheek, I thought. But a good party. (...) There was a curious guest at the party. A tall, sardonic man. No one knew who he was. No one had invited

him. Rebecca writes to me today that after I had gone he followed her into the kitchen and said: 'Wonderful young man, that Michael Arlen. Ah, wouldn't you like to be so well-known as he is!' Rebecca threw a faint on the refrigerator.[10]

A possible reference to the same gathering? Or possibly not.

This may have been the high-water mark of their relationship (be it friendship or more). When West next writes of Arlen, in the late 1920s, the references are to his writing, and they are not flattering. In her long essay 'The Strange Necessity', she elaborates a thesis about the similarities between Pavlov's experiments with conditioned reflexes and the production of works of art. Pavlovian principles, she feels, could be applied to

> certain novels of today which the idiosyncrasy of the author has preserved from participation in the current absorption in character. It would be entertaining to rewrite *The Green Hat* as a timed record of the administration of stimuli to a subject...[11]

Early 1929 brought from West an obituary of Mona Tattersall, *née* Dunn, a society figure who died young. West is under the mistaken impression that Mona was the model for Iris March, the racy heroine of *The Green Hat*:

> It was largely the life she and her friends had led round and about the Embassy Club in London, the Potinière at Deauville, and the Sporting Club at Monte Carlo, which made Michael Arlen write *The Green Hat* and other people read it. (...) Naturally many people who were not in her set wished that they were. Because of the psychic emptiness of England during the exhausted

years following the war, it accepted novels and plays that were based on nothing more important than this wish; though these were plainly as far away from imaginative literature as a manicurist's dream of marrying a millionaire is from creative vision. Today Michael Arlen is no longer the vogue...[12]

In fact, although Mona Dunn was another of Arlen's lady friends – he attended her engagement party at the Embassy Club in December 1924 – the acknowledged inspiration for the fictional Iris was Nancy Cunard, with whom Arlen had a well-documented love affair in the early 1920s.[13]

Our next sighting of Arlen comes on the night of the General Election in May 1929. West and Arlen were both guests at Gordon Selfridge's election night party at his London store. In a published account, West reduces Arlen to caricature. She reports the verdict of those around her, shocked by the possibility of a Labour government: "'The Labour people are in, you know, they're definitely in. Isn't this terribly like the French Revolution with us booing inside and the crowd cheering outside?'" She goes on to describe the incongruous appearance, festooned with emeralds and diamonds, of one of the Dolly Sisters (the Dolly Sisters were a pair of dancers much favoured, and probably bedded, by both Selfridge and Beaverbrook), before lining up her next target: "Nearby stood Mr Michael Arlen, looking in some indefinable way like some Dolly Brother. Almost especially he did not remind me of Versailles."[14]

I suspect West and Arlen lost touch during the Thirties. There was sporadic contact after the War. In 1947 James Thurber attended a *New Yorker* party in West's honour. In a letter he describes an incident at the party when "someone crashed and fell sprawling across my lap. It turned out to be Michael Arlen. We are all poor windlestraws in the stream of time."[15]

By 1955, when West's son Anthony was proposing to publish his autobiographical novel *Heritage*, with its disobliging portrayal of his mother, Arlen proved unsympathetic. He told John Van Druten that West was "bound to get it, as all people who had hurt other people were always bound to get it."[16]

West's last word on her erstwhile friend came in 1971, long after his death, when she reviewed *Exiles*, the memoir by Arlen's son.[17] It's the clearest exposition we have of how she viewed Arlen in retrospect. She describes a talented young man, with refined tastes in literature, whose own writing was "a mixture of the genuine article and advertising copy". To his credit, "he had the essential gift, the power to imagine characters and their reactions". But as success brought him access to "the world of chandeliers and painted ceilings," he became a "notable snob". As for women, his writing made plain that "Venus rising from the foam had nothing on Venus rising from Debrett". All this was distraction: "it took his mind off his game". Then came the "tragedy" of his voluntary "abandonment" of England for America during the War. "It was an act of suicide not to return at the advent of peace." Instead, he and his wife lived out their days in a land where "there was nothing for them... bored stiff like animals preserved by an old-fashioned taxidermist". Arlen in exile was still "gay and funny and generous and kind," but these qualities were now without focus.

It's a partial and somewhat misinformed account of his later life – in fact, apart from an unhappy spell of 'war work' in Coventry, Arlen spent little time in England after 1925; his son's English prep school was evacuated to Canada, which was one incentive for his wife's relocation to North America in wartime – but a clear theme emerges from West's review: someone to whom she once felt close had betrayed his talents and disappointed her.

A fractured relationship, certainly. But a love affair? Who can say?

NOTES

1. Qtd. in George H. Doran, *Chronicles of Barabbas, 1884-1934* (New York: Harcourt, Brace & Company, 1935), pp. 182-3. The attribution was the subject of dispute in the Letters pages of *The Spectator* in 1968. Frances Donaldson (26 July) credited the line to Edna Ferber; A.S. Frere (9 August) suggested that it was Frederick Lonsdale's witticism. According to Dorothy Thompson, it originated with Lord Castlerosse: Vincent Sheean, *Dorothy and Red* (London: Heinemann, 1964), p. 26. Elsewhere it is attributed to Alexander Woollcott, the Algonquin wit.
2. Personal communication, 18 March 2017. In the published memoir of his early life, Michael J. Arlen names several other women his father had been "in love with". One of them, Louise Carnarvon, I have been unable to identify. See Michael J. Arlen, *Exiles* (Harmondsworth: Penguin, 1973 [1971]), p. 140.
3. Pamela Frankau, *I Find Four People* (London: Nicholson and Watson, 1935), p. 131.
4. *Selected Letters of Rebecca West*, ed. Bonnie Kime Scott (New Haven: Yale UP, 2000), p. 50. Marked "circa 1922". In fact, there is so much detail in the letter about people and events that a better dating should be possible. For example, she mentions the death by suicide of Horatio Francis Ninian Scott, which occurred on 10 July 1922; and D.H. Lawrence's arrival in America from Australia – the Lawrences docked at San Francisco on 3 September.
5. Rebecca West, 'Notes on Novels', *New Statesman*, 18 November 1922, p. 206. In his next novel, *The Green Hat*, Arlen takes jocular aim at this review. He introduces a character called Mr Trehawke Tush, "the most successful of the younger novelists," who "had earned from Miss Rebecca West the praise that he was 'the leader of the spats school of thought.'" Tush's contention is that "the whole purpose of a 'bestseller' is to justify a reasonable amount of adultery in the eyes of suburban matrons." See *The Green Hat* (London: Capuchin Classics, 2008 [1924]), p. 95. In her 1922 review West attributed leadership of the "White Spats School" to Stephen McKenna (1888-1967), author of numerous novels focusing on English upper-class society.

6   15 December 1923, qtd. in Gordon N. Ray, *H.G. Wells and Rebecca West* (London: Macmillan, 1974), p. 151. Stacy Aumonier (1877-1928) was a writer and stage performer.
7   *Daily Mirror,* 4 July 1924, p. 9.
8   Sweet to Brownlow, personal communication, 23 June 1983; interview with Blanche Sweet in *Films in Review*, November 1965, p. 560.
9   Max Eastman, *Love and Revolution: My Journey Through an Epoch* (New York: Random House, 1964), p. 438. Eastman reviewed West's *Henry James* in *The Masses* 9(4), February 1917, pp. 30-31.
10 Arlen to Saxton, 28 July 1924 (unpublished).
11 Rebecca West, *The Strange Necessity: Essays and Reviews* (London: Virago, 1987 [1928]), p. 85.
12 Rebecca West, *Ending in Earnest: A Literary Log* (New York: Doubleday, Doran, 1931), pp. 17-18. (Originally published in *The Bookman*.) Mona Tattersall's cause of death was officially recorded as peritonitis, but suspicion pointed to a botched abortion. This echoes the near fatal misfortune that befell Nancy Cunard in 1921 which Arlen ungallantly incorporated into *The Green Hat*. The death in December 1923 of Arlen's actress friend Meggie Albanesi was also the result of complications following an illegal abortion,
13 Anne Chisholm, *Nancy Cunard* (London: Sidgwick & Jackson, 1979), pp. 61-73; *The Sketch*, 31 December 1924, p. 677.
14 *Ending in Earnest*, pp. 112-113. (First published in *The Bookman*.)
15 To Jap Gude, 19 May 1947. *The Thurber Letters: The Wit, Wisdom, and Surprising Life of James Thurber*, ed. Harrison Kinney and Rosemary A. Thurber (New York: Simon & Schuster, 2002), p. 40.
16 Qtd. in Carl Rollyson, *Rebecca West: A Saga of the Century* (London: Hodder & Stoughton, 1995), p. 265.
17 Rebecca West, 'Uprooted Ones', *Sunday Telegraph*, 28 March 1971, p. 14.

AT THE MOVIES

Arlen and the Movies ought to be a topic, but somehow it isn't. He seems to have had little involvement in the film adaptations of his novels and stories. Conversely, his own work in the Hollywood industry was singularly unproductive. A contract to create two scenarios for Pola Negri in 1925 yielded no results, despite massive pre-publicity. A trip to the US in early 1931 was partly to develop *What Fun Frenchmen Have*, the 'talkie' he'd written with Walter Hackett as a vehicle for Ronald Colman; it was never made. When he returned to Hollywood under contract to MGM during the War, his scripts rarely survived the final cut. Much effort was expended on a Katharine Hepburn-Spencer Tracy movie, *Without Love* (1945), before the director decided to start afresh with a new screenwriter. His script for *If Winter Comes* was consigned to oblivion by the time this long-gestated adaptation of the 1921 novel by A.S.M Hutchinson finally emerged in 1947. His contribution to *Mrs Parkington* (1944) was uncredited. Arlen's only on-screen scriptwriting credit from those years was for *The Heavenly Body* (1944), a frothy comedy about an astronomer (William Powell) who is so busy gazing at heavenly bodies through his telescope that he neglects the heavenly body waiting for him at home in the comely form of his wife (played by Hedy Lamarr).¹ "I wrote one-seventh of one seventh-rate picture while I was there," Arlen said later of his Hollywood years. (In the absence of his wife Atalanta, who remained on the East Coast, there were clearly compensations in the many opportunities to escort actresses to fashionable nightspots. Paulette Goddard, "the most civilised girl in Hollywood" in his estimation, was a frequent companion.)

A word is needed, however, about *A Woman of Affairs* (1928), the first and more successful of two adaptations of *The Green Hat*.

Although the Motion Picture Production Code, commonly known as the 'Hays Code', wasn't rigorously enforced until 1934, Hollywood had been self-censoring throughout the 1920s. The fear was that, if the industry didn't police itself, the federal state would step in. Under something known as the 'Formula', the Hays Office drew up a list of books that were not to be adapted for the screen due to their licentious content. *The Green Hat* was on the list. When Greta Garbo, one of MGM's biggest box-office draws in the late Twenties, let it be known that she wanted to play Iris March in her next picture, studio boss Louis B. Mayer therefore had a problem. The solution was to adapt the novel's material, change the title, give the characters new names, and remove all the controversial elements from the original story. Out must go any allusion to homosexuality, bisexuality, alcoholism, drug addiction, syphilis, nymphomania or abortion. That the resulting film is nevertheless a classic is down to Garbo's performance and the skill of the director, Clarence Brown. As Carmen Guiralt has shown in a detailed study of the movie, the filmmakers cunningly exploited the resources of silent cinema to circumvent the censor.² *A Woman of Affairs* has two different storylines running concurrently: on the one hand, the official dialogue approved by the Hays Office and printed

Filming A Woman of Affairs, MGM Studios, July 1928. (Left to right:) Greta Garbo, John Gilbert, Clarence Brown, unknown (Alamy).

on the intertitles; on the other, the story narrated by the images which relates more directly to the original novel. In particular, Brown used objects – almost always filmed in extreme close-up – as symbols to create visual metaphors. A loose-fitting ring is seen to drop off Garbo's finger at points when illicit sexual intercourse is about to take place. In a justly famous sequence at a clinic, Garbo in hospital gown lovingly cradles a bunch of flowers like a baby, signalling that her night of passion has resulted in pregnancy and an abortion. There are many other examples. Even if Arlen had no involvement in the production, he must have been gratified that the rights to his novel had been secured for the then astronomical sum of $50,250. The film's opening credits state "From a story by Michael Arlen" and many reviews referred to *The Green Hat*, despite all MGM's efforts to present the movie as an entirely different property.

By 1934, when another bowdlerized version of *The Green Hat* was trundled out under the title *Outcast Lady*, the gallantry of Irish March had become, in the view of the *New York Times* critic, "the self-conscious and rather stubborn nobility of a silly woman" (3 November 1934). Constance Bennett turns in a creditable performance in the lead role but cannot match Garbo's qualities of mystery and melancholy. This could have been something altogether more interesting. Preston Sturges wrote the original script for what was intended to be a vehicle for producer Irving Thalberg's wife Norma Shearer, but the maverick Sturges was fired, his script unused, and Shearer was diverted into other projects.

Arlen's other outings on screen need not detain the movie buff overlong. Two of the silents – *Dancer of Paris* and *The Ace of Cads*, both from 1926 – do not survive. *These Charming People* (1931), starring Cyril Maude, was Paramount's first 'talkie' to be made in London for the British market. Despite its title, the source was not Arlen's short-story collection of that name but his 1924 stage play *Dear Father*. Maude played a Micawberish English colonel who was always expecting something – generally a loan – to turn up. The *Manchester Guardian* (24 July 1931) praised a "richly comic piece of farcical acting" but opined that the story itself had been "de-Arlenised from a sophisticated to a more ingenuous sentimentality".

Lily Christine (1932), adapted from Arlen's 1928 novel of the same name, received a glitzy charity premiere in London in aid of the League of Mercy, attended by Edward Prince of Wales and his then mistress Thelma Furness. The *Times* of London (2 May 1932) found the whole thing "dull and long and uneventful" but acknowledged that Corinne Griffith, in the title role, did at least "very nearly succeed in making Lily Christine a credible human being".

In *The Golden Arrow* (1936), adapted from one of his stories, Bette Davis plays a forlorn heiress who prevails on an underpaid newspaper man (George Brent) to marry her in order to fend off the fortune-hunters who are snapping at her heels. It turns out she's not an heiress at all but a cafeteria cashier employed by a cosmetics company to keep her name and theirs on the front pages. The *New York Times* (4 May 1936) concluded that the film "derives most of its slight strength from the saucy performance of Miss Davis and the harried, but good-natured expression, of Mr Brent," and it's hard to disagree. Davis herself was less forgiving, recalling later that she was "insulted to have to appear in such a cheap, nothing story".

The Cavalier of the Streets (1937) was summarily reviewed by the London *Observer* (29 August 1937): "A neat pocket drama on the higher ethics of blackmailing... well played by Margaret Vyner, Patrick Barr and Carl Harbord."

One property that attracted interest was Arlen's 1925 story 'The Gentleman from America'. It tells how rich American Howard Puce visits London and makes a £500 bet with two

Englishmen that he can spend the night in a room that is said to be haunted. Under the title *The Fatal Night* (1948) it became the picture that introduced future *Avengers* star Patrick Macnee. *The Cinema* (7 January 1948) singled out this version as "a 55-minute film of unusual excellence". Under the original title, the story then reappeared in 1956 as an episode of the widely distributed TV series *Alfred Hitchcock Presents*.

'Gay Falcon', Arlen's 1940 story about a suave amateur detective, provided the inspiration for a series of sixteen feature films made between 1941 and 1949. The first, *The Gay Falcon*, starring George Sanders, is the closest to Arlen's conception. Sanders had previously played The Saint in adaptations of Leslie Charteris's novel series. Charteris disapproved of the way RKO had been adapting his stories, especially with how George Sanders was playing the title character, and the studio decided to sever ties with him. *The Gay Falcon* was therefore intended to introduce a replacement for The Saint. (Charteris went on to sue RKO on the grounds that The Falcon character was simply "The Saint in disguise." What Arlen made of all these shenanigans is not known.)

Almost no film footage exists of Arlen himself. He reportedly had a cameo role in *Tip-Toes*, a 1927 (silent!) adaptation of the Gershwin musical of the same name, with the action transferred from Florida to London. In a nightmarish sequence Dorothy Gish, the penniless heroine, tossed guiltily on a silken bed in the expensive hotel suite she was occupying under false pretences, and dreamt she saw Michael Arlen talking to 'Shakespeare'.[3] Alas, no print survives. We do have a few seconds of newsreel footage recording his arrival in New York in 1925, and a few more seconds from the Mountbattens' home movies showing Arlen among the *beau monde* at St Moritz in late 1928.

NOTES

1. The *New York Times* reported on 31 May 1944 that Hedy Lamarr's next picture would be *Diamond Rock,* based on the novel *No Truce With Time* by Alec Waugh. It was to be a domestic love-triangle set in the West Indies. In his memoirs Alec Waugh claims that Arlen and Richard Aldington worked on the script. I can find no records to confirm this, and the film was never made. Why not? According to Waugh: "Just when it was to go into production the war ended and the project was shelved". According to Lamarr's biographer, because the star declined the role and elected to make another film, *Her Highness and the Bellboy,* instead. (Alec Waugh, *The Best Wine Last: An Autobiography Through the Years 1932-1969* [London: W.H. Allen, 1978], 173; Christopher Young, *The Films of Hedy Lamarr* [Secaucus, NJ: Citadel, 1978], 187.)
2. Carmen Guiralt, 'Self-Censorship during the Silent Era: *A Woman of Affairs* (1928) by Clarence Brown', *Film History,* 28.2 (2016), 81-113.
3. 'Weird scenes are shown in picture', *The Press Democrat* (Santa Rosa, California), 29 July 1928, p14. (It's unclear from the press report whether this was indeed Arlen himself or an actor playing him.) The original Broadway musical of 1925 borrowed one of its song titles from Arlen: 'These Charming People'.

ARMENIA THE 'COURTESAN'

"A case of pernicious Armenia" – that's how he was wont to describe himself. Arlen's relationship with the land of his ancestors is a complex one. It provides the starting-point for his son's travel memoir *Passage to Ararat*, in which Michael Jr. goes in search of his Armenian heritage, a heritage his father had seemingly done his best to abandon. The son describes family visits to an Armenian restaurant in New York City where his father would read "with a certain offhand professionalism" from the exotic menu; but it was the only place where he recalled his father being half at ease with his Armenian identity. On another occasion an Armenian professor phones up their home to discuss a literary project: "'Tell him I'm out,'" says Arlen Sr. when his son reports who is on the line. "'He'll only want to talk about Armenian problems. He'll go on for hours. They end up boring you to death.'"

Armenians, with their attendant problems, make occasional appearances in Arlen's fiction: the portraits are rarely flattering. In the novel '*Piracy*' (1922), Arlen gives us Sir Aram Melekian, a multi-millionaire of Armenian ancestry perhaps inspired by Calouste Gulbenkian. A wise but bitter old man, a philanthropist and an Anglophile, he's reputed to have financed "several little wars" and earned the dislike of "Mr Belloc and Mr Chesterton". Bizarrely, the character is only introduced as a corpse, laid out in his townhouse, in the novel's final pages. By killing off his character without first granting him life for the reader, the author seems to be placing ironic distance between himself and his Armenian compatriots. In the story 'The Man with the Broken Nose' (1923) two English characters meet a strange dark man in the National Gallery who tells them he is an Armenian nationalist intent on rescuing his sister who has been kidnapped by a Turk and held captive in a London house. In fact, the whole thing is a ruse, into which the two Englishmen are dragged as unwitting accomplices. The vengeful 'Armenian' is none other than gentleman trickster and 'Cavalier of the Streets', Michael Wagstaffe, who is seeking to turn the tables on his father in a convoluted heist. Wagstaffe has hit on the perfect disguise, however, for "no one would say he was Armenian if he wasn't, would he!" At the risk of psychobiography run amok, we might inquire whether this fictional English gentleman who poses as an Armenian is a reverse mirror-image of Dikran Kouyoumdjian, the real-life Armenian who presented himself as an English gentleman.

After the Second World War, William Saroyan embarked on a little project to bring the elder Arlen back into the Armenian fold. He wrote to the editors of the Hairenik Association in Boston promising to persuade Arlen to contribute to their journals. Nothing came of these efforts.

Arlen Sr. never visited Armenia. This didn't stop him telling Claud Cockburn a cock-and-bull story about how he'd once travelled across Armenia on a coach tour. Diverting down a sideroad, the tour guide reportedly stopped the bus and invited the tourists – Arlen among them – to step out and admire a large cairn of rocks by the roadside. This, he informed them, was "the noble tomb of one of the greatest and most resplendent of Armenian thinkers, storytellers and poets – Dikran Kouyoumdjian." (Such mischief-making continues in Ruse, the Bulgarian city of Arlen's birth, where to this day the tourist information centre confidently tells visitors that the town's second-most famous son was nominated for the Nobel Prize for Literature. He was not. A writer with much higher international credibility, the Ruse-born Elias Canetti, won the Prize in 1981.)

And yet, in his earliest writings, Arlen had shown himself ready to espouse the Armenian cause and resist the urge to camouflage himself. In a 1916 essay entitled 'A Very Serious Armenian', he writes: "Until the instinct to hide goes from us, it is difficult to see how we can ever hope to be respected as much as we think we should be." Another article from the same year, 'An Appeal to Sense', seeks to replace the image of the Armenian as victim with that of the fighter, "the father of all patriots, rebels and exiles". Subsequently, in the pages of *The New Age*, he locked horns with Marmaduke Pickthall, noted British orientalist and apologist for the Ottoman cause. And even, later in life – if it suited him – he could still pose as a Very Serious Armenian. In 1930 Arlen was living in Paris and was interviewed by *Haratch*, an Armenian-language exile publication. The periodical had published in translation his short story 'Confessions of a Naturalized Englishman' which was first collected in the 1929 volume *Babes in the Wood*. One passage in particular attracted criticism from Armenian readers:

> Son of an ignoble race, born in the musty twilight of an outcast people, inheritor of centuries of ignoble martyrdoms and mean escapes, what did I deserve but the anxious and helpless solitude of the unwanted servant? What art could come from an Armenian? What greatness? What, even, of worth? O Armenia, O unlovely courtesan, abasing yourself first before one conqueror

and then before another, why could you not die with dignity, why did you not die with Nineveh, Carchemish, Babylon? [...]

The context in the story is that the first-person narrator, named 'Dikran Kouyoumdjian', has been 'stood up' on a dinner date by a young Englishwoman he is romancing, and vents his frustration at her non-appearance by resort to geopolitical metaphor: the girl's rejection of his unworthy self mirrors the world's treatment of his ancestral land. A clue to interpretation may lie in the disclaimer Arlen places at the beginning of *Babes in the Wood*: "The characters in this book are fictitious. The author makes an appearance, but he is fictitious too." Literal-minded Armenian readers, however, read the passage as a national insult and took particular exception to the phrase "unlovely courtesan". The statesman Garegin Nzhdeh published a scathing, nationalistic backlash in Bulgaria in 1930. Hinging on the word "courtesan", Nzhdeh carries on and on in a tirade, insulting Arlen for looking down on his people, as opposed to the Jews and their brilliant Zionist movement. Other figures, such as the writer Arshak Chobanian, weighed in with criticism, and Arlen found it necessary to use his interview with *Haratch* to defend himself. (The problem was compounded by the translator's choice of an Armenian equivalent to the English word "courtesan", which Collins English Dictionary defines as "*A mistress or prostitute, especially of a man of status or wealth*". I've seen the Armenian word variously back-translated as "faker", "deceiver", "teaser", "flatterer" and "love-suitor". Arlen seems to have intended a more positive connotation.)

In fact, in his short story of 1929, Arlen is looping back to his writings of a decade earlier. In 1918, before he was famous and when he was still using his birth name, he published a non-fiction piece in the English magazine *The New Age* under the title 'The Courtesan of the East'. He begins by telling us he once thought of writing a history of Armenia (or 'Hayastan', to use its proper name). After parading his familiarity with those historians who'd previously made the attempt, he admits to "utter helplessness before such a task" and continues:

> ...They call Hayastan "the brain of the East," but she is more truly, *as her greatest writer has said of her,* "*the courtesan of the East.*" Unwillingly she has given herself to master after master, and in her unwillingness to give herself lies the excuse for her faithlessness and treachery to each, for that "extraordinary levity towards her rulers," as Tacitus has described her unceasing rebellion from authority. No new power has swept Lesser Asia but has desired her, and she has given herself to him only for his ruin: but even as he took her, she has cast her eyes, as forced women will, to some rival power, whom she has allured to her help with only a little of the beauty which is still with her for all the blood and carnage which fills her valleys: she has coquetted with Bajazet even while Tamerlane stood and laughed at the pyramids of skulls which he had had built to the glory of the Prophet and she has smiled at the fallen pride of the great Turkish sultan as he was wheeled through her passes in his cage in the train of the Great Mogul. Byzantium and Bagdad, Emperor and Caliph, as Hayastan's own cities crumbled and her princes fought helplessly on for that which fate had long since decided was not to be hers, as in her own fields and valleys "riot cried aloud, and staggered and swaggered in his rank dens of shame," she charmed all strength to weakness, and helped all arrogance to ruin.

> She has accepted no master, Assyrian or Chaldean, Persian or Mogul, but she has brought him down to her own state of misery, and in equal darkness, has laughed at his wretchedness; for she has grown used to chains and bears them lightly, but to them it is a new humiliation. Hayastan, the courtesan still lives! – and now it is the turn of the Osmanli to be dragged down into the darkness, that Hayastan may laugh at his past upstart pride which in five hundred years she has brought down to the dust. [emphasis added]

The "courtesan of the East"? I asked several Armenian literary scholars if they could identify this supposed quotation from their "greatest writer". They could not. It may be more studied indirection on young Arlen's part. Perhaps, as the yarn about the Armenian tomb suggests, he fantasised a future for himself in that role? Certainly, the interview with Hrand Samuel, translated here for the first time, shows Arlen displaying his usual economy with the truth. He states that he insists on his real name appearing in all his books, which was not the case. He also asserts – curiously – that his mother understands no language except Armenian, a claim that doesn't correspond with other people's memories of her.

The French-Armenian writer and literary critic Garo Sasuni used the pages of *Haratch* to mount an eloquent defence of Arlen. This is also reproduced below.

(Note. I'm grateful to Mariana Haladj-Asminian for the translations; to Nareg Seferian for advice on the background; and to Lusine Hambardzumyan-Mueller, whose article on Arlen in *Armenian Review* [Fall-Winter 2015] first alerted me to these obscure sources.)

Hrand Samuel, OUR MEETING WITH MICHAEL ARLEN,
Haratch, March 23, 1930 (translated from the Armenian)

"WITH ALL MY SOUL, I AM AN ARMENIAN"
"IF I WROTE AGAINST ARMENIA OR ARMENIANS, I WOULD BE WRITING AGAINST MYSELF"

A CONVERSATION WHICH HAD STARTED IN ENGLISH CONTINUES IN ARMENIAN

...Now that the 'laureate' and his followers have finished saying their piece after throwing dirt left and right, without having the courage to admit their mistake, let us clarify the truth by hearing it from the actual source.

I am on my way to meet Michael Arlen for an appointment arranged in advance on behalf of *Haratch*.

The Armenian writer has been living in Paris since November, where he will stay for a year. His residence, a private dwelling, is situated on a quiet Parisian street away from any hustle and bustle. An ideal spot for devoting oneself to peaceful literary work.

The doorman informs me that Mr Arlen is already waiting. I climb the wide staircase at the bottom of the patio and I am led to his office by a servant. In the ample room, which is decorated with beautiful furniture you can barely notice the young writer, who is sinking on a big armchair placed in front of a window overlooking the garden. He is writing.

On seeing the reporter of *Haratch* he leaves his work and with a smile that makes him instantly likeable he starts the conversation in English.

I don't waste time in getting to the matter at hand. He asks details about *Haratch* – how many issues do they sell, do they make a profit or loss? He knows that this is the most important and best-selling Armenian paper in France. He asks questions about other Armenian newspapers.

I ask: "Are you aware that nowadays Armenian papers are talking a lot about one of your short stories?"

"Yes, my brother Roupen told me that Mr Chobanian has attacked me in articles he published…"

"Has your story been published anywhere other than *Nash's Magazine*?"

"Of course. *Nash's Magazine* has printed an abridged version of 'A Naturalised Englishman', the first story in my latest book *Babes in the Wood*. They have changed the title to 'And I Was 21'".

And he rushes to bring the book *Babes in the Wood*, printed in America. He reads from pages 56-58 the fragment referring to Armenia and Armenians. I immediately compare it with the first translation published by *Haratch* (2 February) and I see that it matches word for word. Thus,

> *Poor creature! You don't want to die – is that it? God gave you life, and you cherish your faith in God now as you cherished it against Bajazet and Tamerlane. But He doesn't cherish you. Quite the contrary. God is a firm believer in the political principles of the twentieth century, and the political principles of the twentieth century wish you to the devil…*

The conversation, which had hitherto been conducted in English suddenly switched to Armenian, to my great surprise.

He tells me "unfortunately I cannot read or write in Armenian, but I speak it well. I always speak Armenian with my mother and my brother. If I had an Armenian circle, of course I would be able to express myself much better in my mother tongue."

"They accuse you of calling Armenia 'a prostitute' in the story in question, and they attack you in a grotesque manner."

"Armenia, a prostitute! I have never written such a thing. 'Courtesan' does not mean 'prostitute', but a teaser, a 'love suitor', just as *Haratch* has very correctly translated. If I had wanted to say prostitute or tart, I would have written 'whore'. But how can I write anything demeaning about Armenia or against an Armenian? I would be demeaning myself. Because as I have always said everywhere and I repeat it – I am an Armenian with all my soul. I have spoken with praise about Armenians in all my novels. I have constantly tried to represent Armenians as a heroic people who know how to fight for their freedom and not be massacred like slaves. The spirit of the Armenian patriot appears everywhere in my writings. Also, I have always repeated that I am an Armenian and I always insist that they mention in my books that my real name is Dikran Kouyoumdjian. I am sorry that they have not understood the spirit of my writings and they have attributed things that have never even crossed my mind. As an Armenian young man who was thrown into life's battles at the age of 21, I have seen so much sorrow that I have simply burst out about the unfortunate situation to which my motherland and my people have been subjected, a kind of anger against its fate. No disrespectful comment or observation against my race. Those who insist on the contrary either have no knowledge of English or do not understand what they are reading."

Michael Arlen was speaking so candidly that it was impossible to have even the slightest doubt about him. During the conversation he added also that when he married the previous year, he specially called an Armenian priest to officiate the wedding in Nice...

"How many books have you published to date?"

"Ten. I have been writing for 16 years, I am now 34 years old."

"What is your literary ambition?"

"I am a storyteller. I present the lives of people of the world exactly as I see them. I don't follow any political current and I never mix politics in my literature. I write about the English, the French, the Americans, the Hungarians, etc. regardless of their political stance. I am a simple storyteller."

"Which is your favourite book?"

"*The Green Hat*."

"Are you aware that it has been translated into Armenian?"

"Really? What a pleasant revelation, now my mother will be over the moon! The poor thing so wishes to read my work, but she doesn't know any language apart from Armenian. My books are translated into all the European languages, but not into Armenian. I will be very grateful if you could send a copy for my mother."

He leads me into the adjacent room and he shows me ten volumes recently delivered from America – all of them his work – exquisite publications with the same aesthetic binding; his publisher wanted to give him a nice surprise. Further away, a bookcase filled from top to bottom with translations into various languages – French, German, Hungarian, Russian, etc. – of his ten volumes.

There are manuscripts piled up on his desk. He is about to finish a new book.

"What is the title?"

"I haven't decided yet. I always do the same: I give the book a title after completing it."

"It is better that way."

We leave together, accompanied by his distinguished wife. We bid each other farewell in the car, with the promise of meeting again.

Garo Sasuni, THE QUESTION OF MICHAEL ARLEN, *Haratch*, March 12, 1930 (translated from the Armenian)

Haratch, which had considered it a duty to publish the translation of Michael Arlen's well-known novella in its entirety, has also explained in its editorial the whole misunderstanding that ensued.

Indeed, Mr Chobanian's words were unfitting for a book that is so rich in literary novelties and as a whole, very distant from the grotesque mentality attributed to its author.

Following in its footsteps, other newspapers also found unpublished insults; to reproduce them would be shameful.

When you peruse such expressions, you inadvertently get the impression of a Muslim holy war: "dinime sövdü" – "you cursed my faith". And therefore, you can accuse the opponent of anything; you can use any dirty means in order to bring them down.

Of course, none of these can touch Michael Arlen. Firstly, because he does not follow our publication and secondly, because he is absorbed with his writing, undoubtedly portraying something much higher than our festering environment. All that we are left from this lowly moaning is the shame that will stick to Armenian journalism following its slippery mistake.

After all, what is the issue about? In the short story, proud Michael Arlen appears as an Armenian and opposite him he creates the most original Anglo-Saxon girl who represents her nation. The psychological plot that the author has introduced between the Armenian young man and the English girl is complex and delicate. The victories and defeats (mental) follow each other. There is accumulated hatred and derision in the young Armenian's heart towards the people and situations that surround him. He also feels reflective pain and anger for his and his nation's fate. One of the stages of the conflict, which depicts the defeat of the Armenian young man, is an eruption of grief and suffering, or better said, a cry tearing off from the pain in his heart, but not an insult to the nation to which he belongs. There is neither animosity nor contempt in those lines, as the Armenian literary 'heralds' tried to prove.

However, the twists of the short story are not undone and resolved there. The author continues the tragic thread and opens a spontaneous page of conflict in front of us. With a new and unexpected victory, he sets the response to his monologue and makes them go away. In my opinion, the logical development of the text reaches its completion here, shedding a literary light on the fumbling and conditional denials, which the hero of the novel had displayed in his moments of defeat. The essence of the novel is intensified in this resolution of the conflicts where the Armenian comes out victorious.

This is the simple conclusion about Arlen's novella for all those who were able to see through the author's thought process, the criticisms and the mocking comments. Each of his lines, even each of his words has a specific meaning and is tightly woven into the fabric of the whole text, aimed at confirming or supporting a notion that was put beforehand or would be put later. It would be an unforgivable mistake to pick any line or judgment from this architectural whole and to analyse it in isolation. This is where the Armenian journalists stumbled, in a display of perfect literary ineptitude.

However, if we interpret the text in a metaphorical manner and we accept that the Armenian and the English girl represent Armenia and Europe, that is where we find real abhorrence towards so-called civilized humanity. Europe is represented with its deceitful diplomacy, its cruel ambitions and its nervous whims, while Armenia, ever the martyr and left to strive for its dreams by itself, is hopelessly enamoured with civilisation and with Europe. When Armenia finally is close (in bed) to and touches his beloved and inaccessible Europe, he finds that she has ugly hands and nails and is disillusioned from his fantasy...

Why not interpret that Michael Arlen's short story is a call for self-awareness and self-confidence, a call to realise our dreams through our own efforts?

Whatever Michael Arlen expressed in his outburst has often been said in a particularly worse manner in Armenian literature and has been translated into foreign languages. It is as if he had told foreigners an unknown secret, which has put a stain on the whole of our nation's past. We are a curiously extremist people. Sometimes a wind will blow, and you will see that the harness on the Armenian intellectual's mouth will fly away. He will insult the Armenian people in every possible manner; he will attribute every single defect to them. But the wind promptly changes, and pages and pages are filled with praises of our virtues. The last campaign against Michael Arlen proceeds from the latter wind direction.

Aside from this specific phenomenon, when we approach Michael Arlen particularly as a literary man, we see that from the first day he went public as an Armenian, without renouncing his origins. He has stated on multiple occasions up till now, that he is an Armenian thrown into an English environment. We find in him an embodiment of Armenian stubbornness (a positive trait in this case) and the self-confidence learned from Anglo-Saxon education and environment. He does not lean on the English nation and its traditions, or the Jewish geniality that he praises so much, but he remains an Armenian with multiple questions facing him. He continues his journey towards high artistic horizons, burdened by mental dilemmas and experiences. It appears that his resounding success in the artistic arena has become a source of great worry for Michael Arlen, burdened with having to prove that the 'enslaved' and 'corrupted' remnants of the old Armenia are still carrying the former glory of their race.

Michael Arlen's writings and his personal stance most likely tilt the balance on the side of his honour. Meanwhile, a portion of Armenian journalists places him alongside people like Pierre Loti wishing to enlarge the blacklist of the Armenian people at all costs. This is an unfitting and unfair depiction, which needs to be redressed by the press itself, and we think that Mr. A. Chobanian must give the first signal.

Will the complete translation of Michael Arlen's short story provided by *Haratch* prompt the leaders of the Armenian press to refrain from their Armenian stubbornness (unnecessary stubbornness) and for once prove that they too can be *'gentlemen' [English word in original]*?

A FAMILY PHOTO ALBUM

The Kouyoumdjian family, Bulgaria, late 1890s. (Back row) Tacvor, Satinik, Ahavni, Sarkis, Roupen. (Front row) Dikran (Arlen), Krikor.

The matriarch: Satinik Kouyoumdjian.

Arlen in front of the family's Southport home.

Arlen in middle age.

Arlen, Michael John and Atalanta.

Venetia and Atalanta.

A FAMILY PHOTO ALBUM

Arlen with his nephew Sarkis, Southport, 1928.

The High Life, Riviera, 1930s.

A DETAILED TIMELINE

1895
16 Nov – born in Ruse, Bulgaria

1900/1901
The Kouyoumdjians arrived in England (dates are unclear from the official records)

1902
Oct – Ahavni (sister) married Vahan Gulbenkian

1909
Apr – entered Malvern College as a boarder

1913
July – left school
Sep/Oct – enrolled as a student at Edinburgh University

1915
24 Apr – start of Armenian genocide
27 Jul – father died at Grand Hotel, Llandudno
30 Jul – father's funeral

Nov – moved to Redcliffe Rd, London
After 16 Nov – met D.H. Lawrence (via Heseltine?)
Dec – D.H. Lawrence proposed to take him to Florida
13-16 Dec – Visited Garsington with Heseltine
18 Dec – lunch with Frieda Lawrence, Anna Wickham and Monica Saleeby

1916
10-22 Jan – stayed with Lawrences in Porthcothan, Cornwall.
Jan – play 'A Wisp of Straw' typed by Clayton
22 Jan – Clayton returned MS of 'Play'
Mar – 'Pastiche' published in *New Age* under *nom-de-plume*
1 May – encounter with 'Priscilla' in Redcliffe Rd?
1 May – Ahavni married Marco Bakirgian (her second marriage)
Jul – first publication in *Ararat*
Aug – moved from Redcliffe Rd to Market St [Home Office records]. (According to Clayton letters this move was between Feb 1917 and Sep 1918)
3 Aug – republication of 'An Appeal to Sense' in *New Age*
1 Sep – Café Royal incident with Katherine Mansfield *et al*
9 Nov – review of Gilbert Cannan's Mendel in *New Age*
Nov/Dec? – worked with Vickers Aircraft Dept
4 Dec? – staying in Southport for "a few weeks"

1917
Jan-Aug – articles in *New Age*

1918
Aug – 'London Papers' began in *New Age*

1919
22 May – first riposte to Pickthall in *New Age*. Last 'London Paper'

20 Nov – *The London Venture* advertised for publication
Nov? – in Algiers, Hotel St George?
1919-23 – Leonardo Mercati (future brother-in-law) at Balliol College, Oxford

1920
Jan? – *The London Venture* published
Jan – Nancy Cunard moved to Paris
29 Jan – play fragment in *New Age* under both names, 'The Ci-Devant'
Jan/Feb – to Nice and Cannes
1 Apr – last salvo in Pickthall correspondence, under name MA
Apr – meeting with Cunard (in London?)
Summer – Cunard took a villa near Boulogne. July, at La Ducasse
Sep – at Hardelot Plage with Cunard
Nov/Dec – with Cunard in Paris
Dec – Cunard in hospital in Paris, curettage

1921
Jan – in Paris, hoping to "go south"
Jan? – Cunard's hysterectomy
Feb – Cunard in hospital in Paris with infection
Summer – visited Cunard at St-Martin-Eglise; relationship with Cunard fizzled out?
7 Oct – Manouk Kouyoumdjian died, age 53
Oct – *The Romantic Lady* (stories) published
Early Dec – staying at Bowdon Old Hall
Dec – London address: 23 Market Street

1922
16 Jun – became naturalised British subject

Jul – will proved of Manouk Kouyoumdjian, 57 Albert Rd, Southport
Summer – met Ronald Firbank at Café Royal
Sep or Oct – MA and Rebecca West met Gilbert Frankau
26 Oct – *'Piracy'* published
Oct/Nov – met Philip Heseltine again?
Early Nov – at a Mal St Cyr fashion show with Gwen Farrar
7 Dec – to "Africa" (Biskra)?
? – meeting with Beverley Baxter (journalist)

1923
26 Jun? – met Sinclair Lewis in London for tea with Marc Connelly
Jun? – *These Charming People* (stories) published
Jul – visited Nancy Cunard and Iris Tree at Varengeville-sur-Mer
Early Aug – staying with Sinclair Lewis in Seine-et-Marne for 10 days
12 Aug – with Sinclair Lewis to soirée at Gurdjieff Institute
23 Aug? – at home in Southport
30 Aug – staying at Beaumanor; pursuing affair with Mary Howe?
14 Sep? – with Grace Lewis listening to boxing commentary on French radio
30 Sep? – lunch for Mrs Randolph Hearst, London
4 Nov – At Meggie Albanesi's dinner at Embassy, London, for her father
9 Dec – Meggie Albanesi (actress friend of MA's) died
15 Dec – H.G. Wells refers to him in a letter to Rebecca West
Dec? – staying at Bowdon Old Hall for a month?
Address 23 Market St, W1 (electoral roll)

1924

Feb – Osbert Sitwell called him a "beastly little creature" after meeting in street
5 Mar – wrote from Queen St, London, to Raymond Mortimer
24 Mar – at hotel in Paris
16 Jun – *The Green Hat* published in UK
1 Jul? – PEN Club dinner with Rebecca West
Jul – attended party for Radclyffe Hall and Una Troubridge
Late Jul? – meeting with Blanche Sweet, Marshall Neilan and Rebecca West
Late Jul – Rebecca West's "refrigerator" party
Summer? – Gilbert Frankau re-met the original 'Shelmerdene'
Before Sep? – stay at hotel in Algiers [but cf. 'Africa' reference, Dec 1922?]
Sep/Oct – bankrolled *The Vortex* (Noël Coward)
29 Oct – dining with Viscountess Curzon *et al* prior to Selfridge's party
29 Oct – attended Election night party at Selfridge's with Tallulah Bankhead
Oct or Nov – met Sacheverell and Osbert Sitwell in Piccadilly
Nov – took Knightsbridge flat for one month
25 Nov – *The Vortex* (Coward) opened (MA backstage?)
30 Nov – *Dear Father* (play) opened in London
9-11 Dec – attended Grosvenor House Bazaar
18 Dec – settlement of libel action by Cohen & Cohen
Late Dec – attended engagement party for Mona Dunn (with Lois Sturt)
? – advertisements appeared for 'The Dark Angel' (an unpublished title)
? – "weekly" lunches with Daphne Fielding in London
? – on Beaverbrook's yacht
Sep 1924-Jun 1925 – dallying with Janet Aitken (Beaverbrook's daughter)

Address: 14 Queen St

1925
1-16 Jan – in Southport
16 Jan – at opening of Gargoyle Club (Nancy Cunard also there?)
17 Jan – "in front" at *Peter Pan* at Adelphi
Jan or Feb – met A.A. Milne
2 Feb – living at Charles St, London
6 Feb – to South of France with Frederick Lonsdale for 2 weeks
Early Feb – meetings with Sam Goldwyn on Riviera
Mid-Feb? – in Monte Carlo?
Early Mar – watching tennis in Beaulieu
10 Mar – arrived in New York. Stayed at Ritz
10 Mar? – saw Shaw's *Candida* at his insistence
Before 16 Mar – at dinner given by Mr and Mrs Henry B. Sell
17 Mar – guest of Mr and Mrs Gilbert Miller
20 Mar – attended send-off party for Pola Negri
23 Mar – attended first night of revival of *The Little Minister* (J.M. Barrie)
Before 24 Mar – Ray Long gave luncheon for him
24 Mar – guest of Armenian Educational Foundation, New York
24 Mar – Alexander Woollcott party to welcome MA; George Gershwin played
Late Mar? – gypsy-themed party by Mrs W.R. Hearst
Mar? – visited Bebe Daniels on set of *The Manicure Girl* (Long Island)
29 Mar – *The Green Hat* (play) opened in Detroit
11 Apr? – *The Green Hat* (play) opened in Chicago
18 Apr – reserved cabin for this date on *Olympic* liner
20 Apr – Jesse Lasky left NYC for Hollywood
Late Apr/early May – guest of Winchell Smith, Farmington

Early May – spotted at vaudeville matinee in NYC?
May? – attended Alfred Orage talk (or earlier in NYC visit?)
May – Scott Fitzgerald praised MA to Hemingway
19 May – arrived Southampton from NY on Mauretania
11 Jun – *May Fair* (stories) published in UK
Early Jul – at Theatrical Garden Party, London, with Gertrude Lawrence
Summer – guest at Somerset Maugham's house parties in London
Summer – frequented Kate Meyrick's Little Club
Summer? – on Beaverbrook's yacht with Beatrice Lillie *et al*
Aug – lunch to honour James Oliver Curwood
26 Aug – arrived in NY on board *Olympic*
2 Sep – *The Green Hat* (play) opened in London starring Tallulah Bankead
15 Sep – *The Green Hat* (play) opened in NY starring Katharine Cornell
16 Sep – NY opening of Coward's *The Vortex*; MA present
17 Sep – at party for Diana Cooper
19 Sep – *Ziegfeld Follies* of 1925 closed [opened c.6 July?] MA visited Louise Brooks
22 Sep – *Sunny* (musical) opened in NY; MA had a crush on its star, Marilyn Miller
Autumn – *Dancer of Paris* screenplay?
6 Oct – retitled *Dear Father* (now called *These Charming People*) opened in NY
15 Oct – Charlie Chaplin returned to Hollywood
16 or 17 Oct? – MA left for Hollywood by train
20 Oct – arrived in Los Angeles
21 Oct – at Montmartre, LA, with Chaplin *et al*
23 Oct – spoke at Breakfast Club meeting
24 Oct – Pola Negri's dinner dance at the Biltmore
25 Oct – Frank Borzage luncheon

27 Oct – guest of Writers' Club
Late Oct – guest of 250 on arrival in LA. Could be Writers' Club on 27 Oct?
29 Oct – at press lunch for 50 people at Ambassadors
5 Nov – at premiere of *The Big Parade* with Bebe Daniels *et al*
16 Nov – his thirtieth birthday. "Basking" in Anna de Mille's hospitality
13 Dec – arrived in NY from Hollywood
14 Dec? – at NY party in honour of Lady Colefax
Mid Dec – Adolphe Menjou's party for MA at The Colony, NY
20/21 Dec – sailed for England after club-crawl with Noël Coward
Dec – denied rumours he was to wed Pola Negri
28 Dec – arrived Liverpool from NY
28 Dec – Gershwin's *Tip-Toes* opened in NY (starring Fred and Adele Astaire)
Late Dec – in Southport(?) to see sick mother

1926

1 Jan – introduced fictitious character/pseudonym 'Viola Paris' in US *Vogue*
Early Jan – spotted at Gargoyle Club, London, with a "lady in black"
18 Jan – attended James Dunn's wedding in Paris
18 Jan – T.S. Eliot dismissed him in a letter as of no importance
Late Jan or Feb? – photocall with Fred and Adele Astaire in Paris?
28 Feb – *Dancer of Paris* (film) released in US
Early Apr – in Paris, met Gershwin again
25 Apr – pictured in *New York Times* in his flat overlooking Etoile
Late Apr – talking to Cole Porter at Ritz bar, Paris
3 May – in Paris, reportedly "writing another novel"

Spring? – dinner in Paris with Nancy Cunard and Louis Aragon (or was it 1927?)
May? – recuperating at Grosvenor Hotel, Paris, after a "slight op"
3-12 May – The General Strike in UK
14 Jun – first night of Russian Ballet, London
Late Jun – drinking at Ritz, Paris, with Scott Fitzgerald *et al*
Early Jul – to Biarritz
Summer – stag dinner for Will Rogers at Savoy, London, with Bernard Shaw, G.K. Chesterton, J.M. Barrie, Harry Lauder *et al*
22 Jul – staying with Frederick Lonsdale in London
23 Jul – staying with Beaverbrook?
Summer – with Frederick Lonsdale at Salcombe
9 Aug – US West Coast production of *The Green Hat* (play) opened
Summer/autumn – pursuing Audrey Emery in Paris and Biarritz?
Aug – in a "hermit retreat" on "Essex farm" (actually Crawley, Sussex?)
Sep – lunching at The Savoy with Evelyn Fitzgerald (Beaverbrook's brother-in-law)
Mid-Sep – lunching at Embassy with Jean Norton
Autumn – Anthony Powell moved to Shepherd Market
11 Oct – *The Ace of Cads* (film) released in US
Early Nov – at theatre in London with Mary Curzon-Howe
Early Nov (6th?) – at private view of Alvaro Guevara/Edward Wadsworth show, Leicester Galleries, London
Nov – attended first 'bottle party' in London
Nov – flat in Parc Monceau, Paris, now his "HQ"
21 Nov – wedding of Audrey Emery and Grand Duke in Biarritz
27 or 25 Nov – *Why She Was Late for Dinner* (play) in London

30 Nov – at PEN Club fancy dress ball, Hyde Park Hotel; MA as "Don Quixote"
11 Dec – being inoculated with "germs" in Paris
12 Dec – Atalanta's father remarried
? – reencounter with Nancy Cunard in Berkeley Square/Davies Street?
? – had an apartment in Rue Masseran, Paris, in later 1920s?

1927
Jan – "at his flat in Paris", according to *The Tatler*
3 Jan – farewell dinner in Monte Carlo?
Mid/late Jan – threw party for Audrey Emery and Grand Duke, Monte Carlo
Late Jan? – ill with bronchitis in Monte Carlo
30 Mar – planned date of arrival in Rio de Janeiro
Apr – Barbara Cartland married. When did MA proposition her?
29 Apr – *Young Men in Love* published simultaneously in UK and US
30 Apr – "on his way to Peru"?
2 May – appeared on cover of *Time* magazine
7 May – "on a visit to South America"
17 May – *The Zoo* (play, collaboration with Winchell Smith) opened in London
18 May – "on his return voyage from South America"
31 May – arrived Southampton from Buenos Aires
14 Jun – "very ill" and convalescing in Sussex
19 Jun – release of *Tip-Toes* (silent movie)
30 Jun – attended Walker-Milligan prize fight in London
Early summer – lunch in London with Mrs Aria, Osbert Sitwell, Sybil Thorndike & Pamela Frankau
Jul – Australian production of *The Green Hat* (play)
Early Jul (5th?) – to Switzerland

Aug? – staying at a hotel in Como
Summer – US tour of *The Green Hat* (play)
3 Sep – MA reportedly "to undergo an operation in London"?
Sep – in Venice, attended Schneider Cup races, met Atalanta (his future wife)
3 Sep – attended costume ball in Venice (Lady Wimborne?); 'Chips' Channon was "rude" to him
11 Sep – Castlerosse bad-mouthed MA, in his absence, at a party in Berlin. Also present: Tilla Durieux, Diana Manners, Arnold Bennett and Lord Beaverbrook
Mid-Sep – beach party on Lido, Venice, with Elsa Maxwell, the Obolenskys, Noël Coward *et al*
10 Oct – *The Zoo* (play), opened, Pittsburgh, USA
Oct? – cure in Davos after operation for "tubercular tumour"
17 Nov – in Florence: encountered D.H. Lawrence by the Arno
19 Nov – Florence: tea with Lawrence, MA having had "tubercular testicle" removed
23 Nov – scheduled visit to the Lawrences cancelled
29 Nov – Florence: lunched with Lawrence and Norman Douglas
6 Dec – lunch with Maria (and Aldous?) Huxley in Lucca?
Late Dec – to St Moritz for skiing with Noël Coward

1928

Jan – engagement to Atalanta
Feb – E.F. Benson article on 'Green Hattery' and 'Dallowayism'
5 Mar – dinner at Arnold Bennett's house with T.S. Eliot and Hugh Walpole
10 Mar – dinner at P.G. Wodehouse's in London
Mar – Maurice Ravel praised him in an article about jazz
1 Apr – in Paris
Early Apr – dinner for George Gershwin in Paris; Audrey Emery, Grand Duke Dmitri and Alice Obolensky (*née*

Astor) also present
? Apr – drinks with Henry Savage, John Flanagan and Montague Glass, Cannes
1 May – wedding in Cannes, civil ceremony
2 May – wedding, religious ceremony
11-13 May – *A Legend of London*, by MA at Palace, New York
14 May – wrote to Philip Morrell from Villa Edgeroad
May-Oct – living at Villa Edgeroad, Cannes
30 Jun – in Aix-les-Bains visiting his mother
Before 21 Jul – met Ellen Terry
20 Jul-2 Sep – Bernard Shaw holidaying at Cap d'Antibes
29 July – Arlens met Bernard Shaws at Lloyd Osbournes'
Summer? – shot *Why Light Women Float Best* (film) with Beatrice Lillie
12 Aug? – dinner at Antibes with Ordes and Stella Benson
Aug – challenged Somerset Maugham to tennis match
15 Sep – wrote to 'Walter' from Villa Edgeroad, Cannes
11 Nov – interview with Atalanta in *Daily Express*
18 Nov – with wife to lunch with Arnold Bennett
Mid Nov – dining at Embassy with Beaverbrook *et al*
Late Nov – at dinner party for Lt-Col Moore-Brabazon
Nov – *Lily Christine* published
Nov – in London "for a month"
3 Dec – in Southport playing golf with his nephews
4 Dec – photographed in Southport with Atalanta
12 Dec – in Southport; ordered copy of Norman Douglas's smutty *Limericks*
15 Dec – *A Woman of Affairs* (film) released in US
20 Dec – Christmas at St Moritz (with the Mountbattens?)
Late in year? – "accident" (road?) of some sort
? – incorporated himself as a company (or earlier?)

1929

Jan – St Moritz, then back to Cannes
Jan – "tempestuous" weather, snow in Monte Carlo
23 Mar – at a clinic in Freiburg (for smoking?)
30 May – attended Election night party at Selfridge's
Jun – Southport, then Switzerland for 2 months?
2 Jun – dined with wife at Embassy, London
Jun – sat for 'poem-portrait' by Osbert Sitwell
2 Jul – Atalanta contracted to endorse Cutex nail polish
23 Jul – invited to party at Lady Wimborne's
Aug – playing golf in St Moritz
Sep 1929-Sep 1930? – based in Paris?
14 Sep – address Rue de Verneuil?
Sep? – in Paris with Morley Callaghan (tennis)
Oct – wife setting up their new home in Paris
5 Oct? – with Edward Titus *et al* spent afternoon with Hemingway in Paris
8 Oct – dinner party in London at Beaverbrook's
15 Oct – *Babes in the Wood* (stories) published in UK
Mid Oct – Heinemann party at The Savoy; met Graham Greene
22 Oct – saw Edward Titus again
29 Oct – Wall Street crash
Late Oct – Bishop of Southwark criticised him from the pulpit
Later Oct – lunched with Graham Greene
Later Oct – "had a little flutter" (ie. an extramarital affair) in London?
Nov – address Rue Masseran. "Expects" to be in Paris for the next year
Nov – operation for appendicitis in Paris
11 Dec – Daria Mercati (sister-in-law) married André Firmenich in Geneva
? – was heard "singing" at A.P Herbert's home in London

1930

Jan – staying with grandmother-in-law at Villa Fiorentina, Cannes
Mid-Feb – just back in Paris "from the South"
Mar – interview with Hrant Samuel in *Haratch*, Paris
Spring – attended talk on book-collecting in Paris
Before 23 Apr – fallout with Zelda Fitzgerald in Paris?
Early May – at opening of Royal Academy Summer Exhibition?
May – brief visit to his publishers in London
9 Jun – living at 11 rue Masseran, Paris
Jun – met Thomas Wolfe in Paris
1 Jul – visited Noël Coward at Goldenhurst
Aug – comic encounter with 'Countess' (Eileen Duveen) in Paris
26 Aug – at dinner party given by Mr and Mrs Martin Vogel, Boulogne; Prince of Wales guest of honour
Summer – Martha Gellhorn saw him at Lewisohns' on Riviera?
Summer – Richard Aldington "seeing something" of him
25 Sep – arrived in London, staying at May Fair Hotel, looking for a house
Oct – met A.R. Orage in London to discuss *New English Weekly*
Oct – contribution to the retitled *New London Magazine*
Mid Oct – moved into rented house in Stanhope Place, London
22 Oct – dinner with Frederick 'Boy' Browning, Leonardo Mercati and "the Lionel Guinnesses" (= Loel and Joan Guinness?)
23 Oct – lunch with Somerset Maugham at Stanhope Place
27 Nov – attended Thanksgiving party in London with Arnold Bennett *et al*
6 Dec – attended birthday party for Lord Dorling
8 Dec – photo shoot for Bassano Ltd.
9 Dec – Michael John (son) born at Stanhope Place; 'Boy' Browning was godfather

1931
19 Jan – dined with Frieda Lawrence in London
28 Jan – "off to America"
3 Feb – arrived in NY on *Aquitania*
Feb – met Alec Waugh in New York
16 Feb – *Good Losers* (play) opened in London, with Cathleen Nesbitt
25 Feb – sailed from New York on *Bremen*
3 Mar – arrived Southampton from New York
Mar – *Men Dislike Women* (novel) published
18/21 Apr – Dorchester Hotel opened. MA wrote for brochure.
Apr-Aug – meetings with Charlie Chaplin and May Reeves on Riviera
23 Jul – *These Charming People* (film) released
Jul? – party at US Embassy, London, with Daphne du Maurier (or could be earlier in year?)
15 Jul – with wife attended Grace Moore's wedding in Cannes
Aug – centre of attraction at Antibes; "inspired" by Oswald Mosley over dinner at the Mosleys' villa
Aug – moved to Bella Vista, Cannes
Aug? – with Noël Coward at Miramar, Cannes, with Lincoln Gillespie
Autumn? – Osbert Sitwell's *Three-Quarter Length Portrait* published? (but see June 1929)
Sep? – met Dorothy Schiff at Beaverbrook's London salon
Oct – met A.R. Orage re contribution to *New English Weekly* (with Coward?)
13 Oct – at first night of Coward's *Cavalcade*, London
27 Oct – General Election victory for National Government
28 Dec – address Villa Bella Vista, Cannes
? – offered "intimate story of London" to publisher Carrefour? (Exact year unknown)

A DETAILED TIMELINE

1932

25/26 Jan – at Lord Castlerosse's party, Park Lane, London
1 Mar – tea at Princess Karageorgevitch's with Elizabeth von Arnim, Cannes
Apr – first issue of *New English Weekly*
28 Apr – at charity royal premiere of *Lily Christine* (film), London; Prince of Wales and Thelma Furness also attended
18 Jun – tea at Elizabeth von Arnim's, Mougin
23 Jun – hosted Elizabeth von Arnim and H.G. Wells, Cannes
24 July – slight motor accident near St Tropez
Aug – "going to Switzerland for a few weeks"; suffering from "anaemia"
9 Nov – Stalin's wife, Nadezhda Alliluyeva, committed suicide, inspired by a "vile book" (*The Green Hat*)
Nov – in Paris for 2 to 3 weeks?
Nov? – Alec Waugh visited him in Cannes

1933

Jan – in London
Jan – *Man's Mortality* (novel) published in UK
26 Apr – visit from Richard Aldington (cf. 26 June)
May/Jun – golf with Maugham; Atalanta "vomiting"
9 Jun – Venetia (daughter) born in Cannes
26 Jun – met Richard Rumbold and Aldington at Miramar bar, Cannes (cf. 26 Apr?)
7 Jul – to supper with Elizabeth von Arnim
10 Jul – hosted dinner for Elizabeth von Arnim, Somerset Maugham (*et al*?)
16 Sep – wife involved in car accident at Cannes; motorcyclist died as result
Sep/early Oct? – Violet Pakenham saw him, "solitary", in Carlton bar, Cannes
Late Oct – with wife to England

Late Oct – at premiere of *The Private Lives of Henry VIII* (film), London
2 Nov – at opening of *Gay Divorce* (musical), Palace Theatre, London
14 Nov – discussed books with R. Bruce Lockhart in London
22 Nov – met Virginia Woolf at Hutchinsons' dinner party, London
23 Nov – attended opening of Robert E. Sherwood's *Acropolis* (play), London
28 Nov – Atalanta had minor car accident in London
Nov – at publisher's party in London in honour of Beverley Nichols
? – house guest of Cecil Beaton at Ashcombe
? – declined offer to become *Daily Express* drama critic?
? – when attended Lady Mendl's dinner at the Château de la Garoupe?

1934
29 Jan – riots in Nice, anti-Government disturbances
10 Feb – with wife dined with Harold Nicolson and Somerset Maugham in Cannes
19 Apr – libel action by pilot Rupert Bellville, who believed himself libelled in *Man's Mortality*; case settled by MA apologising and paying plaintiff's costs
21 Apr – wedding of Leonardo Mercati (brother-in-law) to Lily Strathatos in Athens
24 Apr – attended London premiere of *Roman Scandals* (film) with Mrs Wardell
25 Apr – attended London premiere of S.N. Behrman's *Biography* (play)
May – Henry Williamson stayed at Winchell Smith's place (dinner guest spoke deprecatingly of MA)
7-9 Jul – visited Noël Coward at Goldenhurst (Sat-Mon)

Mid Jul – discussed financial markets with Harry J. Greenwall (Continental correspondent of the *Daily Express*) at London Ritz

Jul – Syrie Maugham's party; MA danced with Mary Hutchinson

Jul – *Hell! Said the Duchess* published (novel, dedicated to Castlerosse) in UK

Summer – advised Martha Gellhorn about her novel

28 Sep – *Outcast Lady* (second film version of *The Green Hat*) released in US

Sep – "intends" to settle in Vienna for six months

18 Nov – Adolphe Menjou and Veree Teasdale in radio sketch by MA on WEAF (in US)

Late Nov/early Dec – in Budapest

Mid Dec – met Arshag O. Sarkissian and Franz Werfel in Vienna, Hotel Imperial

Christmas – in Vienna

1935

3 Jan – in Vienna, "travelling"

March – in Athens, met journalist R. Selkirk Panton

7 Apr – discussed books with Bruce Lockhart in London

2 May – pre-lunch drink with 'Chips' Channon at Ritz

3 May – at Royal Academy private view, London

Early May – at premiere of Gilbert Miller's *Tovarich* (play)

14 May – lunch with Jean Norton, Ivor Churchill, Daphne Weymouth, 'Chips' Channon

Jul – swimming in Maxine Elliott's pool, Juan-les-Pins

Summer – met Clare Boothe (Luce), Cap-Ferrat?

Sep – lunch at Maxine Elliott's villa with Winston Churchill *et al*

Oct – made public appeal for The Cancer Hospital

Oct – in London with wife and children. Party at Ritz

Early Nov – attended Heinemann's party

14 Nov – waved off returning Greek king from London
14 Nov – at Selfridge's Election night party
Nov – came into his US trust fund?

1936

Feb – gave big party at opening of Ambassadors, Cannes
13 Mar – along with 33 other writers, signed letter to *The Times* calling for reform of libel law to protect authors against "flimsy or malicious charges"
Spring? – announced he was leaving, "he couldn't stand things any more". Soon returned.
1 May? – at Midnight Follies, 'A Little Bit of Hollywood in London', Dorchester Hotel
23 May – *The Golden Arrow* (film) released
Summer – played ping-pong at Grace Moore's villa with Anton Dolin
5 Sep – motor accident in Cannes; cyclist injured
Sep – visited Somerset Maugham at Villa Mauresque
Oct – met Dennis Wheatley in London
Nov – at Embassy Club with Dresden Opera
26 Nov – with wife at a party at Heinemann's (also Somerset Maugham and Richard Aldington)
4 Dec – met Humbert Wolfe (and Pamela Frankau?)
? – Joachim von Ribbentrop, German ambassador to London, interviewed at his home in Germany. Books lining his study included *The Green Hat*.

1937

14 Jan – in bed with a severe chill
Feb – Michael John had tonsils and adenoids out
Feb? – refused to dine in same party as Wallis Simpson (could be earlier in year?)
2 Mar – played golf with Somerset Maugham

Late Apr-17 May – staying at Hotel Lotti, Paris
Jun – in Paris again. Jewellery stolen
19 Jul – to Austria "for 2 months". Semmering?
9 Aug – *The Crooked Coronet* (stories) published in UK
Aug – *Cavalier of the Streets* (film) released in UK
Mid Oct – 'Pendennis' (*Observer* columnist) encountered him in London
Late Oct – at dinner at Garrick for Eugene Saxton
Late Nov – at charity dance in aid of London Fever Hospital (Planetree House, Mrs Stanley-Clarke and Mrs Musker)

1938
18 Jan – mother died at Hesketh Rd, Southport, age 71
21 Jan – attended mother's funeral in Manchester
Feb – London exhibition by Sava Botzaris included sculpted head of MA
Mar – attended Lady Mendl's party in Monte Carlo
Apr – last encounter with Nancy Cunard, in Nice, with Norman Douglas
23 Apr-1 May – HMS *Hood* moored at Golfe Juan. Visited with son
Between Apr and Nov? – dinner at Maud Cunard's with Churchill? Or later?
26 Jun – grandmother-in-law, Princess Daria, died at Villa Fiorentina, Cannes
Jul – took his family to Southport with their Swiss maid
Jul – spotted at The Ritz

1939
Jan – visit to London
Jan – *The Flying Dutchman* (novel) published in UK
Jan? – dinner at Maud Cunard's with Churchill? (cf. Apr-Nov 1938)

Mar – planned to move family to Athens
Apr – in Athens with wife; saw Goebbels
19 May – address c/o Morgan & Co, Paris
Jul – *The Flying Dutchman* published in US
Late Aug – returned with family to England
3 Sep – Britain declared war on Germany
Sep – son started as boarder at Abinger Hill School, Surrey
Nov – began writing weekly column for *The Tatler*
Nov – wife "in the country", MA in London
Christmas – in Southport

1940
Jan? – dinner at Maud Cunard's with Churchill? (cf 1938 and 1939!)
Jan-Mar – wife "still in the country"
23 Feb – radio broadcast of 'Red Anthony' dramatisation on BBC
Mar – visited son at Abinger School?
25 Jun – wife and children sailed to Canada
12 Aug – at May Fair Hotel, London
5 Sep – proposed for membership of Garrick Club
18 Sep – radio broadcast of 'The Three-Cornered Moon' on BBC
15 Oct – lunch with Val Gielgud (BBC producer) in Manchester
19 Oct – George Orwell charged MA with "narcissism" in *New Statesman*
Oct – "pleasant" meeting with Hugh Stewart (BBC producer)
6 Nov – in bed with a chill at Eaton Hall, Chester
Mid Nov – meeting with Val Gielgud?
14/15 Nov – blitz on Coventry. MA at Himley Hall with Lord Dudley
15 Nov – BBC wrote to him at Hesketh Rd, Southport

21 Nov – radio broadcast of 'When the Nightingale Sang in Berkeley Square' on BBC
21 Nov – "doing things about bombs"
Nov – invited to become Public Relations Officer for West Midlands
27 Nov – living at Himley Hall, Worcestershire, for "foreseeable"
26 Dec – staying at Queen's Hotel, Birmingham
? – encounter with J.P. Carstairs in Pall Mall
? – visit to A.P. Herbert on *Water Gipsy* (Herbert's boat) on Thames (or 1941?)
? – did "a hundred push-ups" at Dorchester Hotel, London

1941
Early in year – his assets frozen
2 Jan – became member of Garrick Club
Early Jan – wife supping at El Morocco, NYC, with Jerome Zerbe
17 Jan – wife at opening of El Greco exhibition, New York
30 Jan – parliamentary question asked in Commons about his suitability for war work
10 Feb – wife at Committee of Mercy reception, NYC
11 Feb – parliamentary question to Winston Churchill about MA
Feb – resigned his civil defence position in West Midlands
22 Feb – revival(?) broadcast of 'Three-Cornered-Moon' on BBC
24 Feb – Ritz, London, now his address
Late Feb – "enjoyable" meeting with Val Gielgud
7 Mar – lunch with 'Bendor' Grosvenor and Japanese ambassador?
8 Mar – bomb fell on Café de Paris, London
11 Mar – at launch of *Britain in Pictures* series

28 Mar – wife on committee of Greek Festival for Freedom, NYC
Late Mar-Apr – staying with brother in Southport
13 Apr – radio broadcast of 'The Crooked Coronet' adaptation on BBC
13 Apr – British War Relief Society exhibition, NYC. Greek table setting decorated for wife
24 Apr – wife had guests at dinner dance for benefit of St Clare's Hospital, NYC
6 May – wife sponsored exhibition of paintings for Greek War Relief Association, NYC
8 May – wife a "salesgirl" at Committee of Mercy fashion show, NYC
8-9 May – wife a patroness of bazaar for Greek Relief, NYC
11 May – wife on committee of a Greek Fashion Festival for Greek War Relief Association, NYC
22 May – (repeat?) radio broadcast of 'Red Anthony' on BBC
Late May – wife on committee for 'Bandwagon Ball' on 29 May, NYC
1 Jun – *Lady, Here's A Flower* (radio play) broadcast on BBC
13 Jun – MA undergoing "drastic" cure for 3-4 weeks
2 Jul – at opening night of Noël Coward's *Blithe Spirit* with Earl Mountbatten, Beatrice Lillie *et al*
15 Jul – cocktails at Savoy with Guy Liddell *et al*
30 Jul – staying at Athenaeum Court
Summer? – wife and children vacationed in Edgartown? Northeast? (Or 1940?)
Late Jul/early Aug – met Dennis Wheatley for sherry in London, W8
4 Aug – with Beatrice Lillie at Claygate for National Savings Campaign
6 Sep – sailed from Glasgow to US. His son "seriously ill" (sic)
Late Sep – living at Hotel Volney, NYC
24 Oct – first *Gay Falcon* film released in US

12 Nov – wife a 'hostess' at luncheon to aid Greece, Near East Foundation, NYC
7 Dec – lunched with Cecil Roberts, C.S. Forester and others, NYC
7 Dec – MA and wife assisting with 'Bundles for Britain', NYC
? – first meeting with William Saroyan? (Or later?)
? – visit to A.P. Herbert on *Water Gipsy* on Thames? (Or 1940?)

1942
14 Mar – *Portrait of A Serious Heart* (radio play) broadcast on BBC
Mar – he "has been very ill"
Apr – *Portrait of A Serious Heart* performed on stage, Haymarket Theatre
May – living at Hotel Volney, NYC
22 Jun – lunch with Arthur Hornblow (film producer)
25 Jun – attended Countess Mercati's lunch for Greek King in NYC
Summer? – vacation in White Mountains, New Hampshire?
5-6 Sep – with Countess Mercati at Irving Hotel, Southampton, Long Island
6 Sep – luncheon guests of John A. McVickar at Southampton, Long Island
18 Oct – left New York for Los Angeles
23 Oct – reported to studio in Hollywood
Oct – in Hollywood to write Hedy Lamarr picture
Nov – first draft scripts for *The Heavenly Body*
Nov/Dec? – met Clare Boothe Luce in Hollywood
8 Dec – wife on committee of Friends of Greece; fundraiser tea, NYC
Dec – wife among vice-chairmen of British War Relief Society, NYC
Dec – wife "will join him" in Hollywood after Christmas

When did Michael John spend Christmas in California with his father? 1942 or 1943? Or 1944?

MA in NYC from Sep 1941 to Oct 1942

MA in Hollywood (on and off?) from Oct 1942 to May 1945

1943

Jan – escorted Paulette Goddard and Jinx Falkenburg to nightspots

Jan – photographed outside MGM Studios with John Erskine, John Van Druten and Sinclair Lewis

Jan-Jul – rewrites of *The Heavenly Body*

25 Feb-Mar 3 – script conferences on *The Heavenly Body* with Walter Reisch

Mar – wife had tea with Mrs Cornelius Vanderbilt at Stork Club, NYC

1 Apr – at reception for Madame Chiang Kai-Shek, Hollywood

15 Apr – wife at lunch/fashion show for women's auxiliary of Greek War Relief Association, NYC

May? – signed "long-term" (2-year) contract with MGM

Jun – at Savoy with Paulette Goddard

25 Jul – arrived at The Homestead, Virginia, from Hollywood

30 Jul – Weddells' party at The Homestead

Jul – wife playing gin rummy at The Homestead

Jul? – met young Gore Vidal, whose mother was MA's bridge partner

Aug? – working on script of *If Winter Comes*

23 Sep – with Paulette Goddard *et al* at opening of Ice Follies, Pan-Pacific Auditorium, LA

Sep/Oct – working on script of *Mrs Parkington*

1944

11 Jan – Ann Brokaw (daughter of Clare Boothe Luce) killed in motor accident

15 Feb – "honorary pall bearer" at Edgar Selwyn's funeral
28 Feb – attended wedding reception for Charles Brackett's daughter
Feb-Apr – working on script of *Without Love*?
Mar 22-Apr 6 – script conferences for *Without Love* with Lawrence Weingarten, H.E. Rogers and Katharine Hepburn
31 Mar – dined with Norma Shearer and Sylvia Ashley
Apr – *The Heavenly Body* released in US
19 May – "passing through a time of desperation"
24 May – dined with Paulette Goddard and Burgess Meredith
9 Jun – injured in a car accident in Hollywood
19 Jun – expected to be at The Drake in Chicago but accident prevented travel
18 Jul – "hoping" to leave for The Homestead, Virginia
12 Sep – son started at St Paul's School, Concord, New Hampshire. MA took him?
Oct – *Mrs Parkington* released in US
Autumn – socialised with Kay Francis, Otto Preminger et al
Early Nov – in bedroom fire at Palm Springs, California
19 Nov – dined with Walter Winchell
11 Dec – filed for damages against car driver who caused accident in June
Dec – son visited him in Hollywood? (Or 1942 or 1943?)
? – worked with Richard Aldington on script of film adapted from Alec Waugh's novel *No Truce With Time*? Film never made

1945
Late Jan – visited Paulette Goddard in hospital
Jan – seen with Anita Colby at the Trocadero
Jan – "doing Romanoffs" with Liz Whitney
Early Feb – at a lunch given by Marion Preminger, Beverley Hills
Apr – at Romanoffs with Olivia de Havilland

Early May? – dining with Greer Garson
May – MGM contract expired
15 Jun – with Vincent Sheean at 21, NYC
Jul – at cocktail party in NYC given by Lt Cdr Fairfield
Jul – vacation with family in North Conway, New Hampshire
Sep – encountered Alec Waugh on Fifth Avenue, NYC

1946

26 Feb – back in NY from California and Seattle; address E End Ave, NY
26 Apr – Daria Mercati (sister-in-law) married Paul Palmer in Geneva (her second marriage)
14 Sep – mother-in-law, Harriet Wright, died at Bellerive, Geneva
Sep – invited to 2nd Congress of Soviet Armenian Writers! (Did not attend)
? – addressed pupils of St Paul's School on topic of 'Literature and Life'

1947

5 Apr – death of Count Alexander Mercati (father-in-law) in Athens
25 Apr – death of Tacvor (older brother)
20 May – "sailing to NY on *Queen Elizabeth*"? (Not recorded on passenger list)
May? – attended *New Yorker* party for Rebecca West
May-Jun – claimed to be writing *The Humble Peacock* (play)
17 Sep – lunch with John Golden
Dec – lunch with "Republican politician" in blizzard, NYC

1948

8 Apr – annual dinner dance of Friends of Greece, with wife
Apr – 'Sarkis Kouyoumdjian Ltd' wound up

12 Jul – *The Fatal Night* (film based on 'The Man from America') released in UK
Summer – with wife attended son's graduation from St Paul's
Summer – nephew 'Sarkis'(?) visited family in NY
Aug? – "relieved" to be in London, not Deauville
Autumn – son entered Harvard (graduated 1952)
Oct/Nov – saw Osbert Sitwell in NYC

1949
Apr – still living at Hotel Volney, NYC (cf. 1946)
2 May – with wife at dinner dance for Friends of Greece, Inc
28 Jun – bill introduced in Congress for Arlen family's "relief"
2 Nov – wife and Countess Leonardo Mercati at a fundraiser for poets, NYC
? – mentioned in Royal Commission on the Press as "blacklisted"

1950
Feb – attended cocktail party for Truman Capote in NYC
1 Mar – selected menu for dinner at Sherry-Netherland
Late Mar? – meeting with Hemingway at '21' (wrong date?)
15 Apr – wife flew from NY to Athens with Lily Mercati (her sister-in-law)
25 Apr – TV broadcast of 'The Lovesick Robber' in series *Cads, Scoundrels and Charming Ladies...* (starring Grace Kelly, introduced by MA)
Late Apr? – lunch with P.G. Wodehouse at Colony, NYC
9 Jun – wife arrived NY from Southampton alone
11 Jun – flew from NY to London
29 Jun – staying at Dorchester Hotel
6 Jul – attended dress rehearsal of Noël Coward's *Ace of Clubs*, Cambridge Theatre, London
8 Aug – sailed from Southampton to US

13 Aug – arrived in NY on *Queen Mary*
Oct – bought apartment on Park Avenue. Wife's money?
14 Nov – at fundraiser for Haarlem House Settlement, NYC

1951
4 Feb – wife's stepmother died, NYC
10 Mar – bought Salvador Dali painting ('Oragan' [sic]) at NY gallery
26 Apr – flew from NY to Buenos Aires
3 May – wife attended Greek Easter Ball, NYC
25 May – address: 812 Park Ave
19 Dec – Venetia (daughter) introduced to older family friends
27 Oct – daughter debutante at Tuxedo Ball, NYC
21 Dec – daughter at Debutante Cotillion, Christmas Ball, Waldorf Astoria
27 Dec – son collaborated on a musical, *Seeing Red*, at college
? – "preparation" for "*Knaves and Aces*" TV series in December (Wrong! See 25.4.50)

1952
(Mar? – meeting with Hemingway at '21': wrong?)
Apr – suffering duodenal ulcer
30 Apr – wife sailed from NY to Cherbourg alone
May-Oct – son's romance with 'Amy' (Mary Ellen Flood)
24 Jun – wife arrived NY from Cherbourg alone
Summer – son graduated from Harvard
10 Aug – announcement of son's engagement to Mary Ellen Flood
5 Sep – sailed from NY to Liverpool
13 Sep – arrived Liverpool from NY
13-16 Sep – in Southport
16 Sep – at Bowdon Old Hall
21 Sep – at Dorchester Hotel, London

Sep/Oct? – met Ian Fleming
Oct – interviewed by Ray; poker party at Savage Club; met Joseph Bard?
25 Oct – sailed from Liverpool to US
3 Nov – arrived in NY from England
Late Nov – ill again (in NYC)

1953
Feb – at a lunch to honour H.E. Bates
Apr – met Malcolm Muggeridge in NY
1 May – wife sailed NY to Cannes alone
4 May – his US naturalisation
May – at NY publisher's party for Dylan Thomas, with Gore Vidal
9 Jun – wife flew to NY from Geneva alone
9 Jul – wife's US naturalisation
Son in the army this year?

1954
Apr? – cancer diagnosis
Apr/May? – operation to remove one lung
28 Jun – sailed from NY to Bermuda
3 Sep – arrived in NY from Bermuda
13 Oct – sailed NY to Southampton
18 Oct – arrived Southampton from NY
Oct-Dec – London/Paris
18 Nov – wife sailed from NY to Southampton with daughter
? – last meeting with Alec Waugh? (cf. Feb 1956)
? – Anthony Powell gave him luncheon "*tête-à-tête*"

1955
6 Jan – met J.S. Knapp-Fisher (publisher) at Garrick Club
Jan-May – staying in London and Paris

Spring? – hospitalised in Neuilly
May? – from Paris to South of France
20 Sep – arrived in NY from Cherbourg with wife
Nov – unsympathetic towards Rebecca West over her son's novel, *Heritage*

1956
Feb? – lunch with Alec Waugh (cf. 1954)
29 Apr – 'The Gentleman from America', TV broadcast (in series *Alfred Hitchcock Presents*)
23 Jun – died at home (of cancer)
26 Jun – funeral at Trinity Greek Orthodox Cathedral, NYC
3 Jul – estate valued at less than $5,000, according to the press. Walter Winchell commented: "He took good care of the family. Cut up a million bucks (into trust funds) for Mrs A and the kids."
Autumn? – Atalanta interred MA's ashes in Mercati family plot in Athens

LATER
9 Mar 1957 – son married Ann Warner
Spring 1960 – Ahavni (sister) died, Southport
6 Sep 1964 – wife died of cancer in Athens; interred in Mercati family plot in Athens; "left an estate exceeding a million dollars" (probate)
8 Oct 1968 – BBC TV dramatisation of *Lily Christine* (in series *Jazz Age Tales*)
1969 – daughter Venetia married Bill Brown
1972 – son married Alice Albright (his second marriage)
20 Dec 1974 – Leonardo Mercati (brother-in-law) died in England
28 Sep 1977 – 'Exiles', BBC TV *Play of the Week* (based on son's memoir)

16 Jan 1981 – dramatisation of '*Piracy*' on BBC Radio 4
   (repeated 31/1/1982)
1988? – *Tatler* fashion story on *The Green Hat*
19 Jun 1989 – dramatisation of *The Green Hat* on BBC Radio 4
30 Nov 2011 – daughter died in Quogue, NY

THE EXTANT LETTERS

Correspondents A-Z

Adcock, St. John – NYU
Bagnold, Enid – Yale
Beaverbrook, Lord – Parliament
Belloc Lowndes, Marie – Texas
Brunel, Adrian – misc
Burke, Thomas – Texas
Castle, William R. – Harvard
Churchill, Winston – Churchill
Clayton, Douglas – Texas
Colefax, Sybil – Bodleian
Cond, Miss – misc
Cornell, Katharine – NYPL
Coward, Noël – Birmingham
Craigie, John – NYPL
Creswick, Paul – NYPL
Cunningham, Scott – NYU
Curtis Brown, Albert – Texas
De Mille, Anna – NYPL
Doran, George H. – Yale

Douglas, Norman – Yale
Drinkwater, John – Yale
Emery, Audrey – misc
Evans, C.S. – Heinemann
Firbank, Ronald – NYU
Frere, A.S. – Heinemann
Furlong, Norman Burr – misc
Gerhardie, William – misc
Gielgud, Val – BBC
Gish, Lillian – NYPL
Golden, John – NYPL
Hinton, Percival – NYU
Hutchinson, Mary – Texas
Kahn, Otto – Princeton
Knapp-Fisher, J.S. – Bodleian
Laurie, James – Bodleian
Lewis, Grace – Texas
Long, Ray – NYPL
Longwell, Daniel – Columbia
Luce, Clare Boothe – Lib Congress
Maugham, W. Somerset – Boston
Morrell, Philip – Texas
Mortimer, Raymond – Princeton
Nicolson, Harold – Princeton
Ould, H. – Texas
Pearn, Nancy – BBC
Pinker, Eric – NYPL
Priestley, J.B. – Texas
Savage, Henry – misc
Saxton, Eugene – Texas
Scully, Mary Alice – misc
Sitwell, Georgia – Texas
Sobol, Louis – misc

Stern, G.B. – Boston
Stewart, Hugh – BBC
Stokes, Alan – misc
Stokes, Sewell – misc
Temple, Miss – NYPL
Titus, Edward – Texas
Walpole, Hugh – Texas
Wanger, Walter – misc
Watkins Loomis – Columbia
Waugh, Alec – Texas
Wheatley, Dennis – misc
Wolfe, Humbert – NYPL
Woollcott, Alexander – Harvard
Wykes-Joyce, Max – NYPL

KEY

BBC – BBC Written Archives Centre, Reading
Birmingham – Special Collections, Cadbury Research Library, Birmingham University
Bodleian – Special Collections, Bodleian Library, Oxford University
Boston – Howard Gotlieb Archival Research Center, Boston University
Churchill – Churchill Archives Centre, Churchill College, Cambridge
Columbia – Rare Book & Manuscript Library, Columbia University
Harvard – Houghton Library, Harvard University
Heinemann – Penguin Random House UK, Archive and Library
Lib Congress – Manuscript Division, Library of Congress
Misc – items mostly in private hands, including the present author's
NYPL – Archives, Manuscripts and Rare Books, New York Public Library
NYU – Fales Library, New York University
Parliament – Parliamentary Archives, House of Lords, London
Princeton – Special Collections, Firestone Library, Princeton University
Texas – Harry Ransom Center, University of Texas at Austin
Yale – Beinecke Rare Book and Manuscript Library, Yale University

LETTERS – CHRONOLOGICAL

16 Dec 1915 to mother [Redcliffe Rd]
18, 21 Jan 1916 to Clayton (x2) [Porthcothan]
Jan 1916 – Feb 1917 to Clayton (x15) [Redcliffe Rd]
Sep 1918 – Nov 1919 to Clayton (x4) [Market St]
13 Sep 1920 to Clayton [Hardelot, France]
Dec 1920 – Jan 1921 to Clayton (x2) [Triomph's Hotel, Paris]
18 Oct 1921 (?) to Pinker (could be 1920) [Triomph's Hotel, Paris]
5 Dec 1921 to Clayton [Bowdon]
8 Jan 1922 (?) to Pinker (could be 1921) [Claridge's/Triomph's Hotel, Paris]
Feb 1922 (?) to Pinker [Ritz, London/Market St]
2 Dec 1922 (?) to Adcock [Market St]
1923 (?) to Alan Stokes [n.p.]
Spring 1923 (?) to Pinker [Market St]
12 Aug 1923 Grace Lewis to Stella Wood
23 Aug 1923 (?) to Pinker [Hesketh, Southport]
30 Aug 1923 to Hinton [Beaumanor/Market St]
1924 (?) to Savage [Bowdon/Queen St]
5 Mar 1924 to Mortimer [Queen St]
24 Mar 1924 to Mortimer [Hotel, Paris]

28 Jul 1924 to Saxton [Queen St]
25 Sep 1924 (?) to Saxton [Queen St]
Oct 1924 to Sewell Stokes [Queen St]
18 Oct 1924 (?) to Burke (could be 1923?) [Queen St]
20 Oct 1924 to Cunningham [Queen St]
7 Nov 1924 to Saxton [Knightsbridge]
11 Nov 1924 (?) to Craigie [Knightsbridge]
5 Dec 1924 to Curtis Brown [Queen St]
Dec 1924 (after 5th) to Curtis Brown [Southport]
Dec 1924/Jan 1925 (?) to Belloc Lowndes [Queen St/Bowdon]
Late 1924 (?) to Belloc Lowndes [Queen St]
1-14 Jan 1925 to Curtis Brown (x5) [Southport]
2 Feb 1925 to Curtis Brown [Charles St]
5-8 Feb 1925 to Curtis Brown (x3) [Hotel Bristol, Beaulieu-sur-Mer, France]
26 Feb 1925 to Creswick [Charles St]
Spring 1925 (?) to Woollcott [Ritz, NYC]
30 Mar 1925 (?) to mother [Detroit]
2 Apr 1925 to Katharine Cornell
4 Apr 1925 to Katharine Cornell
13 May 1925 to Woollcott [NYC]
20 Jun 1925 (?) to Firbank [Charles St]
Summer 1925 (?) to Anaïs [Charles St]
7 Nov 1925 to Doran [Lasky Studio, Calif]
8 Nov 1925 Mary Alice Scully to Josephine Chippo
11 Nov 1925 to De Mille [Lasky Studio, Calif]
Dec 1925 (?) to Gish [E 63rd St, NYC]
25 Dec 1925 to Gish [SS Baltic]
26 Dec 1925 to Woollcott [SS Baltic]
30 Dec 1925 (?) to Gish [Southport, telegram]
22 Feb 1926 to Kahn [Mercedes Hotel, Paris]
10 Mar 1926 Kahn to MA
4 Apr 1926 (?) to Gish [Paris, telegram]

16 Apr to Kahn [Grosvenor Hotel, Paris]
Apr/May 1926 (?) to Gish [Grosvenor Hotel, Paris]
3 May 1926 Kahn to MA
Early 1926 (?) to Gish [no address, first page missing?]
Summer 1926 (?) to Emery [Hermitage Hotel en Forêt-le-Fouquet, Paris]
Summer 1926 (?) to Emery [Ritz, Paris]
12 Jul 1926 Kahn to MA
22 Jul to Kahn [Lowndes St, London]
Aug (?) 1926 to Emery [Priors Farm, Crawley]
11 Dec 1926 to Beaverbrook [Rue Fourcroy, Paris]
13 Dec 1926 Beaverbrook to MA
Dec 1926 (?) to Curtis Brown [rue Fourcroy, Paris]
3 Jul 1927 to Colefax [The Grove, Seal, Kent]
9 Jul 1927 (?) to Gerhardie [Palace Hotel, St Moritz]
15 Oct 1927 Beaverbrook to MA
Dec 1927/Jan 1928 (?) to mother [Palace Hotel, St Moritz]
7 Mar 1928 to Belloc Lowndes [Carlton Hotel, London]
25 Mar 1928 to Beaverbrook [Ave de Courville, Paris]
25 Mar 1928 to Curtis Brown [Ave de Courville, Paris]
1 Apr 1928 to Coward [Ave de Courville, Paris]
1 Apr 1928 to Colefax [Ave de Courville, Paris]
5 Apr 1928 Beaverbrook to MA
Apr 1928 to Curtis Brown [Villa Edgeroad]
Late Apr 1928 to Coward [hotel/Villa Edgeroad]
28 Apr 1928 (?) to 'Michael' (Curtis Brown staffer?) [Hotel des Anglais, Cannes]
14 May 1928 to Morrell [Villa Edgeroad]
30 Jun 1928 to Temple [Hotel, Aix les Bains/Edgeroad, Cannes]
15 Sep 1928 to Wanger [Villa Edgeroad]
12 Dec 1928 to Douglas [Hesketh Rd, Southport]
30 Dec 1928 to Beaverbrook [Palace Hotel, St Moritz]
3 Jan 1929 Atalanta to Anaïs [Palace Hotel, St Moritz]

18 Mar 1929 Beaverbrook to MA
23 Mar 1929 (?) to Beaverbrook [Kurhaus, Freiburg]
16 May 1929 Ahavni to Anaïs [Valparaiso]
28 May 1929 to Beaverbrook [May Fair Hotel, London]
1 Jun 1929 Beaverbook to MA
Aug 1929 (?) Atalanta to Anaïs [Royal, Crans, Switzerland]
14 Sep 1929 (?) to Titus [Rue de Verneuil, Paris]
2 Nov 1929 to Beaverbrook [Rue Masseran, Paris]
10 Nov 1929 Beaverbrook to MA
Dec 1929 (?) Atalanta (+ Dikran) to MA's mother [Fiorentina, Cannes]
9 Jun 1930 to Miss Cond [rue Masseran, Paris]
Summer 1930 (?) to Coward [rue Masseran, Paris]
15 Jun 1930 to Coward [rue Masseran, Paris]
19 Jun 1930 to Coward [rue Masseran, Paris]
21 Sep 1930 to Coward [Paris]
2 Oct 1930 to Long (x2) [May Fair Hotel, London]
23 Oct 1930 (?) Anaïs to Tacvor [Stanhope Pl, London]
26 Oct 1930 (?) Atalanta to MA's mother [Stanhope Pl, London]
5 Dec 1930 to Adrian Brunel [Stanhope Pl, London]
Jan 1931 (?) Atalanta to Anaïs [Stanhope Pl, London]
Feb 1931 (?) to Woollcott [Farmington, Connecticut]
4 Mar 1931 to Woollcott [Fiorentina]
30 Mar 1931 (?) to Douglas [Fiorentina]
15 Oct 1931 (?) to Coward [May Fair Hotel, London]
14 Oct 1932 to Walpole [Bella Vista]
8 Nov 1932 (?) to Maugham [Quai d'Orsay, Paris/Bella Vista]
17 Dec 1932 to Priestley [Bella Vista]
1 Feb 1933 to Woollcott [Bella Vista]
14 Jun 1933 to Craigie [Bella Vista]
2 Oct 1933 to Coward [Bella Vista]
23 Nov 1933 to Hutchinson [May Fair Hotel, London]
18 Jun 1934 to Longwell [Bella Vista]

3 Jan 1935 to Furlong [Vienna]
28 Oct 1936 Wheatley to MA [May Fair Hotel]
5 Dec 1936 Wolfe to MA [May Fair Hotel]
15 Dec 1936 to Wolfe [Bella Vista]
11 Jan 1937 Wolfe to MA [Bella Vista]
14 Jan 1937 to Wolfe [Bella Vista; signed by secretary Livesey]
20 Jan 1937 to Priestley (PEN) [Bella Vista]
4 Feb 1937 Ould to MA [Bella Vista]
15 Feb 1937 Ould to MA [Bella Vista]
Feb – Apr 1937 to Evans (x3) [Bella Vista]
16 Mar 1937 to Wolfe [Bella Vista]
Late Apr/May 1937 to Evans [Hotel Lotti, Paris]
May – Jul 1937 to Evans (x6) [Bella Vista]
21 Dec 1937 to Evans [Bella Vista]
3 Jan 1939 to Nicolson [Bella Vista]
20 Jan 1939 Pearn to Gielgud
29 Oct 1939 (?) to Hutchinson [Ritz/May Fair Hotel, London]
26 June 1940 to Priestley [May Fair Hotel, London]
29 June 1940 (?) Priestley to MA
12 Jul 1940 Tacvor to MA [May Fair Hotel]
16 Jul 1940 Tacvor to MA [May Fair Hotel]
12 Aug 1940 to Gielgud [May Fair Hotel]
11 Oct 1940 to Churchill [May Fair Hotel]
19 Oct 1940 Stewart to MA [May Fair Hotel]
6 Nov 1940 to Gielgud [Eaton, Chester]
8 Nov 1940 Gielgud to MA [Eaton, Chester]
15 Nov 1940 Stewart to MA [Hesketh Rd, Southport]
27 Nov 1940 to Gielgud [Civil Defence Birmingham/Himley Hall]
2 Dec 1940 Gielgud to MA [Himley Hall]
10 Dec 1940 to Gielgud [Himley Hall]
12 Dec 1940 Gielgud to MA [Himley Hall]
2 Jan 1941 Stewart to MA [Hesketh Rd, Southport]

8 Jan 1941 to Stewart [Civil Defence Birmingham/Himley Hall]
9 Jan 1941 Stewart to MA [Himley Hall]
30 Jan 1941 Stewart to MA [Himley Hall]
4 Feb 1941 to Stewart [Himley Hall]
11 Feb 1941 Gielgud to MA [May Fair Hotel, London – misdirected?]
24 Feb 1941 to Gielgud [Ritz, London]
24 Feb 1941 Tacvor to MA [Ritz, London]
26 Feb 1941 Stewart to MA [Ritz, London]
1 Mar 1941 to Gielgud [Ritz, London]
4 Mar 1941 Gielgud to MA [Ritz, London]
7 Mar 1941 to Sitwell [Ritz, London]
16 Mar 1941 to Sitwell [Garrick/Athenaeum Ct]
20 Mar 1941 (?) to Wheatley [reported in personal email]
25 Mar 1941 to Gielgud [Garrick]
25 Mar 1941 to Sitwell [Garrick]
31 Mar 1941 Gielgud to MA [Hesketh Rd, Southport]
10 Apr 1941 to Gielgud [Hesketh Rd, Southport]
23 Apr 1941 to Sitwell [Athenaeum Ct/Garrick]
11 Jun 1941 to Sitwell [Garrick]
30 Jul 1941 Gielgud to MA [Athenaeum Ct]
30 Jul 1941 Wheatley to MA
9 Sep 1941 to Gielgud [Port Line Ltd]
23 Sep 1941 Gielgud to MA [Hotel Volney, NYC]
1 Oct 1941 (?) to Woollcott [Hotel Volney, NYC]
1942-65 Watkins Loomis [= business correspondence re. Arlen]
Jan 1943 to Luce [Beverly Wilshire Hotel, Calif]
30 Jul 1943 Castle diary [Homestead, Va?]
1944 (?) to Luce (Thursday) [Beverly Wilshire]
31 Mar 1944 to Luce [Beverly Wilshire]
1 Apr 1944 to Luce [Beverly Wilshire]
8 Apr 1944 to Luce [Beverly Wilshire]
19 May 1944 to Luce [Beverly Wilshire]

24 May 1944 to Luce [Beverly Wilshire]
Late May/early June 1944 to Luce [Beverly Wilshire]
14 Jun 1944 Luce to MA [Beverly Wilshire]
24 Jun 1944 Luce to MA [Beverly Wilshire]
30 Jun 1944 to Luce [hospital, Santa Monica]
3 Jul 1944 to Luce [hospital, Santa Monica]
20 Nov 1944 to Luce [Beverly Wilshire]
Nov 1944 to Luce (flowers) [Beverly Wilshire]
26 Feb 1946 to Luce [186 E End Ave, NY]
11 Sep 1947 Golden to MA [Volney Hotel, NYC]
24 Sep 1947 Golden to MA [Volney Hotel, NYC]
29 June 1950 to Coward (telegram) [Dorchester, London]
16 Sep 1952 to Frere [Southport/Bowdon]
Sep/Oct 1952 (?) to Stern [Dorchester, London]
25 Nov 1952 to Frere [Park Ave, NYC]
3 Sep 1953 to Wykes-Joyce [Park Ave, NYC]
May 1954 (?) to Waugh [Park Ave, NYC]
11 Dec 1954 Laurie to Knapp-Fisher
7 Jan 1955 Knapp-Fisher to MA [Dorchester, London]
25 Jan 1955 Knapp-Fisher to Laurie
7 Sep 1956 Atalanta to Louis Sobol [n.p.]
12 Sep 1970 Michael J. Arlen to Noël Coward
7 Sep 1983 Michael J. Arlen to Kevin Brownlow
Undated to Hutchinson (Friday) [May Fair Hotel]
Undated to Hutchinson [May Fair Hotel]
Undated to Bagnold (later than 1925) [May Fair Hotel]
Undated to Drinkwater (16 Mar, late 1920s?) [Ritz, Paris]
Undated Atalanta to MA's mother, Jan 1934-8 [Bella Vista]
Undated to Coward (later than Sep 1931) [Bella Vista]
Undated to Coward ("can't get hold of you") [May Fair Hotel, London]
Undated to Coward ("think it your best") [May Fair Hotel]

TWO LETTERS TO HIS MOTHER

Few of Arlen's letters to his family survive. The two below, notwithstanding his usual posturing, reveal Arlen as a loving son. In the first the young man returns in high spirits from a visit to Garsington Manor. By the time of the second, the now-successful author has sport at the expense of his prospective in-laws. (His wedding, a grand social affair, took place in the Greek Orthodox church in Cannes in early May 1928.) The letters are written in Arlen's characteristically florid English, which makes sense if he couldn't write Armenian but not if the recipient couldn't speak English. In the official file when she applied for British citizenship in 1923 it's reported that Satinik Kouyoumdjian is "a lady of means and good repute [who] speaks, reads and writes the English language well". Michael J. Arlen writes that his grandmother "could still barely speak English" when he knew her in the Thirties.

46 Redcliffe Rd, SW [London]
Thursday [16 December 1915]

My dearest mother,

Do you by the way remember that on each letter I sent to any of you at home during the last week I put that from Monday till Thursday my address would be Garsington Manor, Oxford?[1] Well on arriving home this evening I find a wire from Roupen[2] on Wednesday asking me to meet Uncle[3] at 10 o'clock on Thursday. But what on earth is the good of my carefully saying where I am going to if no one's going to take any notice of it. Naturally London's caretakers are not gifted with the intelligence of ordinary people, so thinking I was returning on Thursday she did not forward the wire. So much for my dear Uncle. It's late now but I shall call round at the Savoy. I shall listen to his old arguments if he is there – the good old argument between commerce and literature which curiously enough I am not sentimental enough to see – or to appreciate its wisdom. However I suppose we must all stick up for principles. The last four days I have spent away have certainly been the most peaceful I have spent anywhere in my life and certainly in a [quiet?] talkative way the most enjoyable. My dearest mother, Roupen tells me that you have not improved. As a vehicle of truth I see that I shall soon have to give up my mother. He said you were very well while in London. The decision on Florida[4] seems to have brought out a lot of new truths in one way or other. In fact they only seemed to discover that the business was not going as well as it might be when I said I was leaving England. It is curious, Mother, isn't it? To drift and to come up with a bang. To crumble in your hands – and to drop the ashes onto the [proceed?] Thank Heavens my dearest mother I have not lost my sense of humour. I can see in a way the humour of living – the seriousness with which other people try to push themselves at you. I shall leave to my brother Roupen the philosophy of life, to take the common sense of life, to [prick?] the strength of life. I shall keep for myself the humour of it, my mother, for a mind that laughs when others cry. Do you remember still when I used to cry when people were angry with me? It seems as far away as the supposed meaning of the Bible. I may one day dominate the weaker passions. My dearest mother, you must hurry and get well for I have many things to say to you. I can imagine that you are wondering what has come into the mind of your youngest son that she [sic] should write such letters as this. I can imagine my dear mother that you must have been wondering about a lot of things. And so have I. And perhaps Ahavni[5] too. But no, she is one who draws known conclusions without wondering. If these conclusions were right she would be an intellectual woman. But they are not – so she is my sister who loves me, a smart woman with a tendency towards business. Oh, to an end with theory. Let us throw away all that is indefinite and be logical. Let us be Bakirgians. Let us throw up the arts and become as the masses – just to live and eat and smell. And then where will we be? Better or worse, the [gutter?] of money or of ambition? The world says better. I say worse. And the God we worship being the God of self, I am right.

    Goodbye, my dearest mother, and you must get better. My love to [*illegible – looks like 'Stadfiri Elena'*] I suppose they think I'm mad to want to go away. So probably does Iplicjian,[6] and other intelligent observers of humanity? 'He doesn't know what he wants' they say and you say 'He's too young'. But is not his world made for the young?

Your very loving son, Dickran.

Palace Hotel, Biarritz [January 1928]

Darling Mother,

You will be so relieved to hear I am going to marry a nice girl. Her name is Atalanta Mercati. 24 year[s] old. Beautiful. Gentle. Greek-American. Her father Count Mercati, Lord Chamberlain to King Constantine and King George. Her grandmother Princess Karageorgevitch. In fact her whole family are aristocratic fools who bore me to death. But you will like Atalanta as much as you like Anaïs.[7] When we shall get married I am not certain. Very quietly. Anywhere. You will be so glad to hear this, I am certain. Imagine me marrying a really nice girl. Poor girl.

Your loving son Dikran

[PS] The family are terrified of me. They have heard I have had affairs with every woman in Europe. I have told them they are quite right, and in America too.

[PPS] I have *finished* my book.[8]

[PPPS] This is the only photograph I have of her at present. Will send you another. Don't cry too much.

NOTES

1   D.H. Lawrence asked Lady Ottoline Morrell to invite Arlen to her country home. He visited from 13 to 16 December, in company

with Philip Heseltine (aka the composer 'Peter Warlock'). See the chapter on Lawrence earlier.
2. One this older brothers.
3. Manouk.
4. Lawrence was still recruiting volunteers for 'Rananim', his (never-to-be) utopian colony in Florida. See the chapter on Lawrence earlier.
5. His older sister, married to Marco Bakirgian, head of Olivo & Bakirgian.
6. Dikran Iplicjian sat with Arlen's father and Marco Bakirgian on the Manchester Committee of the Armenian General Benevolent Union.
7. Wife of Tacvor, one of Arlen's older brothers.
8. Probably *Lily Christine: A Romance*, which was published later that year.

SOURCES

How (Not) To Write Literary Biography

Writing the Lives of Writers, ed. Warwick Gould and Thomas F. Staley (Basingstoke, Macmillan, 1995); in particular, the essays:
　Martin Stannard, 'A Matter of Life and Death'
　John Haffenden, 'Life over Literature; or, Whatever Happened to Critical Biography?'
　Max Saunders, 'Ford, Eliot, Joyce, and the Problems of Literary Biography'
The Art of Literary Biography, ed. John Batchelor (Oxford: Clarendon Press, 1995); in particular, the essays:
　Richard Holmes, 'Biography: Inventing the Truth'
　John Worthen, 'The Necessary Ignorance of a Biographer'
　Ann Thwaite, 'Starting Again: One of the Problems of the Biographer'
Lee, Hermione. *Biography: A Very Short Introduction*. Oxford: OUP, 2009.
―――, *Virginia Woolf*. London: Chatto & Windus, 1996.
Woolf, Virginia. *Collected Essays*, vol. 4. London; Hogarth Press, 1967.

Early Life

Allen, Roy. *Malvern College: A 150th Anniversary Portrait*. Oxford: Shire, 2014.

Arlen, Michael. 'Confessions of A Naturalized Englishman,' in *Babes in the Wood*. London: Hutchinson, 1929.

———. *The London Venture*. London: Heinemann, 1920.

———. *'Piracy': A Romantic Chronicle of These Days*. London: Collins, 1922.

Arlen, Michael J. *Exiles*. Harmondsworth: Penguin, 1973.

———. *Passage to Ararat*. London: Chatto & Windus, 1976.

Blumenau, Ralph. *A History of Malvern College, 1865-1965*. London: Macmillan, 1965.

Cunard, Nancy. Unpublished memoir. Nancy Cunard Collection 1895-1965, Harry Ransom Center, University of Texas-Austin, Austin, TX.

Gay, Charles. 'Celebrities in Cameo. No. 27: Michael Arlen'. *The Bystander*, December 6, 1933, 451.

George, Joan. *Merchants in Exile: The Armenians in Manchester, England, 1835-1935*. London: Gomidas Institute, 2002.

Hewins, Ralph. *Mr Five Per Cent: The Biography of Calouste Gulbenkian*. London; Hutchinson, 1957.

Hovannisian, Richard G. 'The Historical Dimensions of the Armenian Question, 1878-1923'. In: *The Armenian Genocide in Perspective*, ed. Richard G. Hovannisian. New Brunswick, NJ: Transaction Books, 1986.

Irwin, Margaret. *Knock Four Times*. London: Chatto & Windus, 1942. (First published 1927).

Keyishian, Harry. 'The Armenian Side of Michael Arlen'. *Ararat*, XI, autumn 1970, 6-12.

———. *Michael Arlen* (Twayne's English Authors Series). Boston: Twayne, 1975.

Kouyoumdjian, Dikran. 'Figures in a Room'. *The New Age*, April

5, 1917, 539.

———. 'Michael Arlen: A Fragment of a Novel'. *The New Age*, August 9, 1917, 330-32.

Lang, David Marshall. *The Armenians: A People in Exile*. London: Allen & Unwin, 1981.

Lewis, C.S, *Surprised by Joy*. In Lewis, *Selected Books*. London: HarperCollins, 1999. (First published 1955.)

Mackenzie, Compton. *My Life and Times. Octave 4: 1907-1914*. London: Chatto & Windus, 1965.

Mortimer, Raymond. 'New Novels'. *New Statesman*, June 23, 1923, p.332.

Murry, John Middleton. *Between Two Worlds: An Autobiography*. London: Jonathan Cape, 1935.

Rhodes James, Sydney. *Seventy Years: Random Reminiscences and Reflections*. London: Williams & Norgate, 1926.

Selver, Paul. *Orage and the New Age Circle: Reminiscences and Reflections*. London: Allen & Unwin, 1959.

Shearing, Harriet. 'Arlen Eyebrows Hollywood'. *Photoplay*, February 1926, 72.

Waugh, Alec. 'Michael Arlen in Retirement'. In: *My Brother Evelyn and Other Profiles*. London: Cassell, 1967.

West, Rebecca. 'Uprooted Ones'. *Sunday Telegraph*, 28 March, 1971, p14.

Wilson, A.N. *C.S. Lewis: A Biography*. London: Collins, 1990.

Success: New York, 1925

Cockburn, Claud. *Bestseller: The Books that Everyone Read, 1900-1939*. Harmondsworth: Penguin, 1975.

Cornell, Katharine. *I Wanted to Be an Actress: The Autobiography of Katharine Cornell*. New York: Random House, 1939.

Doran, George H. *Chronicles of Barabbas, 1884-1934*. London:

Methuen, 1935.
Luke, Michael. *David Tennant and the Gargoyle Years*. London: Weidenfeld & Nicolson, 1991.
Mosel, Tad, with Gertrude Macy. *Leading Lady: The World and Theatre of Katharine Cornell*. Boston: Little, Brown, 1978.

D.H. Lawrence

Aldington, Richard. *Portrait of A Genius, But... The Life of D.H. Lawrence, 1885-1930*. London: Heinemann, 1950.
Alpers, Antony. *The Life of Katherine Mansfield*. London: Cape, 1980.
Arlen, Michael. 'Confessions of A Naturalized Englishman,' in *Babes in the Wood*. London: Hutchinson, 1929. 12-77.
_____. *The Green Hat*. New York: George H. Doran, 1924.
_____. *The London Venture*. London: Heinemann, 1920.
_____. *Man's Mortality*. London: Heinemann, 1933.
Arlen, Michael J. *Exiles*. Harmondsworth: Penguin, 1973.
Baldwin, Dean R. *H.E. Bates: A Literary Life*. Selinsgrove, PA: Susquehanna UP, 1987.
Carswell, Catherine. *The Savage Pilgrimage: A Narrative of D.H. Lawrence*. London: Chatto and Windus, 1932.
Delany, Paul. *D.H. Lawrence's Nightmare: The Writer and His Circle in the Years of the Great War*. Hassocks: Harvester, 1979.
Dik-Cunningham, S. [Michael Arlen]. 'Pastiche: Preface and Synopsis.' *The New Age*, XVIII/18 (2 March 1916). 428-9.
Ellis, David. *D.H. Lawrence: Dying Game 1922-1930*. Cambridge: CUP, 1998. [DG]
Frieda Lawrence and Her Circle: Letters from, to and about Frieda Lawrence. Ed. Harry T. Moore and Dale B. Montague. London: Macmillan, 1981.

Gerard, David. *Shrieking Silence: A Library Landscape*. London: Scarecrow, 1988.

Gray, Cecil. *Peter Warlock: A Memoir of Philip Heseltine*. London: Cape, 1934.

Harrison, Andrew. "'A New Continent of the Soul": D.H. Lawrence, Porthcothan and the Necessary Fiction of Cornwall,' *Journal of D.H. Lawrence Studies*, 4/3 (2017), 33-43.

Heald, Tim. *A Life of Love: Barbara Cartland*. London: Sinclair-Stevenson, 1994.

Huxley, Aldous. *Selected Letters*. Ed. James Sexton. Chicago: Ivan R. Dee, 2007.

Huxley, Juliette. *Leaves of the Tulip Tree: Autobiography*. London: John Murray, 1986.

Jobson, Sandra. 'An Incident at the Café Royal,' *Rananim* 2(1), February 1994 (online).

Keyishian, Harry. *Michael Arlen*. Twayne's English Authors Series 174. Boston: G.K. Hall, 1975.

Kinkead-Weekes, Mark. *D.H. Lawrence: Triumph to Exile 1911-1922*. Cambridge: CUP, 1996. [TE]

Kouyoumdjian, Dikran [Michael Arlen]. 'Clever Mr Cannan.' *The New Age*, XX/2 (9 November 1916). 38.

_____. 'Figures in A Room.' *The New Age*, XX/23 (5 April 1917). 539.

_____. 'London Letters I: Ave.' *The New Age*, XXIII/16 (15 August 1918). 253-5.

Lawrence, D.H. *Apocalypse and the Writings on Revelation*. Ed. Mara Kalnins. Cambridge: CUP, 2002. [A]

_____. *The First 'Women in Love'*. Ed. John Worthen and Lindeth Vasey. Cambridge: CUP, 1998. [FWL]

_____. *Lady Chatterley's Lover and A Propos of 'Lady Chatterley's Lover.'* Ed. Michael Squires. Cambridge: CUP, 1993. [LCL]

_____. *Late Essays and Articles*. Ed. James T. Boulton. Cambridge:

CUP, 2004. [LEA]

———. *The Letters of D.H. Lawrence*. Vol. II. Ed. George J. Zytaruk and James T. Boulton. Cambridge: CUP, 1981. [2L]

———. *The Letters of D.H. Lawrence*. Vol. VI. Ed. James T. Boulton and Margaret H. Boulton with Gerald Lacy. Cambridge: CUP, 1991. [6L]

———. *The Letters of D.H. Lawrence*. Vol. VII. Ed. Keith Sagar and James T. Boulton. Cambridge: CUP, 1993. [7L]

———. *Reflections on the Death of a Porcupine and Other Essays*. Ed. Michael Herbert. Cambridge: CUP, 1998. [RDP]

———. *Studies in Classic American Literature*. Ed. Ezra Greenspan, Lindeth Vasey and John Worthen. Cambridge: CUP, 2002. [SCAL]

———. *Study of Thomas Hardy and Other Essays*. Ed. Bruce Steele. Cambridge: CUP, 1985. [STH]

———. *The Virgin and the Gipsy and Other Stories*. Ed. Michael Herbert, Bethan Jones and Lindeth Vasey. Cambridge: CUP, 2005. [VG]

———. *Women in Love*. Ed. David Farmer, Lindeth Vasey and John Worthen. Cambridge: CUP, 1987. [WL]

Mansfield, Katherine. *The Collected Letters of Katherine Mansfield*. Vol. I. Ed. Vincent O'Sullivan and Margaret Scott. Oxford: OUP, 1984.

Maxwell, Elsa. '"Green Hat" Author Now War Worker.' *Philadelphia Inquirer*, 16 October 1941, p. 13.

Meyers, Jeffrey. 'Katherine Mansfield, Gurdjieff, and Lawrence's "Mother and Daughter".' *Twentieth Century Literature*, 22 (1976), 444-53.

Miller, Jane Eldridge. '"The penumbra of its own time and place and circumstance": Modern Women, the Edwardian Novel, and *Sons and Lovers*,' *D.H. Lawrence Review*, 39.2 (2014), pp. 77-96.

Murry, John Middleton. *The Letters of John Middleton Murry to*

Katherine Mansfield. Ed. C.A. Hankin. London: Constable, 1983.

_____. *Reminiscences of D.H. Lawrence*. London: Cape, 1933.

Nehls, Edward, ed. *D.H. Lawrence: A Composite Biography*. Vol. 2. Madison, WI: University of Wisconsin P, 1958.

_____. *D.H. Lawrence: A Composite Biography*. Vol. 3. Madison, WI: University of Wisconsin P, 1959.

Obolensky, Serge. *One Man in His Time: The Memoirs of Serge Obolensky*. New York: McDowell, Obolensky, 1958.

Ottoline at Garsington: Memoirs of Lady Ottoline Morrell 1915-1918. Ed. Robert Gathorne-Hardy. London: Faber and Faber, 1974.

Smith, Barry. *Peter Warlock: The Life of Philip Heseltine*. Oxford: OUP, 1994.

Warlock, Peter. *The Collected Letters of Peter Warlock*. Vol II. Ed. Barry Smith. Woodbridge: Boydell, 2005.

_____. *The Collected Letters of Peter Warlock*. Vol III. Ed. Barry Smith. Woodbridge: Boydell, 2005.

Waugh, Alec. 'Michael Arlen in Retirement', in *My Brother Evelyn and Other Profiles*. London: Cassell, 1967. 255-70.

Ernest Hemingway

Arlen, Michael. *Babes in the Wood*. London: Hutchinson, 1929.

_____. *The Green Hat*. New York: George H. Doran, 1924.

_____. *Man's Mortality*. London: Heinemann, 1933.

_____. 'Riviera'. *The Bystander*, 1 May 1929, pp. 247-50, xvi; 8 May 1929, pp. 303-06, 322.

_____. *The Romantic Lady*. London: Collins, 1921.

_____. *Those Charming People*. London: Collins, 1923.

Arlen, Michael J. *Exiles*. Harmondsworth: Penguin, 1973.

'Artists' Revels Prove a Great Success at Covent Garden Last

Week.' *The Tatler*, 18 March 1914, p. 301.

Baker, Carlos. *Ernest Hemingway: A Life Story*. New York: Scribner's, 1969.

Bloom, Harold, editor. *Brett Ashley (Major Literary Characters)*. New York: Chelsea House, 1991.

Bruccoli, Matthew J. *Some Sort of Epic Grandeur: The Life of F. Scott Fitzgerald*. London: Hodder & Stoughton, 1981.

Chamberlin, Brewster. *The Hemingway Log: A Chronology of His Life and Times*. Lawrence, KS: Kansas UP, 2015.

Chisholm, Anne. *Nancy Cunard*. London: Sidgwick & Jackson, 1979.

Hemingway, Ernest. *The Fifth Column and Four Stories of the Spanish Civil War*. New York: Scribner's, 2008.

———. *The Letters of Ernest Hemingway. Vol. 3: 1926-1929*, edited by Rena Sanderson, Sandra Spanier and Robert W. Trogdon. Cambridge: Cambridge UP, 2015.

———. *A Moveable Feast*. London: Jonathan Cape, 1964.

———. 'Notes on life and letters: or a manuscript found in a bottle.' *Esquire*, 1 January 1935, pp. 21, 159.

———. *Selected Letters, 1917-1961*, edited by Carlos Baker. New York: Scribner's, 1981.

———. *The Sun Also Rises*. London: Arrow, 2004.

———. *The Torrents of Spring*. Harmondsworth: Penguin, 1976.

Hotchner, A.E., *Hemingway in Love: His Own Story*. London: Picador, 2016.

Keyishian, Harry. *Michael Arlen*. Twayne's English Authors Series 174. Boston: G.K. Hall, 1975.

Lawrence. D.H. *The Letters of D.H. Lawrence*, Vol. VII, edited by Keith Sagar and James T. Boulton. Cambridge: Cambridge UP, 1993.

Leff, Leonard J. *Hemingway and His Conspirators: Hollywood, Scribners, and the Making of American Celebrity Culture*. Lanham, MD: Rowman & Littlefield, 1997.

Marcus, Jane. *Hearts of Darkness: White Women Write Race.* New Brunswick, NJ: Rutgers UP, 2004.
Mayfield, Sara. *Exiles from Paradise: Zelda and Scott Fitzgerald.* New York: Dell, 1971.
Mosel, Tad, with Gertrude Macy. *Leading Lady: The World and Theatre of Katharine Cornell.* Boston: Little, Brown, 1978.
'Royal Ascot.' *The Tatler*, 21 June 1922, p. 437.
Sarason, Bertram D. *Hemingway and 'The Sun' Set.* Washington, DC: NCR Microcard Editions, 1972.
Saroyan, William. 'The Armenian who Almost Didn't Want to be an Armenian,' *Ararat*, vol. XI, autumn 1970, pp. 2-5.
_____. *The Daring Young Man on the Flying Trapeze and Other Stories.* Random House, 1934.
Soto, Michael. *The Modernist Nation: Generation, Renaissance, and Twentieth-Century American Literature.* Tuscaloosa, AL: Alabama UP, 2004.
Spilka, Mark. *Hemingway's Quarrel with Androgyny.* Lincoln, NE: Nebraska UP, 1990.
Stewart, Donald Ogden. *By A Stroke of Luck! An Autobiography.* New York: Paddington, 1975.
Tyler, Lisa. *Student Companion to Ernest Hemingway.* Westport, CT: Greenwood, 2001.
'Woman Artist's Failure.' *The Times* (Law Reports), 3 October 1928, p. 5.

F. Scott Fitzgerald

The Ace of Cads. Dir. Luther Reed. Paramount, 1926. (Film.)
Arlen, Michael. *These Charming People.* New York: Doran, 1924.
_____. *The Green Hat.* New York: Doran, 1924.
_____. *Lily Christine: A Romance.* New York: Doubleday, 1928.
_____. *The London Venture.* New York: Doran, 1920.

_____. *May Fair*. New York: Doran, 1925.
_____. *Men Dislike Women: A Romance*. London: Heinemann, 1931.
_____. '*Piracy*': *A Romantic Chronicle of These Days*. New York: Doran, 1923.
_____. *The Romantic Lady*. London: Collins, 1921.
Arlen, Michael J. *Exiles*. Harmondsworth: Penguin, 1973.
Atkinson, J. Brooks. 'The Play: Careless People and Gatsby.' *New York Times*, February 3 1926: 22.
Bruccoli, Matthew J. *Some Sort of Epic Grandeur: The Life of F. Scott Fitzgerald*. London: Hodder and Stoughton, 1981.
_____, and Margaret M. Duggan, eds., with the assistance of Susan Walker. *Correspondence of F. Scott Fitzgerald*. New York: Random House, 1980.
_____, and Jennifer McCabe Atkinson, eds. *As Ever, Scott Fitz – Letters between F. Scott Fitzgerald and His Literary Agent Harold Ober, 1919-1940*. Philadelphia: Lippincott, 1972.
Bryer, Jackson R., and Cathy W. Barks, eds. *Dear Scott, Dearest Zelda: The Love Letters of F. Scott and Zelda Fitzgerald*. New York: St. Martin's P, 2002.
Carter, Angela. *Shaking A Leg: Collected Journalism and Writings*. Ed. Jenny Uglow. London: Vintage, 2013.
Chisholm, Anne. *Nancy Cunard*. London: Sidgwick & Jackson, 1979.
Cline, Sally. *Zelda Fitzgerald: Her Voice in Paradise*. London: John Murray, 2002.
Collins, Joan. *Past Imperfect: An Autobiography*. London: W.H. Collins, 1978; rev. ed. New York: Berkley Books, 1985.
Cunard, Nancy. Unpublished memoir. Nancy Cunard Collection 1895-1965, Harry Ransom Center, University of Texas-Austin, Austin TX.
Dean, James W. 'In New York.' *The (Franklin PA) News-Herald* April 1, 1925: 4.

SOURCES

De Courcy, Anne. *Five Love Affairs and a Friendship: The Paris Life of Nancy Cunard, Icon of the Jazz Age*. London: Weidenfeld & Nicolson, 2022.

Duhamel, Marcel, *Raconte pas ta vie*. Paris: Mercure de France, 1972.

Fitzgerald, F. Scott. *All the Sad Young Men*. Ed. James L.W. West III. New York: Cambridge U P, 2007.

_____. *The Basil, Josephine, and Gwen Stories*. Ed. Ed. James L.W. West III. New York: Cambridge UP, 2009. [BJG]

_____. *F. Scott Fitzgerald: A Life in Letters*. Ed. Matthew J. Bruccoli. New York: Scribner, 1994.

_____. *The Great Gatsby: A Variorum Edition*. Ed. James L.W. West III and Don C. Skemer. New York: Cambridge UP, 2019.

_____. *The Letters of F. Scott Fitzgerald*. Ed. Andrew Turnbull. New York: Scribner's, 1963.

_____. *My Lost City: Personal Essays, 1920–1940*. Ed. James L.W. West III. New York: Cambridge UP, 2005. [MLC]

_____. *Taps at Reveille*. Ed. James L. W. West III. New York: Cambridge UP, 2014. [TAR]

_____. *Tender Is the Night: A Romance*. 1934. Ed. James L.W. West III. New York: Cambridge UP, 2012. [TITN]

Hemingway, Ernest. *Ernest Hemingway: Selected Letters 1917-1961*. Ed. Carlos Baker. New York: Scribner's, 1981.

_____. *In Our Time*. New York: Boni and Liveright, 1925.

_____. *The Letters of Ernest Hemingway, Vol. 3: 1926-1929*. Ed. Rena Sanderson, Sandra Spanier and Robert W. Trogdon. New York: Cambridge UP, 2015.

_____. *A Moveable Feast*. New York: Scribner's, 1964.

_____. *The Sun Also Rises*. New York: Scribner's, 1926.

_____. *The Torrents of Spring*. New York: Scribner's, 1926.

Keyishian, Harry. *Michael Arlen*. Boston: G.K. Hall, 1975.

Kuehl, John, and Jackson R. Bryer, eds. *Dear Scott/Dear Max: The*

Fitzgerald-Perkins Correspondence. New York: Scribner's, 1971.

Mayfield, Sara. *Exiles from Paradise: Zelda and Scott Fitzgerald*. New York: Delacorte, 1971.

Mosel, Tad, with Gertrude Macy. *Leading Lady: The World and Theatre of Katharine Cornell*. Boston: Little, Brown, 1978.

'Mr. Arlen's Syrup.' *New York Times Book Review*, November 18, 1928: 6.

'Mr. Shaw and Mr. Menjou; Full Report of Talk of Author and Actor in a London Hotel.' *New York Times*, June 3 1928: 10:8.

Rascoe, Burton. 'Contemporary Reminiscences.' *Arts and Decoration* 23 (May 1925): 45, 85-87.

Sutherland, John. *Bestsellers: A Very Short Introduction*. Oxford: Oxford UP, 2007.

Taylor, Kendall. *Sometimes Madness Is Wisdom: Zelda and Scott Fitzgerald: A Marriage*. London: Robson, 2002.

Waugh, Alec. *My Brother Evelyn and Other Profiles*. London: Cassell, 1967.

A Woman of Paris. Dir. Charlie Chaplin. United Artists, 1923. (Film).

Yardley, Jonathan. *Ring: A Biography of Ring Lardner*. New York: Random House, 1977.

Further sources

Where no sources or details are given, the interested reader is welcome to contact the author for further information (if available). Visit https://michael-arlen.blogspot.com, click on 'About Me' and then go to the email tab. The blog also has additional photographs.

ABOUT THE AUTHOR

Philip Ward is a writer, translator and (occasional) composer. He worked for many years in the House of Commons Library. A member of the Society of Authors and the Biographers' Club, he lives in Cambridge, UK, where he is a Senior Member of Wolfson College.

https://brushondrum.blogspot.com
https://michael-arlen.blogspot.com

This book is printed on paper from sustainable sources managed under the Forest Stewardship Council (FSC) scheme.

It has been printed in the UK to reduce transportation miles and their impact upon the environment.

For every new title that Matador publishes, we plant a tree to offset CO_2, partnering with the More Trees scheme.

For more about how Matador offsets its environmental impact, see www.troubador.co.uk/about/